BUSINESS ENGLISH

WRITTEN BY
María Isabel Castro Cid, PhD
Teachers College, Columbia University
and Enrique Montes

EDITED BY
Helga Schier, PhD
Merrick Walter
Suzanne McQuade

LIVING LANGUAGE®

Published in the United States by Living Language, an imprint of Random House, Inc.

www.livinglanguage.com

ISBN 978-1-4000-0661-8

Library of Congress Cataloging-in-Publication Data available upon request.

This book is available at special discounts for bulk purchases for sales promotions or premiums. Special editions, including personalized covers, excerpts of existing books, and corporate imprints, can be created in large quantities for special needs. For more information, write to Special Markets/Premium Sales, 1745 Broadway, MD 6-2, New York, New York 10019 or e-mail specialmarkets@randomhouse.com.

PRINTED IN THE UNITED STATES OF AMERICA

10 9 8 7 6 5 4 3 2

ACKNOWLEDGMENTS

I wish to thank each and every one of my dear friends for their love and constant encouragement, and for their great senses of humor. I also wish to extend my deepest gratitude to my family for their patience, endurance, and love. Many thanks to my editors, Merrick Walter and Helga Schier. Thanks to the Living Language® staff: Tom Russell, Nicole Benhabib, Christopher Warnasch, Suzanne McQuade, Shaina Malkin, Elham Shabahat, Sophie Chin, Linda Schmidt, Alison Skrabek, Carolyn Roth, and Tom Marshall.

TABLE OF CONTENTS

INTRODUCTION   1

LESSON 1: Arriving in the United States   5
    A. Dialogue: Where Is My Luggage?   5
    B. Notes   6
    C. Grammar and Usage 1. The Elements of a Sentence
       2. Personal Pronouns 3. *There + To Be*   8
    D. Idiomatic Study: Introductions   11
    E. Strictly Business 1. Entry Forms 2. Social Etiquette
       3. Vocabulary   12
    F. Exercises   14

LESSON 2: Family Relations   17
    A. Dialogue: "Conversations with Camila"   17
    B. Notes   19
    C. Grammar and Usage 1. The Simple Present 2. The Present
       Continuous   22
    D. Idiomatic Study: Asking for Clarification, Clarifying   27
    E. Strictly Business 1. Family Structure in the United States
       2. Vocabulary   28
    F. Exercises   29

LESSON 3: Computers in the Workplace   31
    A. Dialogue: The Company That Wasn't   31
    B. Notes   33
    C. Grammar and Usage: 1. Nouns 2. Articles 3. Quantity
       Expressions 4. *Few* vs. *a few* and *little* vs. *a little*   34
    D. Idiomatic Study: Invitations   39
    E. Strictly Business 1. The Virtual Office 2. Vocabulary   40
    F. Exercises   43

LESSON 4: Insurance Policies   45
    A. Dialogue: The Accident   45
    B. Notes   47
    C. Grammar and Usage 1. The Simple Past 2. *Used to*
       3. The Past Continuous   49
    D. Idiomatic Study: Descriptions   55
    E. Strictly Business 1. Health Insurance in the United States
       2. Other Insurance 3. Vocabulary   57
    F. Exercises   59

LESSON 5: Discrimination in the Workplace   61
    A. Dialogue: An Interview   61
    B. Notes   63
    C. Grammar and Usage 1. The Present Perfect 2. *For* and *since*
       3. The Present Perfect Continuous 4. The Past Perfect 5. The
       Past Perfect Continuous   64
    D. Idiomatic Study: Voicing a Complaint   68
    E. Strictly Business 1. Against Discrimination 2. Vocabulary   68
    F. Exercises   71

READING I: Online Etiquette for Newbies   73

LESSON 6: Business Expansion   76
    A. Dialogue: A New Store   76
    B. Notes   77
    C. Grammar and Usage 1. The Future with *to be going*
       2. The Future with *will* 3. Using the Future Tense 4. The Future
       with Time Expressions 5. Using the Present Tense to Express
       the Future   79
    D. Idiomatic Study: Expressing Agreement, Expressing
       Disagreement   82
    E. Strictly Business 1. The Latest in Retail Sales 2. Vocabulary   83
    F. Exercises   84

LESSON 7: Banking in the United States   87
    A. Dialogue: A New Bank Account   87
    B. Notes   89
    C. Grammar and Usage 1. The Conditional 2. Homonyms   90
    D. Idiomatic Study: Asking for a Favor   94
    E. Strictly Business 1. Banks in the United States 2. Vocabulary   95
    F. Exercises   98

LESSON 8: Health Care   101
    A. Dialogue: A Visit to the Emergency Room   101
    B. Notes   103
    C. Grammar and Usage 1. The Verb *to Be* 2. The Verb *to Have*
       3. The Verb *to Do* 4. *To Do* vs. *to Make*   106
    D. Idiomatic Study: Giving Warning   109
    E. Strictly Business 1. Medical Services 2. Emergency Services
       3. Vocabulary   110
    F. Exercises   112

LESSON 9: Social Etiquette   115
    A. Dialogue: Are We Dating?   115
    B. Notes   117

    C. Grammar and Usage 1. Modal Verbs: Form 2. Modal Verbs:
     Usage   118
    D. Idiomatic Study: Asking for Permission   122
    E. Strictly Business 1. Social Etiquette 2. Vocabulary   123
    F. Exercises   125

LESSON 10: Real Estate   127
    A. Dialogue: Looking for Office Space   127
    B. Notes   129
    C. Grammar and Usage 1. The Comparative 2. The Superlative
     3. Sentence Structures of Equivalence 4. *Good* vs. *Well*   130
    D. Idiomatic Study: Expressing Preferences   133
    E. Strictly Business 1. Real Estate 2. Roommates 3. The Lease
     4. Vocabulary   134
    F. Exercises   137

READING II: Give Me the Splendid Silent Sun   139

REVIEW QUIZ 1   141

LESSON 11: Getting Around   144
    A. Dialogue: Pizza Delivery   144
    B. Notes   146
    C. Grammar and Usage 1. Negation 2. Adverbs of Negation
     3. The Usage of *Not* and *No* 4. *Some* vs. *Any*   148
    D. Idiomatic Study: Placing an Order over the Phone   150
    E. Strictly Business 1. Relying on the Automobile 2. Vocabulary   151
    F. Exercises   153

LESSON 12: Politics   155
    A. Dialogue: I'm an American Too!   155
    B. Notes   156
    C. Grammar and Usage 1. Possessive Nouns 2. Possessive
     Adjectives 3. Possessive Pronouns 4. Reflexive Pronouns
     5. Impersonal Pronouns 6. Words Ending in *-ever* 7. Expressions
     with *Other*   157
    D. Idiomatic Study: Expressing Intentions   161
    E. Strictly Business 1. Lawmaking in the United States
     2. Vocabulary   162
    F. Exercises   164

LESSON 13: Sports and Exercise   166
    A. Dialogue: Ballroom Dancing   166
    B. Notes   167

C. Grammar and Usage 1. The Gerund 2. Present and Past
Participles   169
D. Idiomatic Study: Complimenting, Expressing Displeasure,
Expressing Congratulations   171
E. Strictly Business 1. The Business of Sports and Athletes
2. Vocabulary   173
F. Exercises   174

LESSON 14: The Media   176
A. Dialogue: Nothing to Watch   176
B. Notes   177
C. Grammar and Usage 1. The Infinitive   178
D. Idiomatic Study: Apologizing   181
E. Strictly Business 1. The Power of the Mass Media
2. Vocabulary   182
F. Exercises   184

LESSON 15: Social Problems in the United States   186
A. Dialogue: An Encounter with the Homeless   186
B. Notes   188
C. Grammar and Usage 1. The Passive Voice   189
D. Idiomatic Study: Taking Leave   192
E. Strictly Business 1. Social Responsibilities 2. Vocabulary   193
F. Exercises   195

READING III: How Young Is Too Young for CEOs?   196

LESSON 16: Import and Export   198
A. Dialogue: A Late Shipment of Sugar   198
B. Notes   199
C. Grammar and Usage 1. Direct vs. Indirect Speech   200
D. Idiomatic Study: Expressing Certainty or Uncertainty   203
E. Strictly Business 1. Importing Products into the United States
2. Vocabulary   203
F. Exercises   206

LESSON 17: Higher Education in the United States   208
A. Dialogue: Registering at the Local College   208
B. Notes   209
C. Grammar and Usage 1. Prepositions   211
D. Idiomatic Study: Offering Help   214
E. Strictly Business 1. Higher Education in the United States
2. Vocabulary   215
F. Exercises   218

LESSON 18: Marketing and Advertising   221
  A. Dialogue: Like Good Wine   221
  B. Notes   222
  C. Grammar and Usage 1. Relative Pronouns 2. Coordinating
    Conjunctions 3. Coordinating Adverbs 4. Subordinating
    Conjunctions   224
  D. Idiomatic Study: Asking for and Giving Advice   227
  E. Strictly Business 1. Marketing 2. Vocabulary   228
  F. Exercises   230

LESSON 19: The Environment   232
  A. Dialogue: The Ozone Layer   232
  B. Notes   233
  C. Grammar and Usage 1. Phrasal Verbs 2. The Subjunctive   235
  D. Idiomatic Study: Expressing Probability or Improbability   237
  E. Strictly Business 1. Environmental Protection 2. Vocabulary   238
  F. Exercises   240

LESSON 20: A Nation of Immigrants   242
  A. Dialogue: Touring Ellis Island   242
  B. Notes   244
  C. Grammar and Usage 1. Capitalization 2. Prefixes 3. Suffixes   246
  D. Idiomatic Study: Asking Someone to Repeat Something   250
  E. Strictly Business 1. Immigrants in the United States
    2. Vocabulary   250
  F. Exercises   252

READING IV: You Hate When They Call, But Their Stocks
Look Good   254

REVIEW QUIZ 2   255

ANSWER KEY   259

APPENDIXES   269
  A. Pronunciation Table   269
  B. Grammar Summary   271
  C. Irregular Verbs   283
  D. Writing Letters   285

VOCABULARY LIST   291

INDUSTRY-SPECIFIC TERMS   305

INDEX   325

INTRODUCTION

If you have mastered the basic structures in English, whether it is because you studied the language in school, practiced it while traveling, or studied it through other Living Language courses, then *Business English* is an ideal course for you.

The complete course includes this textbook and four hours of recordings. If you already know English pronunciation, you may use the book by itself.

Business English teaches readers to speak, understand, read, and write idiomatic English. The program also introduces cultural aspects and business etiquette in the United States. You will be able to participate in interesting conversations about a wide variety of topics; you will also be able to respond to formal and informal speaking styles.

The course will transport you to different places, from Ellis Island to a virtual office, so you become acquainted with different expressions and the English vocabulary that is required of most businesspeople. You will read newspaper articles and analyze financial reports. You will also learn more about the subtle cultural differences in interpersonal relations, such as when you should insist on paying for a meal and when you should let others pay. These tips will help you when you are traveling to or doing business in an English-speaking country.

COURSE MATERIALS

MANUAL

The *Business English* manual consists of twenty lessons, four reading passages, and two review quizzes. The reading passages appear after every five chapters. There are two review quizzes, one after Lesson 10 and the other after Lesson 20. We suggest that you read and study each lesson before listening to the recordings.

DIALOGUE: Each lesson begins with a dialogue that contains standard, idiomatic language that depicts a typical real-life situation—a job interview, an apartment search, registering for a university course—in the United States.

NOTES: The notes generally refer to expressions and phrases that are specific to the dialogue. They give you a specific cultural or historical background and allow you to see grammatical rules and vocabulary "in action."

GRAMMAR AND USAGE: After a brief review of basic English grammar, the course focuses on more advanced grammatical structures and their usage. You will learn how to better express yourself using idiomatic phrases in English.

IDIOMATIC STUDY: This section presents idiomatic expressions in English. You will learn how to express disagreement and how to make a complaint in the same way that a native English speaker does. You will also learn some popular colloquial expressions in English. This detailed vocabulary study will not only help you use the right colloquial expression, but it will also help you avoid common mistakes made by speakers of English as a second language.

STRICTLY BUSINESS: This section reviews different areas of the U.S. economy as well as historical and cultural information related to business etiquette. We discuss imports and exports and business attire and advertising. We provide useful information that will show you how to do business in the United States.

EXERCISES: This section reviews the grammar and the vocabulary that was introduced during the lesson. You may check your answers in the Answers section that appears after Lesson 20 in the book.

READING: Four readings appear in this book, after Lessons 5, 10, 15, and 20. You will be able to infer the meaning of the readings using background information from previous lessons.

REVIEW: Two review sections appear after Lessons 10 and 20. They are similar in structure to the exercises. These review sections integrate and evaluate the material presented in previous lessons.

APPENDIXES: There are four appendixes: a pronunciation table, a grammar review, a list of irregular verbs, and a section on correspondence.

VOCABULARY LIST: The vocabulary list at the end of the book is a reference guide that includes the vocabulary that has been presented in the book.

INDUSTRY-SPECIFIC TERMS: This list of industry-specific terms offers more vocabulary unique to various business industries.

INDEX: The manual ends with an index that contains all the grammatical points that are discussed in the lessons.

The appendixes, vocabulary lists, and index make this manual an excellent source for reference and future study.

RECORDINGS

This course has four hours of recorded practice material. By listening and imitating the pronunciation of the native speakers, you will improve your own pronunciation and comprehension as you learn new phrases and grammatical structures.

The recordings are designed to give four hours of listening practice in English, and they follow the dialogues presented in the twenty lessons. The recorded material is printed in bold type in the manual. Listen to the native speakers as they converse in English at a normal conversational pace. Next, you will hear the same dialogue a second time, when you will be able to repeat each phrase after the pauses in the recording.

To practice your comprehension, listen to the recording without reading along in the manual. Write a summary of what you have heard and then listen to the recording again, this time following the script in the book.

New York
45
15 fifteen

cloudy sky   (Adj + noun)
sign up sheet   (compound noun)
              noun + noun

JFK Aeroynas

LESSON 1
Arriving in the United States

A. DIALOGUE

WHERE'S MY LUGGAGE?

Gloria is a sales representative for a leather company in Argentina. This is her first trip to the United States. She's arriving in New York where she will have to clear customs and take a connecting flight to Missouri,[1] her final destination. She's sitting next to Herman, a businessman from San Francisco whom she's never met before.[2]

*friendly
pleasurable
free of trouble
calm
peace*

CAPTAIN: Ladies and gentlemen, this is the captain speaking. We will be landing in approximately 15 minutes. The current temperature at JFK[3] is 45 degrees, under cloudy skies. Flight attendants will be handing out customs declaration forms and I-94 forms.[5] Please complete them before landing.

GLORIA: Excuse me, do you have a pen I could borrow?[6]

HERMAN: Here you are.

GLORIA: Thanks. Oh, it's so bumpy. It's difficult to write. I'm sorry to bother you again, but do you happen to know the flight number?

HERMAN: Umm, it's Flight 351. *sniper end*

GLORIA: Thanks. By the way, I'm Gloria.

HERMAN: I'm Herman. Nice to meet you. Is this your first trip to the States?

GLORIA: As a matter of fact, it is. I'm very excited[7] about it. Are you from New York? *short pause*

HERMAN: No, I'm from San Francisco. I have to catch another flight in about an hour, and we still have to go through customs.

GLORIA: I understand it's a nightmare.

HERMAN: Actually,[8] it's not that bad.

FLIGHT ATTENDANT: Ladies and gentlemen, please make sure all your forms are filled out and ready along with your passport when you leave the plane. We hope you've enjoyed your trip. Thank you for flying United.

GLORIA: Thanks for the pen, and have a good trip to San Francisco.

5

HERMAN: You, too. Enjoy your stay.

Later at the Baggage Claim area.

GLORIA: Excuse me, where did you get that cart?

ANOTHER PASSENGER: Sorry, lady, I'm afraid I can't help you. I've got to get my bags. Why don't you ask the skycap[9] over there?

GLORIA: Excuse me, I need to get one of those carts.

SKYCAP: They're on the other side of the hall under the sign that says Baggage Carts.

GLORIA: Thanks. Do they cost anything?

SKYCAP: A dollar fifty.

GLORIA: Oh, no. I don't have any change.[10] Do you have change for a twenty?

SKYCAP: I'm afraid not. There's a currency exchange counter over there, on the right, ma'am. I'm sure they'll be able to help you.

GLORIA: Thank you. You've been very helpful.

Gloria gets some change, picks up a cart, and waits near the baggage carousel for a long time without seeing her suitcases.

HERMAN: Hi there! You look a little worried. Anything I can help you with?

GLORIA: Well, I've been standing here forever, and my suitcases are nowhere to be found. They're filled with leather bags and shoes for the trade show in St. Louis tomorrow. I just can't afford to lose them. Look, almost everyone else already has their stuff!

HERMAN: The problem is you're standing at the wrong carousel. This one is for Flight 361; ours was 351.

GLORIA: I'm so embarrassed![11] I should have worn my glasses. Thank you so much.

HERMAN: No problem. Come on, I'll help you get your baggage.

B. NOTES

1. The state of Missouri is located in the Great Plains, to the west of the Mississippi River. One of the most famous cities of this area is St. Louis, also known as the Gateway to the West, because of its gigantic landmark arch. The city was founded in 1784 by French explorers.

Today, it is the headquarters of large companies such as Anheuser-Busch and McDonnell Douglas, among others.

2. The city of San Francisco is in the state of California. It is a relatively small city, famous for its architecture, hills, steep streets, and the impressive Golden Gate Bridge. Among its neighborhoods are the famous Chinatown; Nob Hill with its huge mansions; SoMa, or South of Market, known for its art galleries; and the Financial District, with its skyscrapers and beautiful views of the bay.

3. Most Americans use the abbreviation *JFK* to refer to John F. Kennedy International Airport in New York. The New York metropolitan area has two other large airports: La Guardia Airport in Queens and Newark Liberty International Airport in Newark, New Jersey.

4. In the United States temperature is measured in degrees Fahrenheit. The formula for converting from Fahrenheit to Celsius and vice versa is:

$$(°F - 32) \times \tfrac{5}{9} = °C \qquad 10°C = 50°F$$
$$(°C \times \tfrac{9}{5}) + 32 = °F \qquad 21°C = 70°F$$
$$32°C = 90°F$$

5. Form I-94 is the Department of Immigration record of entries and departures from the United States. The form confirms that you have been legally admitted into the United States. It also shows the amount of time that you are legally allowed to stay in the country. You must show this document again when you leave the country.

6. *To borrow* means "to obtain or receive something on loan." It is important not to confuse this verb with *to lend,* which means "to give or to allow someone to use something temporarily."

7. *To be excited* means "to have strong feelings or emotion." It expresses anticipation and extreme happiness. *To be excited by* often has a sexual connotation, so the expression should be used with care.

8. The adverb *actually* means "in fact" or "in reality." It is not to be confused with *currently,* which means "at the current time or presently."

9. A *skycap* is a person who helps travelers with their luggage at an airport. A similar term is *porter.* A porter works in a building or in a hotel.

10. The noun *change* describes the money of smaller denomination received in exchange for money of higher denomination. It normally refers to coins.

11. *To be embarrassed* means to feel self-conscious, ill at ease, or ashamed.

C. GRAMMAR AND USAGE

1. THE ELEMENTS OF A SENTENCE

Sentences in English have a subject and a predicate. English is stricter than other languages when it comes to word order.

English sentences may consist of a subject and a verb:

(S)	(V)
Birds	*fly.*

They may have a subject, a verb, and an object (direct or indirect):

(S)	(V)	(O)
The passenger	*called*	*the flight attendant.*

(S)	(V)	(DO)	(IO)
The passenger	*gave*	*his bag*	*to the immigration officer.*

You may add complements to the beginning, middle, or end of a sentence, but you must always follow the order of subject + verb + objects.

(S)	(V)	(DO)
The passenger, (who didn't speak English,)	*couldn't understand*	*what the official was saying.*

2. PERSONAL PRONOUNS

Pronouns are used to replace a noun, a phrase, or another pronoun in a sentence. There are two types of pronouns: those that replace the subject of the sentence, and those that replace the object of the verb.

a. Subject Pronouns

SINGULAR:	first person	*I*
	second person	*you*
	third person	*he/she/it*
PLURAL:	first person	*we*
	second person	*you*
	third person	*they*

Unlike in other languages, you cannot omit the subject of a sentence in English. It is absolutely necessary to state the subject pronoun.

Gloria called the flight attendant. She wanted a glass of water.
The flight attendant asked passengers to put their seats in the upright position. She was preparing the plane for landing.

The passengers were a little nervous when they realized they were in the middle of a storm.

The impersonal pronoun *it* is used to refer to animals, places, or objects. The impersonal pronoun is also used in expressions of time, distance, and temperature. *It* can also be used to refer to a baby whose gender you do not know.

Where is the baggage claim area? It's on the other side of the room.
Look at that dog! It's an airport police dog.
That baby looks sick. It cried throughout the entire trip.

You can use the pronoun *it* with impersonal expressions, especially those related to the weather:

It's raining.
What time is it? It's six.
What's today's date? It's the third of March.
What day is it? It's Monday.

The pronoun *it* is used when the subject of a sentence is a verb in the infinitive form. In that case, *it* refers to the verb that appears after the pronoun:

It's easier to work as a flight attendant than as a waitress in a restaurant.

The subject of this sentence is: *to work as a flight attendant.* This sentence could be constructed without using the pronoun *it:*

To work as a flight attendant is easier than to work as a waitress in a restaurant.

Similarly:

It's a pity to go to New York for only three days.
To go to New York for only three days is a pity.

When the subject of the sentence is a phrase, the pronoun *it* can replace the phrase:

It never occurred to me that flying with a cold would be dangerous.

The subject of this sentence is the phrase *that flying with a cold would be dangerous.* The same sentence could be constructed without using the pronoun *it:*

That flying with a cold would be dangerous never occurred to me.
It's odd that he hasn't called to let us know he arrived.
That he hasn't called to let us know he arrived is odd.

Finally, the pronoun *it* is used to refer to a phrase or verb that was used previously in the sentence:

Although smoking on the plane is not allowed, he did it anyway.
He suggested flying, but I thought it would cost too much.

b. Object Pronouns

		DIRECT AND INDIRECT OBJECTS
SINGULAR:	first person	*me*
	second person	*you*
	third person	*him/her/it*
PLURAL:	first person	*us*
	second person	*you*
	third person	*them*

In English, object pronouns are different from subject pronouns in all cases except the second-person singular and plural forms. The subject and object pronouns have the same form: *you.*

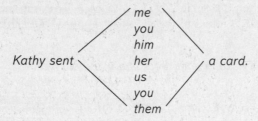

Kathy sent — *me / you / him / her / us / you / them* — *a card.*

In English the indirect object may be placed before the direct object:

(S)	(V)	(IO)	(DO)
I	*gave*	*the immigration officer*	*my passport.*
I	*gave*	*him*	*my passport.*

When the indirect object follows the direct object, the indirect object is preceded by the preposition *to* or *for:*

(S)	(V)	(DO)	(IO)
I	*gave*	*my passport*	*to the immigration officer.*
I	*gave*	*my passport*	*to him.*
I	*gave*	*it*	*to him.*

(S)	(V)	(DO)	(IO)
She	*bought*	*a round-trip ticket*	*for Mary.*

| She | bought | a round-trip ticket | for her. |
| She | bought it | for her. | |

3. THERE + TO BE

The phrase *there + to be* is used to indicate the existence of something.

There is a customs declaration form you have to fill out.
There is a mistake.

Notice that although the word *there* appears to be the subject of the sentence, the real subject is the noun that appears after the verb *to be*. If the noun following *there + to be* is singular, the verb *to be* takes the singular form, if it is plural, it takes the plural form.

There were twenty passengers who lost their luggage.
There was a mistake.

D. IDIOMATIC STUDY

INTRODUCTIONS

When you meet someone for the first time, it is customary to give a firm handshake. When you want someone to meet a person that you already know, you use the verb *to introduce*.

FORMAL INTRODUCTIONS
I'd like to introduce you to _____.
Let me introduce you to _____.
I'd like you to meet _____.

INFORMAL INTRODUCTIONS
This is _____.
I'd like to introduce you to one of my colleagues, Mr. John Smith. John, this is Sarah Jones, our new director.

FORMAL ANSWERS
(I'm) pleased to meet you.
(I'm) happy to meet you.

INFORMAL ANSWERS
(It's) nice to meet you. (It's) nice meeting you.
(I'm) glad to meet you.
It's been a pleasure meeting you.

When you initiate a conversation with someone you do not know, you may use one of these phrases:

(Excuse me, but) I don't think we've met. My name is _____.
Allow me to introduce myself.

English speakers generally use short phrases when greeting someone. You are not expected to give a long and detailed answer:

Good morning.	*How are you doing?*
Good afternoon.	*How have you been?*
Good evening.	*Fine, thanks.*
How do you do?	*Very well, thank you.*
How are you?	

Other common phrases that are more informal include the following:

Hello.	*How are things?*
Hi.	*All right.*
What's up?	*Okay.*
What's new?	*Not bad.*
How's it going?	

E. STRICTLY BUSINESS

1. ENTRY FORMS

Foreigners who plan to visit the United States must have a valid current passport. When you arrive in the United States, it is recommended that you register your passport with the consulate or embassy of your country. If you register, you will be able to get a replacement more easily in the event that your passport is lost or stolen. The U.S. government requires that your passport be valid for at least six months past the date of your initial entry into the country.

You are also required to obtain a valid visa. Visas are issued by a government official in the United States embassy or consulate in your country. You will be issued either a permanent visa (as the spouse or relative of a United States citizen) or a temporary visa. The visa indicates the date that you will be allowed to enter the country and the number of visits that you are entitled to after that date. The United States Citizenship and Immigration Services officer who examines your passport when you enter the United States is the person who will determine how long you will be allowed to stay in the country. There are several different types of temporary visas, depending on the reason for your visit:

• F-1 Academic Student Visa. This visa is for full-time students who have been accepted by American universities or colleges.

- M-1 Vocational Student Visa. This visa is for full-time students who have been accepted by technical or vocational schools.
- J-1 Exchange Visitor Visa. This visa is for exchange students (generally for students following a graduate program) who need to be in the country to do research or complete academic studies.
- H-1 Temporary Work Status for Foreign Nationals. This type of visa is for foreigners who come to the country to work on a provisional, non-permanent basis.

For more information regarding the different types of visas and the requirements for each, visit the Department of State's Web site (www.travel.state.gov/visa_services.html).

2. SOCIAL ETIQUETTE

The United States has a particularly complex and diverse society. When you travel from one region to another, you will find that different regions have some major differences in etiquette. However, some customs are standard to the whole country. Americans are very particular when it comes to their physical space. It is important to maintain a certain distance when speaking to someone, especially in a more formal situation. You should also avoid touching or patting the person to whom you are speaking. Americans feel uncomfortable if the person speaking to them is standing too close to them. The appropriate distance is one meter between the two speakers. Physical contact is only appropriate when the person wants to show affection in a more informal situation with friends and family.

It is customary to shake hands when meeting someone for the first time. Hugging and patting on the back are not appropriate in this type of situation. When greeting someone, you may want to extend your hand, but normally the greeting is done only in a verbal manner without physical contact. When saying goodbye in a formal or business situation, you may shake hands but you should avoid hugs, pats on the back, or other forms of physical contact.

In formal or business situations with people who are older than you, it is customary to use the person's title—Mr., Mrs., or Ms.—followed by the person's last name, unless that person tells you that he or she prefers to be called by his or her first name.

A: Good morning, Mr. Smith.
B: Good morning, and please call me John.

Generally, women prefer the title Ms., which can be used to refer to women who are either single or married. This term is useful when you are not aware of the woman's marital status.

3. VOCABULARY

abroad	to declare
actually	departure
arrival	duty-free
baggage	gate
baggage carousel	ground transportation
baggage claim	immigration
to be embarrassed	to land
to be excited	luggage
to board	skycap
to borrow	to take off
change	visa
customs	

EXERCISES

1. Complete the following sentences using the appropriate subject or object pronouns.

Immigration Officer:	May _(a)_ see your passport, please.
Passenger:	Yes, of course.
Immigration Officer:	Are these your bags?
Passenger:	Yes, _(b)_ are.
Immigration Officer:	Who packed _(c)_?
Passenger:	I did.
Immigration Officer:	Do _(d)_ have any agricultural products?
Passenger:	No, _(e)_ don't.
Immigration Officer:	Are _(f)_ carrying currency worth more than $10,000 dollars?
Passenger:	No, _(g)_ only have traveler's checks.
Immigration Officer:	Could _(h)_ please put your bag on this counter and open _(i)_ for me? Are these gifts?
Passenger:	Yes. I bought _(j)_ for my family.
Immigration Officer:	What is the total value of all the goods _(k)_ purchased abroad?
Passenger:	About $700.
Immigration Officer:	Are any family members traveling with _(l)_?
Passenger:	Yes, my son. _(m)_ already went through customs and is waiting for _(n)_ over there.
Immigration Officer:	_(o)_ seems that everything is in order. Thank you and welcome to the United States.

2. Replace the underlined nouns with pronouns in each of the following paragraphs.

When you arrive at the airport you can have a taxi drive you to your hotel. The taxi dispatcher will give you the taxi's identification number. (a) The identification number can be used to identify the taxi in case there is a problem.

Every major airport has a currency exchange counter. (b) The currency exchange counter is the place where you should go to exchange currency or get change.

Your passport is your most important identification document when you are outside your country of residence. (c) The passport is normally issued in your country. When you arrive in a foreign country, an immigration officer will ask you to give (d) the passport to him/her. (e) The immigration officer will review (f) the passport. (g) The officer will also check that you have a current visa.

One of the passengers on this morning's flight got sick. He was described as a male in his late forties. Cathy, the flight attendant, took care of (h) *the sick passenger* until the paramedics arrived. (i) The flight attendant gave the man some oxygen. (j) The man had suffered a heart attack. The doctor said (k) the heart attack was not serious. The doctor also said (l) the man would be well soon.

3. Complete the following sentences with *there + to be.*

   a. _____ no agricultural products in my bag.
   b. _____ several flights landing at the same time.
   c. _____ a different form for U.S. citizens.
   d. _____ not enough time for me to make my connection.
   e. _____ a few delays at the airport due to the weather.
   f. _____ some questions we'd like to ask you.
   g. _____ no reason for you to empty the contents of my suitcase.
   h. _____ a rent-a-car counter at the end of the hall.
   i. _____ public buses and trains you can take to the airport.
   j. _____ a mistake on this form.

4. Fill in the blanks with the appropriate word (not all words will be used).

lend	excited	actually	present	embarrassed
presently	borrow	exciting	actual	

   a. I was so _____ when I couldn't remember the name of Tom's wife.
   b. My car won't start. May I _____ yours?
   c. The _____ retail price of that dress is $150. I'm giving it to you for the bargain price of $80.
   d. Ann is very _____ about her trip to Europe.

e. I don't like to _____ my clothes to anyone.
f. Two of our dearest friends are _____ visiting us.

5. Rewrite the following sentences to show the real subject.

EXAMPLE:
It's scary to fly through a storm.
To fly through a storm is scary.

a. For most international flights, it's required to arrive at the airport two hours prior to departure.
b. It's annoying to have to wait for a connecting flight.
c. It's necessary to make flight reservations ahead of time during the holiday season.
d. It's important to eat something before getting on the plane.

LESSON 2
Family Relations

A. DIALOGUE

"CONVERSATIONS WITH CAMILA"

The popular television talk show[1] Conversations with Camila is taped in Los Angeles, California.[2] It airs every day at 4 P.M. and is watched[3] by millions across the country. Unlike many other talk shows, this one focuses on family matters.

CAMILA: Welcome to *Conversations with Camila.* In the past we've done several shows on moms.[4] Well, today's show focuses on dads[4] instead. Many of you are familiar with today's very special guest, psychologist Alfonso Cassid. His latest and very controversial book, *Fatherly Instincts,* has just been published to critical acclaim and commercial success. Dr. Alfonso Cassid is the founder of the Center for Fathers in Richmond, Virginia, where he offers counseling services. Please give a warm welcome to Dr. Alfonso Cassid.

The audience applauds and cheers.

CAMILA: Welcome to our show Dr. Cassid.

DR. CASSID: Thank you. It's a pleasure to be here.

CAMILA: Tell us a little bit about the Center for Fathers.

DR. CASSID: Well, our center has been operating since 1991. It's basically a place for men[5] to learn more about fatherhood.[6] You see, most men who become fathers find themselves woefully[7] unprepared. Many of today's fathers act as absentee benefactors, leaving their wives[5] to deal with the more important aspects of parenthood.

CAMILA: Do you mean to say that men[5] are poor[8] fathers because historically it's been the woman's[9] role to nurture and raise the kids?

DR. CASSID: Well, I can only speak of what's happened in the United States. The historical situation and development may be quite different in other countries. But if you look at the history of this country, fathers were intimately involved with their children up until the Industrial Revolution.[10] They worked at home as farmers, smiths, or carpenters. Therefore, they were around to take part in their children's upbringing by teaching them their art or craft.

CAMILA: In other words, fathers were in charge of their children's[9] professional education.

DR. CASSID: Exactly. The industrial revolution caused changes in family relationships. Fathers were forced to look for work outside their homes, and women had to take over the burden of nurturing and educating the children all by themselves. The father's role became that of the financial provider. Emotional support became the mother's domain.

CAMILA: Somebody from the audience is raising his hand. Yes, sir. What is your question?

PERSON IN THE AUDIENCE: I'm a father of two, and I work full-time. I find it very hard to set aside time for my family. Do you think that most of the problems we as fathers have today are due[11] to a lack of time or a lack of emotion?

DR. CASSID: Neither, actually. While it is true that some fathers often have less time to spend with their[12] kids than mothers do, it is not true that they lack emotion. The problem is that most fathers do not have a role model. Most of the men who come to me have fathers who were never there[12] for them emotionally, and often not even physically.

CAMILA: Most of our fathers were concerned about putting food on the table[13] and making ends meet.[14]

DR. CASSID: You're absolutely right. Our fathers didn't know any different. So, while I believe that fathers today want to have an active part in their children's upbringing, they feel that they're moving into a territory they don't have a map for.

CAMILA: What do you think are the most difficult times for a father?

DR. CASSID: Many men come to counseling during the initial stages of fatherhood. A first-time father often feels a sense of loss when his baby arrives. All of a sudden his wife is giving all of her attention to the newborn.

CAMILA: A tinge of jealousy?

DR. CASSID: Correct. However, with the wife's reassurance, these

18

problems are easy to overcome. Another extremely difficult time for a father to go through is his son's or daughter's adolescence.

CAMILA: You mean that fathers, like mothers, find it difficult to let go?

DR. CASSID: Some men might find it difficult to let go. Men feel they are losing[15] their youth. All of a sudden they look at themselves in the mirror and realize[16] they're getting old. Also, at this time most men are going through their midlife crisis. So, it becomes a particularly tough time for all.

CAMILA: There's another comment from the audience. Yes, ma'am . . .

PERSON IN THE AUDIENCE: I'm a single mother of three children and I'm going through the same thing. I think most mothers also feel that way.

DR. CASSID: I'm sure they do. Most parents, but particularly fathers, go through power struggles with their adolescent children about curfews, dating, drinking, and the like. This destabilizes the entire family and increases the sense of loss most parents feel when their children become adults. Parents realize that not only their children are entering a new phase of life, but they themselves are as well. Traditionally women have been more adept at dealing with this than men.

CAMILA: We have to take a commercial break. When we come back we'll talk to a single father of three who says Dr. Cassid has changed his life. Stay tuned.

B. NOTES

1. Talk shows are very popular television programs in the United States. These programs follow a question and answer format where both the host and the audience participate in the questioning of the guests. Some of the more popular talk shows are hosted by Oprah Winfrey, Jenny Jones, and Ricki Lake, but more are constantly being added and cancelled. Talk shows generally deal with social issues or family relations. Typically, these shows feature a guest who is an expert in his field; he or she is invited to give his or her opinion and guidance regarding the topic that is being discussed.

2. Los Angeles is a city in the state of California, on the west coast of the

United States. This city is famous for its beaches and, of course, its movie industry. Many famous artists live in the Los Angeles area. Los Angeles is also home to many groups of immigrants, which makes it one of the most ethnically diverse cities in the United States. The city has other important attractions, such as the Contemporary Art Museum, Chinatown, and the Hollywood area, where you'll find the Capitol Records building and the Walk of Fame, featuring the names of famous stars in the world of entertainment. Many motion pictures, such as Universal Studios, Warner Brothers, and Walt Disney Pictures, have headquarters here.

3. There is a difference between the verbs *to see* and *to look. To see* means "to perceive with the eye" whereas *to look* means "to direct one's eyes in one direction." In other words, the verb *to look* denotes intention while *to see* is a more passive action.

   After the surgery, she could not see for a few days.
   I looked at him and realized that he did not know what to do.

   There is also the verb *to watch,* which means "to observe or to look with attention." This verb also means "to act as guard or sentinel," "to take care of," or "to look after."

   to watch a movie/the news/a film/a program
   I was watching the ten o'clock news when the phone rang.
   Please, watch the children while I go to the store.

4. The words *mom* and *dad* are more informal ways of referring to your mother and father.

5. Some nouns such as *man* and *wife* have irregular plural forms: *men, wives.* Please see Lesson 3 for a more detailed explanation.

6. The suffix or ending *-hood* is used to designate a period or stage in the life of a person. Fatherhood refers to the stage after a man becomes a father. The suffix *-hood* could be added to other nouns. Here are some examples:

parent	→	*parenthood*
mother	→	*motherhood*
adult	→	*adulthood*
child	→	*childhood*

   There are also the words *sisterhood* and *brotherhood,* which refer to religious congregations or societies (in Lesson 20 we will discuss suffixes and prefixes further).

7. *Woe* is a noun that means "deep distress or misery." The adverb form is *woefully,* which means "awfully."

8. In this context the adjective *poor* does not refer to poverty or lack of money. In this context it means "deficient or inadequate."

9. Note that the possessive form in English is formed by adding an apostrophe and an -*s* to the end of the word. For a more detailed explanation about this topic, see Lesson 12.

   the woman's role
   the children's professional education

10. The industrial revolution refers to the social and economic changes that took place in the 19th century as a result of the development of new machinery and tools. These new technological changes led to rapid industrial growth.

11. *Due,* when used as an adjective, means "payable immediately," "owed as a debt," or "anticipated." When it is used before the preposition *to,* it means "because of."

    The due date for that project is March 1.
    With all due respect, I think you're making a mistake.
    The train is due at six.
    Due to bad weather, the airports are closed.

12. It is important to learn to differentiate the homophones *their, they're,* and *there. Their* is the possessive pronoun of the third-person plural. *They're* is the contracted form of *they are.* (For a more detailed explanation about the difference between possessive pronouns and possessive forms using a contraction, go to Lesson 12.) *There* is an adverb that expresses direction; it is the opposite of *here. There* can also be used with the verb *to be* (*there is/are/was/were*) to indicate the existence of something. (For a more detailed explanation, go to Lesson 1.)

    Their fathers never supported them emotionally.
    They're coming to the center next week.
    There are about 50 fathers working there now.

13. *To put food on the table* is a common colloquial expression. It means "to provide for" or "to be the main provider." It implies that the person who is the main provider is generally the person who pays for food and household expenses.

14. *To make ends meet* is a colloquial phrase that is used frequently to indicate that the person is living with just enough income to take care of the basic necessities. The phrase generally suggests that the money being earned is not enough, and the person needs more.

15. The pronunciation of the verb *to lose* is similar to the adjective *loose;*

this normally confuses students of English as a second language. The difference is that the verb form is pronounced with a stronger and more sonorous s (similar to a z sound), while the adjective maintains a softer s sound.

16. The verb *to realize* means "to comprehend completely."

    I realize that you have been working very hard on this project.

C. GRAMMAR AND USAGE

1. THE SIMPLE PRESENT

a. Form

AFFIRMATIVE CASE

In its affirmative case, the simple present form of a verb has the same form as the infinitive. To create the simple present, remove *to* from the infinitive form. This form is also known as the simple form of the verb. It is important to remember that you need to add an -s to the third-person singular form *(he/she)*.

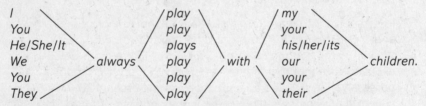

The verbs *to have, to be,* and *to do* are exceptions that we will study in Lesson 8.

Add -es to the third-person singular form of the verb if the verb ends in *o, ss, sh, ch,* or *x.*

to go	She goes to school Monday through Friday.
to fix	My mother always fixes dinner for us on Sundays.
to teach	Every Sunday he teaches his son how to play chess.

There is a different rule for verbs that end in a consonant followed by *y.* In those cases, change the *y* to *i* and add -es. If the verb ends in a vowel followed by a *y,* add an -s.

to carry	He carries his books in his backpack.
to obey	She never obeys the teacher.

NEGATIVE CASE

The negative of the present simple is formed by conjugating the auxiliary verb *to do* and adding the main verb in its simple form. The format for the negative form is the following:

> subject pronoun + *do/does* + *not* + main verb in its simple form

Notice the contracted form in parenthesis.

I do not (don't) read stories to them.
You do not (don't) need to be a psychologist to be a good dad.
He does not (doesn't) understand the importance of spending a few hours a day with the children.

THE INTERROGATIVE CASE

The short answer interrogative case is formed by following this format:

> *Do/Does* + subject pronoun + main verb in its simple form . . . ?

Do you read stories to your children before they go to bed?
Yes, I do./No, I don't.
Does he think that men are poor parents because they lack a role model?
Yes, he does./No, he doesn't.

For long answer questions follow this format:

> *When/what/where/why/who/how* + *do/does* + subject pronoun + main verb in its simple form . . . ?

Where do your parents live now?
They live in Los Angeles.
How does your father communicate his emotions?
He cries when he's sad.

b. Usage

The present simple is used to express events that happen with frequency or habitually. Generally you use adverbs of frequency such as:

always
every day/year
sometimes
often
frequently

seldom
never

My husband always takes the kids to school.
The show airs at 4 P.M. every day.

The simple present is used to state a general fact.

Most toddlers play with blocks.
Parents make a lot of sacrifices for their children.

Finally, it is used for planned events that will occur in the future.

The plane leaves tomorrow at 8 A.M.

2. THE PRESENT CONTINUOUS

a. Form

AFFIRMATIVE CASE
The present continuous is formed by using the simple present of the verb *to be* and the present participle of the main verb:

$$am/is/are + verb + -ing$$

Note the contracted form in parenthesis:

You are (you're) watching a TV show now.
They are (they're) talking about what it takes to be a good parent.
I am (I'm) taking a course in child psychology.

NEGATIVE CASE
The negative case is formed by following this format:

$$Subject + am/is/are + not + verb + -ing$$

The contracted form appears in parenthesis.

I am (I'm) not counseling them now.
She is not (isn't) taping any shows this summer.
They are not (aren't) taking the program seriously.

INTERROGATIVE CASE
Short answer questions are formed by changing the word order of the sentence:

$$Am/Is/Are + subject\ pronoun + verb + -ing \ldots ?$$

Are you teaching them to be better parents?
Yes, I am. / No, I'm not.
Is he watching the program?
Yes, he is. / No, he isn't.
Are they going to take the course on how to survive a midlife crisis?
Yes, they are. / No, they're not.

For questions with complete answers:

> *When/what/where/why/who/how + am/is/are*
> *+ subject pronoun + verb + -ing . . . ?*

What are you watching?
I'm watching Oprah.
How is the psychologist helping you?
He's not helping me at all.

SPELLING RULES

If the verb ends in *e*, you need to eliminate the *e* and add *-ing*. If the verb ends in *ee*, you do not eliminate the last *e*.

hope	*hoping*
become	*becoming*
prepare	*preparing*
flee	*fleeing*

If the verb consists of only one syllable and ends in one vowel followed by a consonant (except *w* and *x*), duplicate the final consonant and add *-ing.*

stop	*stopping*
rob	*robbing*
beg	*begging*

If the verb consists of only one syllable and ends in two vowels followed by a consonant, add *-ing*.

rain	*raining*
dream	*dreaming*
sleep	*sleeping*

If the verb consists of two syllables with the stress on the first syllable, add *-ing*.

cancel	*canceling*
offer	*offering*
travel	*traveling*

If the verb consists of two syllables and the stress is on the second syllable, then duplicate the final consonant and add -ing.

begin	*beginning*
prefer	*preferring*
control	*controlling*

If the verb ends in two consonants or in *y*, add -ing.

start	*starting*
demand	*demanding*
enjoy	*enjoying*
buy	*buying*

If the verb ends in *ie*, then you need to replace the *ie* with a *y* and add -ing.

die	*dying*
lie	*lying*
tie	*tying*

b. Usage

The present continuous is used to express an action or event that is occurring at the same moment you are speaking or writing.

The television crew is preparing the stage for the next show.
The audience is clapping and cheering because the host has just walked onto the stage.

It can also be used to emphasize an action or event that is not permanent.

They are taping the show on location for a few weeks.

Finally, it can be used to refer to an action that will occur in the future.

Our neighbors are leaving on vacation tomorrow morning.
He's going to the Center for Fathers on Tuesday for counseling.

c. Exceptions

There are certain verbs that do not use the present continuous. These are verbs that describe feelings or state of being and do not express a continuous action.

VERBS THAT EXPRESS MENTAL STATE OF BEING

to believe	*to prefer*
to doubt	*to realize*
to feel	*to recognize*
to forget	*to remember*
to imagine	*to suppose*

to know	to think
to mean	to understand
to need	to want

VERBS THAT EXPRESS EMOTIONAL STATE OF BEING

to appreciate	to hate
to care	to like
to envy	to love
to dislike	to mind
to fear	

VERBS THAT EXPRESS POSSESSION

to belong
to possess
to own

VERBS THAT EXPRESS SENSES

to hear	to see

OTHER CASES

to consist of	to include
to contain	to look like
to cost	to owe
to exist	to seem

D. IDIOMATIC STUDY

ASKING FOR CLARIFICATION

There are times when you don't understand something and need to request clarification. The following phrases are useful for asking someone to explain something to you:

What do you mean (by that)?
What does that mean?
Could you clarify that for me?

You may also use these phrases, which are less direct and a bit more formal:

I'm afraid I'm not following you.
I'm not really sure what you're getting at.
I'm not quite clear as to what you mean (by that).

Or you may want to paraphrase what you just heard:

Do you mean (to say) _____?

Are you saying _____?
Does that mean _____?

CLARIFYING
The following phrases are useful to explain or clarify what you are trying to say:

Let me put it this way.
Let me put it another way.
What I'm (really) saying is . . .
What I mean is . . .
What I'm getting at is . . .
In other words . . .

E. STRICTLY BUSINESS

1. FAMILY STRUCTURE IN THE UNITED STATES
Every ten years the Census Bureau of the United States gathers information about the residents of the country and investigates the changes that have transformed American families over the decade. The department analyzes this information to examine important aspects such as the size, habits and structure of the American family. After studying the data, the bureau has concluded that the traditional family is a thing of the past.

According to Census 2000, the traditional family composed of a father, mother, and children under the age of 18 is disappearing. In 1970, 40 percent of families were traditional families; in 1980 the number fell to 31 percent while in 1990 only 26 percent of all families consisted of a father, mother, and children. According to the last census of 2000, more than 70 percent of families in the United States were made of single parents and their children, divorced parents with their children, couples without children, parents with older children, or adults with no blood relations sharing a house. Even more surprising was the increase in the number of single fathers (as opposed to single mothers) as heads of household. The number of families led by a single father increased 62 percent over the last decade, while the number of families led by a single mother increased by 25 percent. Although the number of single fathers living with children is less than the number of single mothers, the growth rate was more than double that of single mothers. The number of single-father homes grew from 1,354,540 in 1990 to 2,190,989 in 2000.

According to social workers and other experts, this increase should not come as a surprise. Men have greater interest these days in exerting their parental rights. Also, as more women are incorporated fully into the labor force, they do not feel as guilty as they were made to feel decades ago for not being the primary parent figure in the house. There has also been greater interest in the importance of the father's role in raising children. That is why more judges than ever before grant parental custody to single fathers.

For more information about Census 2000 and other interesting facts, visit the U.S. Census Bureau's Web site at www.census.gov.

2. VOCABULARY

absentee	to nurture
adolescence	out of wedlock
adulthood	parenthood
baby-sitter	parents
childhood	relatives
dad	siblings
day-care center	single
divorced	talk show
home	upbringing
married	U.S. Census Bureau
mom	widow
motherhood	widower

EXERCISES

---

1. Complete the following sentences using *their, they're,* or *there.*

   a. _____ fathers were men who worked at home as carpenters, smiths, or farmers.
   b. _____ coming to the center to find out more about parenthood.
   c. _____ are a number of men who are truly concerned about _____ children's emotions.
   d. The center is _____ to help fathers deal with _____ fears and expectations about fatherhood.
   e. _____ two of the best psychologists I know. We're lucky _____ working for us.
   f. _____ fathers were never _____ physically or emotionally.

2. Complete the following sentences using *to lose* or *loose.*

   a. When my father sits on the couch he _____ the _____ change in his pockets.
   b. I never _____ any sleep over my problems.
   c. Many parents feel they will _____ their children when they become adults.

d. My father doesn't like me wearing _____ clothes.

e. If you _____ your father when you're young, you also _____ one of your best role models.

3. Use either the simple present or the present continuous to complete the following sentences.

   a. Dr. Cassid _____ (to write) another book this year.

   b. Today, more than ever, fathers _____ (to try) to improve their parenting skills.

   c. We _____ (to begin) each day with a group session. Each man _____ (to talk) a little about his experiences with his own father and his children. We _____ (to want) them to open up and to feel comfortable talking about their feelings.

   d. Today, the roles of men and women _____ (to change) very quickly. Men _____ (to begin) to understand that they _____ (to need) to be there both financially and emotionally for their children.

   e. When children become adolescents, fathers _____ (to feel) a sense of loss and abandonment. They _____ (to realize) that they _____ (to get) old.

4. Change the following sentences to the negative form. Use contractions where possible.

   a. Most of the problems fathers have today are due to a lack of time.

   b. The host is interviewing fathers for her show today.

   c. Fathers today want to provide financial support.

   d. My husband is going through a midlife crisis.

   e. Many fathers find it difficult to let go of their children.

   f. The television crew is taping two shows today.

   g. Most fathers give their children emotional support.

   h. This show airs every day at 4 P.M.

   i. Some people in the audience know Dr. Cassid.

   j. He wants to ask him a question.

   k. The center solves all of your problems.

LESSON 3
Computers in the Workplace

A. DIALOGUE

THE COMPANY THAT WASN'T

Frank Williams is a recent college graduate with a degree in business administration. A few weeks ago, he sent his resumé to several companies in his hometown of San Antonio, Texas.[1] Today he has an interview with Alamo Mutual Funds, a respected investment firm.

RECEPTIONIST: May I help you?

FRANK: Yes, my name is Frank Williams, and I have a ten o'clock appointment with Judy Dobbs.

RECEPTIONIST: Please have a seat. She'll be with you shortly.

JUDY: Frank? Good morning! I'm Judy Dobbs. Nice to meet you.

FRANK: Nice to meet you, too. Sorry I'm a little late . . .

JUDY: That's all right. Traffic can be pretty bad.

FRANK: Actually, there wasn't much traffic. I wasn't sure if I had the right address or not. I guess I was expecting a large office building. . . .

JUDY: Well, we used to have our own building downtown. But about six months ago, we created this virtual office environment. We still have over a hundred investment brokers working for us, but now just about everybody works from home.

FRANK: Oh yeah! I heard about these types of companies in one of my management courses. Exactly how does a virtual office work?

JUDY: It's pretty simple, really. In this business, just about everything is done with a computer and a telephone. All we had to do was move the equipment we had in the old building to the homes of our employees and hook them up to our network.

FRANK: But don't people ever need to come into the office?

JUDY: No, not really. Since our brokers spend most of the day on the phone, they can do their job just as easily from home. They can also access up-to-the-minute information on stocks, bonds, and mutual funds via the Internet. Whenever they do[2] have a scheduled meeting, they almost always go to their client's home or office.

31

FRANK: But what about your own staff meetings?

JUDY: We rely on teleconferencing. We can hear each other and hold[3] open discussions on the phone just as well as we can in person. Managers just have to send out e-mail with the time for everyone to dial in.[4]

FRANK: Speaking of managers . . . how do they monitor their employees?

JUDY: That wasn't much of a concern for us. Since most of our employees earn commission, they have to work hard regardless of where they are. However, we were surprised to see our quarterly earnings increase by almost ten percent in the first three months.

FRANK: That's pretty amazing. What brought that on?[5] Higher interest rates and stock dividends? Are people just investing more now that the economy is picking up?[6]

JUDY: Those factors have some bearing,[7] I'm sure. But most importantly, our brokers simply work better from home. Based on the needs of their clients, our employees decide how much they have to work and when. They really enjoy this flexibility, and they work with greater efficiency.

FRANK: So, what's this office for?

JUDY: Management decided that we still needed an office, although a very small one. The network mainframe is here, so MIS[8] is here as well. We also have an 800 number[9] for new clients, so we rotate a few brokers in every day to handle inquiries and generate new leads. And, of course, we still have people drop by with deliveries and mail, so a receptionist is needed as well. — extra info

FRANK: Wow! It seems so strange, but I guess there's really no reason for your employees to come to work in an office.

JUDY: Not at all. It's an arrangement that more and more companies are seriously considering. It makes sense financially because it cuts down on operating costs. And it makes all the employees happy because they can make better use of their time to do what they really enjoy doing.

FRANK: This is very interesting.

JUDY: Now, what about this job interview I was supposed to be conducting here? You've been doing all the interviewing!

FRANK: I'm sorry . . .

JUDY: Don't worry about it. I like an employee who can ask a good question every once in a while!

B. NOTES

1. The state of Texas is in the southwest United States. The state capital is Austin. San Antonio is one of the most beautiful cities in Texas. The Alamo is located in San Antonio. It stands as a monument to the 189 volunteers who died in 1836 during the 13-day blockade of Mexican dictator General Santa Ana. Another important city in Texas is Houston. Houston, the fourth largest city in the United States, is an important center or international commerce.

2. As we have seen in previous chapters, the verb *to do* is generally used as an auxiliary verb with other verbs to produce the negative form and the interrogative form. If you use the verb *to do* in the affirmative form, it emphasizes the action of the main verb.

   I don't know much about the Internet, but I do know there are different service providers.
   He doesn't know about computers, but I do.

3. The verb *to hold* in the context of the dialogue means "to have a meeting or session." It can also have other meanings:

   to have an official job title
   He holds the office of governor.

   to make someone fulfill an obligation
   They held him to his promise.

   to believe
   We hold these truths to be self-evident.

   to host, to facilitate, to conduct, to organize
   Athens will hold the next Olympic games.

   to be true, valid, or certain
   The theory that there once was life on Mars still holds.

4. Notice that *to dial* means "to make a phone call." However, with new technological advances, the verb's meaning has shifted to incorporate the use of computers. In this case, it is used with the preposition *in* and it means "to communicate/have access to." It can also be used with the preposition *up* to mean "to use a phone line to connect a computer to the Internet." As the number of computers using cable lines to maintain constant connectivity to the Internet increases, this phrase is becoming increasingly rare.

5. *To bring on/about* means "to cause" or "to accomplish something." There are other expressions that use the verb *to bring:*

to bring back	"to return"
to bring down	"to cause a downfall, to capture, to kill"
to bring forth	"to produce"
to bring up	"to rear, to educate a child, to introduce a subject into conversation"
to bring down the house	"to make the audience applaud or cheer in approval"

6. In the context of the dialogue, the verb *to pick up* means "to get better." It may also mean "to raise" or "to start a conversation with a stranger, usually with romantic intentions." Other expressions with the verb *to pick* are:

to pick out	"to choose"
to pick on someone	"to bother or tease someone"
to pick at something	"to pull something with your fingers"

7. The expression *to have bearing* means "to have importance."

8. *MIS* is the acronym for Management Information Services. Generally it refers to the department that is in charge of administering and maintaining the communication systems of a company.

9. In the United States any company can order a toll-free number for its clients. These numbers are generally known as 800 numbers because the original area code given to toll-free numbers was 800. These numbers have become so popular that more three-digit area codes were added to accommodate the demand for toll-free numbers. Other three-digit toll-free area codes are 866, 877, and 888. To find the toll-free number for a particular company, visit www.inter800.com.

C. GRAMMAR AND USAGE

1. NOUNS
There are two broad categories of nouns in English: countable and noncountable nouns.

a. Countable Nouns
As the name implies, countable nouns are those that can be counted as independent units. These nouns have singular or plural forms. The plural of most countable nouns is formed by adding an *-s* to the end of the noun:

computer(s)
desk(s)
street(s)
page(s)
cable(s)

If the noun ends in *sh, ch, ss,* or *x,* add *-es* to the end of the noun:

wish(es)
match(es)
business(es)
fax(es)

If the noun ends in a consonant followed by *y,* change the *y* to an *i* and add *-es:*

technology	*technologies*
industry	*industries*
country	*countries*

If the noun ends in *fe* or *f,* change the ending to *v,* and add *-es:*

wife	*wives*
knife	*knives*
calf	*calves*
half	*halves*
leaf	*leaves*
life	*lives*
self	*selves*
shelf	*shelves*
thief	*thieves*
wolf	*wolves*

There are a few exceptions to this rule:

belief	*beliefs*
chief	*chiefs*
cliff	*cliffs*
roof	*roofs*

The plural of nouns that end in *o* is formed by adding an *-s* or an *-es* to the ending of the noun. Unfortunately, there is no rule that governs which to use; it is something you have to learn with each individual word:

tomato(es)
potato(es)
hero(es)

echo(es)
mosquito(es)
zoo(s)
radio(s)
studio(s)
piano(s)
soprano(s)
photo(s)
auto(s)

With the following nouns you can form the plural by using either one of the two forms:

zero(es)/zero(s)
volcano(es)/volcano(s)
tornado(es)/tornado(s)

There are other nouns that have plural forms that are completely irregular:

man	*men*
woman	*women*
child	*children*
person	*people*
ox	*oxen*
mouse	*mice*
louse	*lice*
foot	*feet*
goose	*geese*
tooth	*teeth*

Some words that are derived from Latin also have irregular plural forms:

memorandum	*memoranda*
phenomenon	*phenomena*
cactus	*cacti*
radius	*radii*
medium	*media*

There are some nouns that do not change in the plural form:

deer	*deer*
fish	*fish*
sheep	*sheep*
offspring	*offspring*
species	*species*

b. Noncountable Nouns

Noncountable nouns are those that denote the following:

liquids: *water, milk, soup, coffee, tea*
solids: *ice, bread, cheese, meat, glass, paper*
gases: *air, oxygen, smoke*
particles: *rice, flour, sugar, sand, salt*
abstract concepts: *luck, time, beauty, happiness, truth, wealth*
languages: *Italian, German, French, Spanish*
fields of study: *chemistry, biology, math, history*
sports: *soccer, football, baseball, basketball*
natural forces: *light, rain, snow, fog, heat, wind*
a group of items composed of similar parts: *furniture, clothing, jewelry, garbage, food*

These nouns cannot be counted since they refer to indivisible units. Because they express units, noncountable nouns do not have plural forms. The only way to express plural is by placing the mass that these nouns refer to in containers. If we separate the mass into containers, then we can count the individual parts. We can count *bottles of wine, bags of sand, moments of truth, ounces of meat, pieces of information, drops of rain,* or *grains of rice.* In some instances, you may see a plural ending added to noncountable nouns when a variety of types are being described:

Today's coffees are Colombian, kava, and hazelnut.
The cheeses that we carry from France are Camembert, Brie, and Roquefort.

2. ARTICLES

In English there are definite and indefinite articles.

INDEFINITE ARTICLE

a + noun that begins with a consonant or vowel that is pronounced like a consonant
an + noun that begins with a vowel or a silent *h*

a printer	*a university*
a cable	*a European town*
an icon	*an hour*
an error	*an honorable man*

The indefinite article *(a/an)* is used with countable nouns to refer to a nonspecific item. You do not need any articles in front of a nonspecific countable or noncountable noun.

You do not use any articles in front of the plural form of a countable or noncountable noun.

DEFINITE ARTICLE

$$\boxed{the + noun}$$

The definite article *(the)* is used in front of countable and non-countable nouns when they refer to specific items.

The following chart summarizes the usage of articles:

	NONCOUNTABLE NOUNS	COUNTABLE NOUNS	
		SINGULAR	PLURAL
GENERAL/INDEFINITE	Ø	a/an	Ø
SPECIFIC	the	the	the

NONCOUNTABLE NOUNS (GENERAL/INDEFINITE)
Software is changing our lives.
There's additional space here.

COUNTABLE NOUNS (SINGULAR, GENERAL/INDEFINITE)
A secondhand machine will not be as fast.
In an ideal situation, we'd have ten computers.

COUNTABLE NOUNS (PLURAL, GENERAL/INDEFINITE)
Color printers are more expensive than black ink printers.
Newer applications run on Windows XP.

NONCOUNTABLE NOUNS (SPECIFIC)
We need to review the software we ordered.
The space in my office is too small.

COUNTABLE NOUNS (SINGULAR, SPECIFIC)
The machine on the right is down.
The situation is more critical than I thought.

COUNTABLE NOUNS (PLURAL, SPECIFIC)
The printers are downstairs.
The applications run faster on these machines.

Notice that the indefinite article in English does not have gender or number as it does in other languages. The closest word to a plural indefinite article is *some*.

I have some documents I'd like you to take a look at.

3. QUANTITY EXPRESSIONS

When you use expressions that indicate quantity, you need to determine whether the quantity is modifying a countable or noncountable noun. Notice the cases below:

NONCOUNTABLE NOUNS	COUNTABLE NOUNS (PLURAL)
much	many
a little	a few
a lot of	a lot of
some	some
any	any
no	no

Notice that these expressions cannot be used with singular countable nouns.

How much memory does each machine have?
How many computers do we need to buy?
There is little space in this office for a computer workstation.
There are a few programs I want you to look at.
I need some time to install the software.
Some printers are not working.

4. *FEW* VS. *A FEW* AND *LITTLE* VS. *A LITTLE*

When you use an indefinite article with the expressions of quantity *few* and *little*, the phrase has a positive implication. When the article is omitted, it has a negative implication.

POSITIVE IMPLICATION
A few computers are hooked to a printer.
We have a little money left to purchase additional software.

NEGATIVE IMPLICATION
Few computers are hooked to a printer.
We have little money left to purchase additional software.

D. IDIOMATIC STUDY

INVITATIONS
These are useful phrases to use when you want to invite someone to join you:

Would you care/like to meet us for happy hour?
Would you be interested in joining us for lunch?
How about if we meet for a drink after work?

We'd like to invite you to have dinner at our place.
I'd love it if you could join me for dinner this evening.

After you invite the person, you may want to emphasize the invitation with these phrases:

I hope you can come.
We hope you can make it.
I hope you'll be able to join me/us.
Please try to come.
See you soon.
We look forward to having you over.

Here are some possible responses to an invitation:

I'd love to.
We'd like to.
I'd be happy to.
We'd be glad to come.
Thanks for inviting me.
Thank you for the invitation.
We're looking forward to it, too.
I'd love to, but I won't be able to make it.
We'd like to, but we already have a previous engagement.
I'd be delighted, but I made plans earlier.
I'm afraid I won't be able to come.

E. STRICTLY BUSINESS

1. THE VIRTUAL OFFICE

Many technological advances that took place during the 1980s revolutionized the way that Americans work in their offices. The traditional equipment that had existed for decades consisted of typewriters and traditional telephone systems. During the technological revolution of that decade, these machines were replaced with computers and technologically advanced telephones that allowed people to send voice messages and data to coworkers. Just as Americans were getting used to the new technologies, a new trend started to emerge, and it threatened to end the traditional concept of an office. The concept of the virtual office has its origins in a time when large companies with offices throughout the country implemented changes that allowed them to function in a more cohesive way. Organizational development was a goal pursued by many companies in the field of airlines, banking, and finance. These large firms wanted both clients and workers to have access to information, regardless of their location. With the widespread use of fax, telephone, and computers, employees were able to work on the same project even if they were thousands of miles away from each other. With the introduction of high-speed Internet connections, employees can now access documents and information quickly from anywhere in the world.

The success of this type of organizational style has led many smaller companies to follow the example of the larger institutions. As office space became more expensive to rent, some executives realized that they could save money if they asked their employees to work out of their own homes. Initially, many people thought the idea was too radical. After all, employees and executives were used to a daily trip to an office where they would work regardless of productivity. Until recently, few people could imagine having an office that had no predetermined physical space.

Naturally, there are certain elements that are necessary to have a successful virtual office. The main factor is technology, especially having access to high-speed Internet. To do his or her job in an efficient way, an employee must have a computer at home with easy access to the company's network. The connection to the company's network makes it possible to send and receive information to colleagues regardless of where they are. It is also possible to have phone or Internet conferences (with live image) with other employees. Technology also allows employees to communicate with other companies at a worldwide level. Companies and employees use the Internet to advertise or sell products and to obtain information about any subject. It is essential to have a sophisticated telephone system in order to establish a successful virtual office.

Unfortunately, the virtual office is only applicable to a limited number of professions. However, it has proven to be a successful organizational model for many companies that offer financial or legal services or those companies that specialize in publishing or sales. The virtual office seems to benefit both the company and the employee. The cost of the virtual office is very reasonable, because most companies that have adopted this type of organization already owned the necessary technology. Additionally, many firms have benefited from a lower employee absentee rate. It is difficult to find an explanation for this, but many experts believe that employees devote more time to work in a virtual office because they are happier in their environment. Because employees do not have to spend so much time traveling to and from work, they are better able to enjoy their free time. Although the virtual office is still an exception to the rule, it is an organizational system that many companies are considering. If this trend continues, there will be more employees who will find themselves working in a similar environment.

2. VOCABULARY

to bring on/about	*Internet*
bug	*mainframe*
code	*network*
computer	*to pick up*
conference call	*print*
cursor	*RAM (random access memory)*
data	*save*
debug	*software*
download	*switchboard*
efficiency	*traffic*
e-mail	*typewriter*
flexibility	*virtual office*
font	*voice mail*
hard drive	*workplace*
to hold	*word processor*

The following table shows many of the most popular computer terms that you will probably need to know:

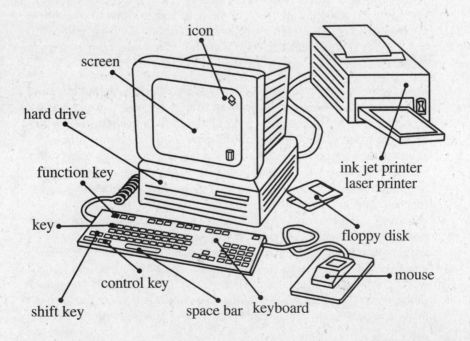

EXERCISES

1. Complete the following dialogue by filling in the blanks with the appropriate article *(a/an/the/Ø)*.

Cody:	Hello, PC Warehouse. This is Cody. How can I help you?
Ms. Bailey:	I'd like to place __(a)__ order, please.
Cody:	O.K. Will you be ordering from __(b)__ catalog?
Ms. Bailey:	Yes.
Cody:	Do you have __(c)__ catalog in front of you?
Ms. Bailey:	As a matter of fact, I do. I'm interested in __(d)__ Power Center Series on __(e)__ page 21.
Cody:	Are you interested in __(f)__ Power PC desktop model or __(g)__ Profile model?
Ms. Bailey:	__(h)__ desktop model.
Cody:	That model comes with 128MB of RAM and __(i)__ 2.5 GHz hard drive. It is currently quoted at $795.
Ms. Bailey:	How much would it be with 256MB of Ram?
Cody:	$995.
Ms. Bailey:	Would you be able to give me __(j)__ discount if I purchased 15 computers?
Cody:	I believe so. Let me check. Yeah, you'll get __(k)__ 20 percent discount on __(l)__ order of that size.
Ms. Bailey:	Okay. We also need some network software and __(m)__ connectors.
Cody:	__(n)__ machines already come with built-in modem support and Internet software.
Ms. Bailey:	Great! Will this include __(o)__ installation?
Cody:	No. But, we can arrange for __(p)__ technician to come to your office and set everything up. It will cost $30 per machine.
Ms. Bailey:	That would be wonderful! I'll write up __(q)__ purchase order and send it out this afternoon. Should I call and make __(r)__ appointment with __(s)__ technician?
Cody: No.	When we're ready to ship your purchase, __(t)__ technician will call you.
Ms. Bailey:	Very well. Thanks.

2. Choose the correct word to complete each sentence.

   a. How _____ *(much, many)* memory should I buy to upgrade my computer?

b. There are _____ (a little, a few) printers that need to be repaired.
c. _____ (A lot of, Many) the work in this office is done with a computer.
d. I need _____ (any, some) information on how to run this program.
e. Are _____ (any, no) of these computers not working?
f. No, there's _____ (any, no) problem with the monitor. It's the keyboard that's not working.
g. _____ (Much, Some) CD-ROMs are quite expensive.
h. Does this printer use _____ (a lot of, a few) ink?
i. We need _____ (a few, some) paper for the printer.
j. I'm sure I'll learn this program in _____ (a few, a little) days.

3. Decide whether the noun in parentheses should be in the singular or the plural form.

a. Most _____ (business) are moving toward newer _____ (technology).
b. The United States is a country formed by _____ (people) with different _____ (belief), _____ (custom), and _____ (language).
c. I walked so much this morning that one of my _____ (foot) hurts.
d. Most _____ (child) today learn how to use _____ (computer) in kindergarten.
e. The _____ (echo) you hear is produced by sound _____ (wave) that hit against that rock.
f. _____ (Dentist) are using innovative ways to prevent _____ (tooth) decay.
g. One of her _____ (parent) is traveling around Europe.
h. The astronauts who returned from the moon kept talking about a series of strange _____ (phenomenon) they witnessed.
i. According to some psychologists, _____ (man) and _____ (woman) express fear in different ways.
j. We went fishing last week, and I caught five _____ (fish).

4. Match each of the words in List A with its synonym in List B.

A	B
innovate	erase
delete	remove
save	go back
return	renew
withdraw	add
insert	keep

LESSON 4
Insurance Policies

A. DIALOGUE

THE ACCIDENT

Patricia Brien is a student at Harvard University.[1] Two weeks ago[2] she witnessed a traffic accident while she was having coffee with a friend at an outdoor café. The police took her name and number and gave it to the insurance companies of the parties[3] involved.

HANS: Hello, Ms. Brien. My name is Hans Shole. I work for Boston Auto Insurance, and I represent one of the parties involved in the accident you witnessed on[4] the 13th of July. For the purpose of our investigation, I need to get a statement from you.

PATRICIA: I'd be[5] happy to. I saw what happened very clearly.

HANS: First could you please state your name for the record?[6]

PATRICIA: My name is Patricia Brien.

HANS: Do I have permission to record your statement?

PATRICIA: Yes, you do.

HANS: Before we begin, do you have any questions?

PATRICIA: Yes, who did you say you represent?

HANS: I'm afraid[7] I can't tell you that. I need your statement first. I hope you understand.

PATRICIA: Well, I guess it's all right.

HANS: Do you remember what time the accident happened?

PATRICIA: Well, it must've been about 1:30 in the afternoon. We had just finished lunch and had already ordered coffee.

HANS: And what were the conditions like? Was it sunny or rainy? Were the roads wet?

PATRICIA: I remember that it was really hot that day, so there's no way the roads could have been wet.

HANS: Where, exactly, did this accident take place?[8]

PATRICIA: At the intersection of Chestnut and Charles Streets.

A friend and I were sitting outdoors on the patio at the Season's Café. I was facing Charles Street, so I was able to see everything.

HANS: Can you describe the vehicles that were involved?

PATRICIA: Well, one of the cars was a green BMW. The other car was red, but I don't remember the model.

HANS: Okay . . . now to the best of your knowledge, could you please describe exactly what happened?

PATRICIA: Sure. I remember seeing the red car make a left turn onto Charles. Then, suddenly, the BMW broadsided[9] it in the middle of the intersection.

HANS: What direction was the BMW heading?

PATRICIA: Let's see . . . It was coming toward me from the left . . . so it must have been heading west on Chestnut.

HANS: And the red car?

PATRICIA: The BMW was heading west . . . so that means the red car was driving east on Chestnut . . . then it made a left turn . . . so it was turning to head north on Charles when it was hit.

HANS: Was there a traffic light controlling the intersection?

PATRICIA: There sure was.

HANS: Did you see who had the green light?

PATRICIA: I'm pretty[10] sure the red car did, because right after the accident, I saw the green left-turn arrow.

HANS: Are you saying that the BMW ran a red light and broadsided the red car?

PATRICIA: As far as I could tell, yes. I believe so.

HANS: Then what happened?

PATRICIA: Well, the red car spun[11] around and ended up[12] on the sidewalk in front of the café. The BMW was stuck in the intersection. (no streets mentioned)

HANS: What did you do next?

PATRICIA: I ran inside the café and asked the owner to call 911.[13] Then I went back outside. I saw the driver of the red car wandering around the street, so I went to help her. She was pretty shaken up.

HANS: Can you describe the driver of the red vehicle for me? Could you tell if she was hurt or not?

PATRICIA: The driver was an African-American[14] woman in her forties.[15] I don't think she was hurt physically, but she was definitely in shock. She was shaking all over.

HANS: Did you see any passengers in the car?

PATRICIA: There was another woman. She seemed to be more in control of herself. She was also African-American.

HANS: What about the people in the other car? Can you describe the driver?

PATRICIA: I didn't quite see them. It all happened so fast. Later, I saw a white man in a red shirt sitting on the sidewalk. I don't know if he was the driver. He was holding a towel or something to his head. I think he was the only person in the car.

HANS: All right. I think that's about it, unless there's anything else you'd like to add?

PATRICIA: No, I think I told you everything. I'd like to know which party you represent, though.

HANS: The woman in the red car.

PATRICIA: Good! I hope the information I've given you is helpful.

HANS: It sure is. Thanks for your time.

B. NOTES

1. Harvard University is located in Cambridge, near Boston, in the state of Massachusetts. It was founded in 1636 and it has two important museums. The more famous of the two is the Fogg Art Museum, which has an impressive collection of 80,000 works of art from all over the world. The Arthur M. Sackler Museum specializes in Greco-Roman, Egyptian, Islamic, and Chinese art. South of Harvard is the famous Massachusetts Institute of Technology, or MIT. Boston is one of the largest cities in New England, an area that comprises several states, including Maine, New Hampshire, Vermont, Massachusetts, Rhode Island, and Connecticut. Boston is also the cradle of independence in this country, and many of the city's buildings are famous for their historical significance. Several personalities in American history such as John Hancock, Paul Revere, and Samuel Adams (heroes of the American Revolution) inhabited its streets and made the city famous. Boston is also one of the most important financial, technological, and cultural centers in the country.

2. Note the usage of the adverb of time *ago*. Also notice that unlike some other languages, the adverb comes after the expression of time.

   Two weeks ago she was still living in Boston.

3. The noun *party* changes meaning depending on the context where it is being used. The most common usage is that of a celebration or gathering of people. In the dialogue, it refers to a group of people. It can also refer to a political group, such as the Republican or Democratic Party.

4. Notice the usage of the preposition *on* with a date or specific day:

   on Monday   on the 12th   on Christmas Day

5. The contraction *I'd* is the short form of *I would*.

6. *Record* is a noun that means "register" in this context. When you pronounce the noun form, the stress goes on the first syllable (**ré**-kord). "*To record*" is a verb that means "to register or to transfer music or data onto a disc or cassette." The verb places the stress on the second syllable (re-**kórd**).

7. *I'm afraid (that)* is a common colloquial expression. It is used to express that the person is sorry about something he or she is about to say or announce:

   I'm afraid I won't be able to make it to your wedding next week.

8. *To take place* means "to happen or to occur." *To take* is an irregular verb:

PRESENT	PAST	PAST PARTICIPLE
take	took	taken

   Tell me what took place yesterday.
   Tell me what had taken place when you arrived.

9. The verb *to broadside* is often used to describe a car accident that involves a lateral impact. Other car collision terms are *to rear-end* ("to hit from behind"), *to sideswipe*" ("to hit from the side") and *to crash* ("to have an impact or collision"), or *to have a head-on collision* ("when two cars hit front to front").

10. The word *pretty* works as an adverb in this case. When it is used as an adverb it means "almost." When it is used as an adjective it means "beautiful or good-looking."

11. *To spin* is an irregular verb:

PRESENT	PAST	PAST PARTICIPLE
spin	spun	spun

12. The verb *to end up* is used when you want to express the result or outcome of an action. Other similar expressions are *to wind up* and *to turn out*.

13. The telephone number 911 is the emergency number for immediate assistance in the United States. Generally, a call to 911 is answered by a trained employee who summons the police, firemen, or ambulance, and offers assistance until these services arrive on the scene.

14. *African-American* is the term that is used in the United States to refer to Americans who are black. The term *black* may also be used. The term *Negro* should be avoided because it is considered to be insulting.

15. When you are uncertain about a person's age, you may want to approximate the person's age by using the plural. *A woman in her twenties* means that you think that the person is at least twenty years old, but not yet thirty.

C. GRAMMAR AND USAGE

1. THE SIMPLE PAST

a. Regular Verbs
To express the past form of a regular verb, add *-ed* to the infinitive form.

to represent	*represented*
to need	*needed*

If the infinitive ends in *e*, add *-d* to the ending of the verb.

to name	*named*

If the verb ends in *y*, change the *y* to an *i* (except with diphthongs such as *obey* and *relay*) and add *-d* or *-ed*.

to say	*said*
to try	*tried*

Unlike some other languages, all regular verbs in English use the same form with all subjects.

I witnessed an accident last week.
She helped the injured passenger until the ambulance arrived.
You paid the hospital in advance.

Spelling rules of regular verbs:

If the infinitive form ends in *e*, add *-d*.

hope	hoped
date	dated
prepare	prepared

If the verb is a one-syllable verb that ends in a vowel followed by a consonant (except *w*, *x*, and *y*), duplicate the consonant and add *-ed*.

stop	stopped
rob	robbed
beg	begged

If the verb is a one-syllable verb that ends in two vowels followed by a consonant, add *-ed*.

| rain | rained |
| dream | dreamed |

If the verb is a two-syllable verb that has the pronunciation stress on the first syllable, add *-ed*.

cancel	canceled
offer	offered
travel	traveled

If the verb is a two-syllable verb that has the stress on the second syllable, duplicate the final consonant and add *-ed*.

| prefer | preferred |
| control | controlled |

If the verb ends in two consonants, add *-ed*.

| start | started |
| demand | demanded |

If the verb ends in a vowel followed by a *w*, *x*, or *y*, add *-ed*.

tow	towed
enjoy	enjoyed
pray	prayed

Some common exceptions to this rule are:

say	said
lay	laid
pay	paid

If the verb ends in a consonant followed by a *y*, change the *y* to *i* and add *-ed*.

study	studied
try	tried
reply	replied

If the verb ends in *ie*, add -*d*.

die	*died*
lie	*lied*
tie	*tied*

b. Irregular Verbs

Irregular verbs do not follow a particular conjugation pattern. Each verb has its own form which is used for all subjects. For a more complete list, see the appendix.

to buy	*bought*
to run	*ran*
to see	*saw*
to begin	*began*

He saw the accident from the other side of the street.
They bought a new insurance policy.
We ran inside to call 911.
The policeman began to ask the potential witnesses some questions.

c. Negative Case

The negative of regular and irregular verbs is formed by using the simple past of the auxiliary verb *to do*. Here is the format of the negative past tense:

> *did* + *not* + simple form of the verb

The contracted form of *did not* is *didn't*. *Did not* and its contraction should be used with all subjects.

I did not (didn't) pay the hospital in advance.
One of the witnesses did not (didn't) want to be identified.
You did not (didn't) buy a new insurance policy.

d. Interrogative Case

The interrogative case of regular and irregular verbs is formed by using the simple past of the auxiliary verb *to do*. The main verb remains in its simple form. Unlike some other languages, in English it is very important to maintain the specific order of the format of the question. The format of the interrogative form is the following:

For questions with short answers, affirmative or negative:

> *Did* + subject + infinitive . . . ?

Did you have an accident?   *Yes, I did./No, I didn't.*

For questions with complete answers:

> When/where/why/who/how + did + subject
> + verb in its simple form . . . ?

When did the accident occur?
How did it happen?
Where did you go?

e. The Verb *to Be*
The simple past of the verb *to be* follows a different format. The form of the verb varies according to the subject:

AFFIRMATIVE

I	*was*
You	*were*
He/She/It	*was*
We	*were*
You	*were*
They	*were*

I was at the café when a truck hit the stop sign.
They were around the corner.

NEGATIVE

The verb *to be* does not need an auxiliary verb to form the negative case:

I	*was not/wasn't*
You	*were not/weren't*
He/She/It	*was not/wasn't*
We	*were not/weren't*
You	*were not/weren't*
They	*were not/weren't*

She wasn't at the corner when the accident happened.
You weren't there.

INTERROGATIVE

The verb *to be* does not need an auxiliary verb to form the interrogative case:

SHORT ANSWERS

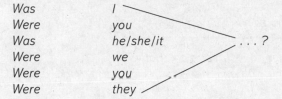

Was   *I*
Were   *you*
Was   *he/she/it*   . . . ?
Were   *we*
Were   *you*
Were   *they*

Were you in the car when Mary was rear-ended?

COMPLETE ANSWERS

> *When/Where/Why/Who/How + was/were . . . ?*

Where were you yesterday morning?
What were the road conditions?
Who else was in the car?

f. Usage of Simple Past

The simple past is used to refer to events or actions that took place and were completed in the past. Many times, even though it may not be specified, it is assumed that the event or action was completed in the past.

Last year he had an accident that left him paralyzed below the waist.
She didn't drive for a long time after the accident.

The simple past is also used to refer to a habitual or customary event in the past. It can also be used with adverbs of frequency *(always, never, sometimes)* to specify the period of time involved.

I always crossed that intersection carefully because I knew it was not safe.
I never liked to drive at full speed.

2. USED TO

The expression *used to* + verb in its simple form is used to express a habit or a customary action in the past.

She used to work in the intensive care unit at the local hospital.
When I was single, I used to go to that café.

Do not confuse this form with *to be used to*. As mentioned above, *used to* refers to a habitual action in the past. *To be used to* means that the person is accustomed to something. Also notice the difference in the way that the phrases are constructed:

> used to + verb in its simple form
> vs.
> to be used to + verb + -ing

Peter used to work for an insurance company.
She is used to dealing with emergencies because she works as a 911 operator.

There is also the expression *to get used to,* which means "to get accustomed to something."

I lived in Canada for twenty years, but I never got used to the long winters.

3. THE PAST CONTINUOUS

a. Form

The past continuous is formed by using the simple past form of the verb *to be* + the present participle of the main verb (verb + *-ing*).

I was working.

AFFIRMATIVE CASE

The affirmative case is formed by using the following construction:

> personal pronoun + the past of the verb *to be* + the present participle of the main verb (verb + *-ing*)

I was working on my report when the phone rang.
Nancy was driving too fast, so she got a ticket.

NEGATIVE CASE

The negative case is formed by using the following construction:

> personal pronoun + the past of the verb *to be* + *not* + the present participle of the main verb (verb + *-ing*)

He was not (wasn't) paying attention to the road when he crashed.
We were not (weren't) eating outside, so we didn't see the accident.

INTERROGATIVE CASE

The short answer question is formed by using the following construction:

> the past of the verb *to be* + personal pronoun + the present participle of the main verb (verb + *-ing*)

Were they watching television when the police arrived?
Was the BMW speeding when it hit you?

Complete answer questions:

Where were you going last night?
How was she doing when you saw her?

b. Usage
The past continuous is used to express past actions or events of an unknown duration.

Last year at this time, I was recovering from an accident.
The car was speeding north on Charles Street.

The past continuous is used to express two actions or events that occurred simultaneously in the past.

While the police were taking her statement, the suspect was trying to escape.
The police were trying to calm her down, while the nurse was treating her injuries.

The past continuous and the simple past are used in the same sentence to express that one ongoing action was interrupted by another action.

We were having dinner when we heard the crash.
I was going to look for help when the ambulance arrived.

D. IDIOMATIC STUDY

DESCRIPTIONS
When describing a person or an object you use the verb *to be* followed by an adjective:

His hair is red.
Her nose is long.

You may also use the verb *to have*. The verb *to have* is used to describe a quality or aspect that the person or object has.

He has red hair.
She has a long nose.
The house has a brick roof.

Sometimes you may have to use more than one adjective to make the description more realistic and interesting.

It was a cold and damp winter night. A tall, young girl was standing at the bus stop waiting for the bus to come. She was alone and frightened.

You may want to make comparisons to make the description more precise:

His stomach was as round as a ball.
I think he looks like his grandfather.

English adjectives follow a distinct order, and the adjective is always placed before the noun. Notice the following examples:

He bought three beautiful, big, old, brown, French marble tables.
Her handsome, tall, 30-year-old, English, Catholic uncle got married.

Observe how adjectives are used to give descriptions in the following dialogue:

After looking for his missing friend all afternoon, Andy Winter approaches a police officer and asks for assistance.

ANDY WINTER: Excuse me officer. Could you help me find a missing friend of mine?

POLICE OFFICER: Certainly. Could you describe your friend for me?

ANDY WINTER: He has dark hair.

POLICE OFFICER: What color is his hair?

ANDY WINTER: It's black.

POLICE OFFICER: Is it straight or curly?

ANDY WINTER: It's straight and quite long.

POLICE OFFICER: How long?

ANDY WINTER: I would say it's at least as long as yours.

POLICE OFFICER: Do you remember anything else about him?

ANDY WINTER: Yes, he has a funny walk.

POLICE OFFICER: What do you mean "funny"?

ANDY WINTER: Well, he walks as if one of his legs is shorter than the other.

POLICE OFFICER: So, he limps?

ANDY WINTER: Yes, I guess you could say that.

POLICE OFFICER: What was he wearing?

ANDY WINTER: Nothing.

POLICE OFFICER: Nothing?

ANDY WINTER: No. Nothing at all.

POLICE OFFICER: Anything else you'd like to add?

ANDY WINTER: Yes. The last time I saw him he was chasing a white cat.

POLICE OFFICER: Chasing a cat?

ANDY WINTER: Yes. Like most dogs, he hates cats.

POLICE OFFICER: A dog! We're looking for a dog?

E. STRICTLY BUSINESS

1. HEALTH INSURANCE IN THE UNITED STATES

In the United States there is no national health insurance plan that pays for hospital care in case of emergency. Most of the health-care sector is controlled by private companies, which is why it is essential for Americans to have a private health insurance plan. Generally, the employer pays for at least part of the insurance fees for their employees and their families. However, many people still have to pay for their insurance out of their own pockets while others simply do not have any health insurance plan at all, either because they are unemployed or because their employers do not contribute to their plan. A grave illness or serious accident may result in a financial disaster to any uninsured person who suddenly has to pay for hospital care. If you think that insurance premiums are too high for your budget or that having insurance is unnecessary, think again: The cost of hospital care and doctor bills in the United States could easily cost many thousands of dollars. The cost of hospital and medical care does vary greatly throughout the country, but one thing is certain: Prices are constantly going up. Generally, urban areas are more expensive (and sometimes provide better service) than rural areas.

You probably already have an insurance plan in your country of origin. Unfortunately, most of these plans are not valid in the United States since many hospitals and companies simply do not accept foreign health insurance plans. In most cases you would have to pay out of your pocket and try to charge your insurance company in your country to get some of the money back. It is important to ask your insurance company if they cover expenses in the United States. Otherwise, it is recommended to get a basic insurance plan in the United States during your stay. Generally, these basic insurance plans cover the cost of doctor visits during an illness, in addition to hospitalization and expenses related to surgery. These basic plans generally do not cover doctor visits for non-emergency conditions or minor illnesses. Other insurance companies offer family health plans or plans for long-term illnesses. This last type of insurance covers long-term conditions as well as emergencies.

Many plans use a deductible clause. This means that you are expected to pay a certain amount of the costs, while the insurance company pays any amount above that minimum. Deductibles are generally between $500 and $1,000, depending on the type of insurance and insurance policy. The insurance companies may pay from $5,000 (an insufficient amount) to $1,000,000. It is recommended to have a minimum coverage of $25,000.

LIMITATIONS

Most insurance plans stipulate the type of services that they pay, from type of hospital room to the number of days covered. These stipulations depend on the company and type of insurance you select.

EXCLUSIONS

Most insurance plans do not cover the following:

- Maternity—Maternity health care must be purchased separately before pregnancy. Most insurance plans only cover two days of hospital care. The normal cost of pregnancy is from $3,850 to $6,000.
- Dental Care—Only a few companies cover the cost of dental care. It is a good idea to see your dentist before you travel to the United States. Dental care can be one of the most expensive services in the health-care field. Anyone who is planning to stay in the United States for a prolonged period of time should get a separate dental insurance plan.
- Eye Care—If you wear eyeglasses, make sure you get an eye exam before coming to the United States. It is recommended that you get an additional pair of glasses and bring your prescription with you to the United States. Most insurances cover injuries, but not preventive care.

2. OTHER TYPES OF INSURANCE

LIFE INSURANCE
In case of death, the designated beneficiary receives the payout. There are several companies that offer different types of life insurance coverage.

AUTO INSURANCE
In most of the United States it is mandatory to have car insurance. The extent of the coverage varies by state. If your car is not insured, the owner of the car is responsible for any accident or damage related to the car, as well as personal injury and property damage. The legal cost of an accident can be extremely high, which is why it is important to have an insurance policy even if it covers only the minimum amount.

3. VOCABULARY

beneficiary	health
to broadside	health plan
to charge	life insurance
collision	long-term
conditions	mandatory
costs	maximum
coverage	medical insurance
to crash	minimum
deductible	party
dental insurance	plan
dentist	pregnancy
to end up	pretty
to have a head-on collision	preventive care
hospitalization	premium
illness	to rear-end
injury	record
insurance	to record
insurance policy	to represent
to insure	sickness
insured	to sideswipe
intensive care unit (ICU)	statement
glasses	to take place

EXERCISES

1. Complete the following paragraph using the simple past tense of the verbs in parentheses.

   Last year I __(a)__ (to turn) 55 years old, and I __(b)__ (to decide) it was time to get some kind of life insurance. I __(c)__ (to think) that it would be a good idea to leave my spouse and children something they could depend on in case I died. I __(d)__ (to go) to Boston Life Insurance to obtain some information. They __(e)__ (to make) an offer I __(f)__ (can not) resist. Without spending a lot of money, their life insurance plan would provide my family with adequate health insurance and pay for education and other ongoing living expenses. The quote they __(g)__ (to give) me __(h)__ (to seem) very reasonable and affordable, so I __(i)__ (to sign up).

2. Complete the following sentences using used to, to be used to, or to get used to.

   a. When I was in medical school, I _____ not sleeping much. I often got up at 5 A.M. to study.

b. It's strange to drive an automatic car. I _____ driving a stick-shift.

c. Rita _____ work at an insurance company for a long time, but now she doesn't.

d. Doctors _____ seeing blood all the time. I don't think I would ever _____ it.

e. My insurance policy _____ cover all dental problems. Now it's been changed and it only covers dental surgery.

f. Insurance companies _____ cover pre-existing conditions, but now they don't.

3. Use the simple past or the past continuous of the verb in parentheses to complete each sentence.

a. The paramedics _____ (to try) to get the old man to breathe.

b. I _____ (not to hear) the fire alarm go off because I _____ (to sleep).

c. Stanley _____ (to climb) the stairs when he _____ (to trip) and _____ (fall). Luckily, he _____ (not to hurt) himself.

d. When the insurance company _____ (to call), I _____ (to have) lunch with Mark.

e. They _____ (to record) my statement when the lights _____ (to go) out.

4. Suggested Activity. Write a paragraph describing a time when you were in an accident or when you witnessed an accident. What happened? What did you see?

LESSON 5

Discrimination in the Workplace

A. DIALOGUE

AN INTERVIEW

Teresa Miron, a reporter for Business magazine in Washington, D.C.,[1] is conducting an interview with Mr. Ted Chiarri, a retired businessman.

TERESA: Age discrimination[2] has long been a fact of corporate life in the United States. Wall Street[3] has always emphasized youthful, dynamic management. Why do you think it's advantageous for a company to suggest early retirement[4] to highly paid older executives?

TED: I think it's very tempting for a company to cut expenses. Salary costs and pension liabilities are reduced if managers ask older employees to retire. At the same time, they are making room at the top for young achievers. And, of course, early retirement is a viable way for a company to avoid massive layoffs—if the employees agree to retire voluntarily.

TERESA: What can an aging executive do if he or she suspects age discrimination has had something to do with being fired or asked to retire?

TED: If an employee does not want to retire, he or she should fight back. In fact, many executives have done just that by invoking[5] the protection of the Age Discrimination in Employment Act, also known as the ADEA.[6] There are quite a few corporations with age bias cases pending against them. Many have lost suits,[7] while many others have paid huge amounts of money to settle out of court.

TERESA: What is the success rate in cases like these?

TED: Very high. Because most cases go to a jury trial, the odds are in favor of the employee. When an employee confronts a large corporation on an issue in court, the jury tends to identify with the plaintiff.

TERESA: I understand this can become quite an expensive affair[8] for a company!

TED: You're absolutely right. The more people hear about these

61

cases as more victims speak out, the bigger the problems will be for such corrupt corporations.

TERESA: You've experienced this type of discrimination firsthand. Would you mind telling us about your case?

TED: Not at all. I was the director of financial affairs at a major broadcasting corporation[9] for over ten years. I was just about to turn 60 when I was fired. Along with my job, I lost my salary, my benefits, and a little bit of my self-esteem.

TERESA: On what grounds were you fired?

TED: My employer had been building up a dossier[10] of the little mistakes I had made in my years of employment there. At first, I felt they were right to have fired me. But then, I remembered that other executives before me had been forced out when they were around my age. Suddenly it dawned on[11] me that the issue at hand had never been my performance, but my age. That is discrimination.

TERESA: What did you do then?

TED: I got a lawyer who helped me prove that my performance was more than adequate and that the company could not show just cause for firing me.[12]

TERESA: How much time does an employee have to file an age discrimination claim?

TED: There's a six-month deadline, but some states allow 300 days.

TERESA: What are some of the signs of age discrimination that an employee should watch out for?

TED: The signs are usually very subtle. Check your company's policy toward older employees in general—whether many older people are fired or whether the ones who leave voluntarily really want to retire. Make sure your colleagues keep you in the loop.[13] Having your responsibilities slowly taken away from you is a sure sign that you're being forced out. Then it's time to act.

TERESA: What is your advice for older employees?

TED: Build up your own dossier, keep notes and copies of all commendations, speak up if you suspect age discrimination, and most of all, do your job well. If your performance cannot be criticized, you have no reason to worry.

TERESA: Mr. Chiarri, thank you very much for this interview.

B. NOTES

1. Washington, D.C. (District of Columbia), the capital of the United States, was founded in 1791. The city has many tourist attractions, including important government buildings such as the Capitol and the White House. Washington, D.C., has one of the largest museums in the country, the Smithsonian. The city also has many other museums, including the National Art Gallery and the National Museum of American History, among others.

2. The Age Discrimination Law of 1967 prohibits discrimination when hiring, laying off, or compensating workers between the ages of 40 and 69.

3. Wall Street is in the heart of New York City, at the southern end of Manhattan. The New York Stock Exchange is located in this area. Wall Street is the most important financial center in the country. When people refer to Wall Street, they are referring not only to the geographic area encompassing Wall Street and the district surrounding it, but also to the financial institutions and powerful executives that exert such strong influence on the markets and the economy.

4. Generally an executive retires at the age of 65. Some companies offer retirement to their employees at an earlier age to save the company money. Some of them allow the employee to retire after 30 years of service regardless of whether they have reached 65 years of age.

5. In this context the verb *to invoke* means "to utilize" or "to use." It can also mean "to call," "to beg," or "to implore."

   The sorcerer was invoking the spirit of the old man's wife.

6. ADEA is the acronym for the Age Discrimination in Employment Act.

7. In this context the noun *suit* refers to a trial. The verb form, *to sue,* means "to litigate in order to obtain financial compensation."

   If you harass me again, I'll sue you.

   The noun *suit* also refers to a set of clothes or a type of symbol (diamonds, hearts, clubs, or spades) appearing on playing cards.

   She bought a blue suit for her interview on Monday.
   You have to play any card of the same suit.

8. The noun *affair* refers to a social or business event. It can also be used to describe a love encounter or relationship, usually illicit or forbidden.

   That account is my affair, so let me handle it.
   He was fired because he was having an affair with his boss's wife.

9. There are many television corporations in the United States. The most important national networks are ABC, NBC, CBS, CNN, and FOX.

10. A company's personnel department keeps a file on each employee's employment history, including evaluations, recommendations, and other documents related to the employee's performance.

11. *To dawn* is an intransitive verb that literally refers to the moment when the sun comes up at the beginning of the day. When it is used with the preposition *on* or *upon* it means "to realize."

    It never dawned on her that she had been fired unjustly.

12. The verb *to fire* means "to terminate employment because of unsatisfactory performance." The verb *to let (subject) go* is also used to convey the termination of employment.

13. The phrase *to be in the loop* is used frequently in work-related contexts; you will often hear businessmen and women saying "keep me in the loop on this one, Bob." The expression means "to be receiving the necessary information" or "to belong to a group receiving information on a specific topic." If you are *out of the loop,* you have not been receiving information on the specific topic.

C. GRAMMAR AND USAGE

1. THE PRESENT PERFECT

a. Form
The present perfect is formed by using the present of the auxiliary verb *to have* and the past participle of the main verb.

AFFIRMATIVE

> subject + *have/has* + past participle

I have (I've) experienced this type of discrimination firsthand.
Wall Street has always emphasized youthful, dynamic management.
They have (They've) been to our office before.

NEGATIVE

> subject + *have/has* + *not* + past participle

She has not (hasn't) found a lawyer to take her case.

Although he's a victim of discrimination, he has not (hasn't) filed a suit yet.
I have not (haven't) been in the office all week.

INTERROGATIVE
With a question word:

> *What/when/where/why/whom/how* + *have/has* + subject
> + past participle . . . ?

The contraction can also be used in the question form. The contraction is not made with the subject pronoun but with the question word (except for negative questions).

Where have (Where've) you been?
What has (What's) he done?
Why have they not gone in yet? (Why haven't they gone in yet?)

Without a question word:

> *Have/Has* + subject + past participle . . . ?

Contractions are not used with this construction (unless it is in the negative form).

Have you filed this report yet?
Has he ever experienced discrimination firsthand?
Has he not had (Hasn't he had) time to conduct your performance review?

b. Usage
The present perfect is used to express something that took place recently or something that happened in the past whose precise time is unspecified or unimportant.

This corporation has forced six employees to retire early.
Have you ever known someone who was fired because of his or her age?

If the time is specified, then the simple past should be used instead. Compare the previous sentences with the following:

Last month, this corporation forced six employees to retire early.
You knew about the layoffs yesterday?

Events expressed in the present perfect generally have an effect on the present.

*They have been to see the boss. (They are probably not still
in his office.)*
He hasn't heard from his lawyer yet. (So, he's still waiting.)

Events that are expressed using the simple past do not have an effect
on the present. In other words, the events occurred in the past and
their present time effects are unknown.

They went to see the boss.
He didn't hear from his lawyer.

The present perfect is also used to refer to an event that occurred
repeatedly before the present time. The exact moment in which it
occurred is unimportant.

I have had three evaluations so far.
I have called her several times.
I have met many people at the employee lounge.

It is important to point out that the simple past should be used if the
moment that the event took place is mentioned. Compare:

I had three evaluations last semester.
I called her several times this morning.
Yesterday, I met many people at the employee lounge.

2. *FOR* AND *SINCE*

The present perfect is used with expressions using the prepositions *for*
and *since* to indicate that an action started in the past and continues
into the present. The preposition *for* is used with expressions that refer
to a period of time.

I have worked here for ten years. (And I still work here.)
I have been traveling on business for two months. (I'm still traveling.)
I have had this computer for two years. (I still have it.)

The preposition *since* is used with expressions of time that indicate a
particular starting time for that action.

He has been on a leave of absence since December.
We have been in charge of this project since 1993.
He has not felt well since last Monday.

3. THE PRESENT PERFECT CONTINUOUS

You may use the present perfect continuous to emphasize the duration
of a recent event. The present perfect continuous is formed by using
the auxiliary verb *to have*, the past participle of the auxiliary verb *to
be*, and the main verb in its present participle form (verb + *-ing*):

$$\text{subject} + \textit{have/has} + \textit{been} + \text{verb} + \textit{-ing}$$

I have been thinking about making a career change.
The company has been hiring new accountants since March.

There is a difference between the present perfect and the present perfect continuous. When the present perfect is used without a phrase that indicates time, it is assumed that the action has ended and that it may not be a very recent one. On the other hand, when the present perfect continuous is used, it is assumed that the action has not ended yet or has ended very recently.

I have read the newspaper.
I have been reading the newspaper.
I have interviewed a candidate for the job.
I have been interviewing a candidate for the job.

4. THE PAST PERFECT

The past perfect is used to express an action that ended before another action in the past. It uses the following format:

$$\text{simple past of the verb } \textit{to have (had)} + \text{past participle} \\ \text{of the main verb}$$

I had never heard about age discrimination until it happened to one of my colleagues.
The meeting had already begun when I arrived.

You do not need to use the past perfect if the sentence uses the adverbs *after* or *before*.

I felt better after I talked to a lawyer about my case.
I went to see my therapist before I made up my mind.

5. THE PAST PERFECT CONTINUOUS

The past perfect continuous is used to emphasize the duration of an action that was in progress in the past. It follows this format:

$$\text{simple past of } \textit{to have (had)} + \textit{been} + \text{main verb} + \textit{-ing}$$

The employee had been building up a file to prove his adequate performance before taking his case to court.
The company had been firing people, but no one suspected discrimination.

It is also used to illustrate an action that was in progress at the onset of another action in the past.

The man was out of breath because he had been running to make it on time.
I hadn't been paying attention to what the chairman was saying, so I couldn't give him an answer to his question.

D. IDIOMATIC STUDY

VOICING A COMPLAINT
It is important to be polite when voicing a complaint or expressing dissatisfaction with services you have received. The following phrases are very useful:

I'm sorry, but I have a complaint about the constant noise from your apartment. It really disturbs my sleep.
I hate to say this, but this product does not work to my satisfaction.
I don't want to sound rude, but this situation is unacceptable.
You may disagree, but I feel that you are not treating me fairly (I feel that I am not being treated fairly).
Excuse me for being so direct, but I do not deserve this kind of treatment.
I hope you'll forgive my criticism, but I'm very disappointed in your work lately.

E. STRICTLY BUSINESS

1. AGAINST DISCRIMINATION
During the 1960s and 1970s, many civil rights groups mobilized to demand changes in the way minorities were treated. As a result, many laws and regulations were created to monitor how employers treat their workers. These laws prohibit companies of any size from discriminating against a person based on race, religion, nationality, age, or handicap. Additionally, there is a growing number of companies that prohibit discrimination on the basis of sexual orientation. Most employment discrimination legislation comes from federal and state laws. The Constitution of the United States as well as the constitutions of individual states guarantee certain rights to employees. The Equal Pay Act of 1963 is one of these protective laws. It is a product of an amendment to a previous law. The Equal Pay Act prohibits a company from instituting any difference in wages based on gender. This law focuses only on the gender of the employee and does not cover other types of discrimination. The law states the following:

"No employer having employees subject to any provisions of this section shall discriminate, within any establishment in which such employees are employed, between employees on the basis of sex by paying wages to employees in such establishment at a rate less than the rate at which he pays wages to employees of the opposite sex in such establishment for equal work on jobs the performance of which requires equal skill, effort, and responsibility, and which are performed under similar working conditions . . ."

Title VII of the Civil Rights Act of 1964 expanded the types of discrimination that are prohibited by law. The Title VII Act applies to any company with more than fifteen employees that has business ties in more than one state. The law prohibits discrimination based on race, gender, religion, or national origin. This law also extended protection to pregnant women who are about to give birth or women with very young children.

The Age Discrimination in Employment Act (ADEA) prohibits discrimination against people who are over 40 years old. The extent of the law is similar to the protection offered by the Title VII Act. The Nineteenth Century Civil Rights Act is very similar to the Title VII Act. The most recent amendment to this act was passed in 1993.

The Rehabilitation Act promotes and expands employment opportunities to those people with physical disabilities. The companies who are affected by this law are those that receive federal aid or those that have business contracts with the federal government in excess of $2,500. This law also applies to all agencies of the federal government.

The American with Disabilities Act (ADA) was created to eliminate job discrimination against people with disabilities. It outlaws discrimination on the basis of physical or mental disabilities. This law is more detailed and extensive than the Title VII Act.

The Black Lung Act was designed to protect mine workers who suffer from pneumoconiosis. The Equal Employment Opportunity Commission (EEOC) is the agency that is responsible for interpreting and implementing employment discrimination laws such as the Equal Payment Act, Title VII, ADEA and the Americans with Disabilities Act. In 1980 the commission published a series of regulations and guidelines that defined what is now known as sexual harassment. Sexual harassment refers to any kind of unsolicited sexual advances or sexual propositions; its nature may be physical or verbal. It is illegal for any employer to sexually harass an employee. If you are a victim of sexual harassment, you should keep track of the date and nature of any inappropriate behavior and report the situation to the personnel office in your company or contact an attorney. The personnel department will indicate which steps you need to follow. It is also illegal for an employer not to give a raise or promotion to a person because of gender, marital status, or other personal circumstances aside from the person's experience and achievements. If you are going on a job interview, keep in mind that the interviewer may not ask you whether you plan to have children, ask for a photograph, or inquire about your religious views. The law also prohibits questions regarding your parents' nationality or any questions regarding your ethnic origin, political affiliations, age, marital status, or sexual orientation.

For more information regarding your rights, visit the EEOC's Web site at www.eeoc.gov. Their Web site offers information in English, Spanish, Arabic, Vietnamese, Korean, and Haitian Creole.

2. VOCABULARY

advantageous	law
affair	lawsuit (suit)
age bias	lawyer
attorney	to let go
attorney-at-law	marital status
to be in the loop	minority
to be out of the loop	pension
bias	personnel department
civil rights	plaintiff
claim	political affiliation
to complain	to prohibit
to dawn	prosecutor
disability	race
discrimination	regulation
dossier	to retire
ethnic origin	salary
to fire	sexual harassment
gender	sexual orientation
guideline	to sue
handicapped	suit
to harass	trial
to invoke	unsolicited
judge	wages
jury	

1. Complete the following sentences with the verbs in parentheses. You must decide whether the verb should be in the present perfect tense or the simple past tense.

MEMORANDUM

TO: Jane Bloom, Director of Human Resources
FROM: Catherine Howard, President
DATE: November 5, 1995
RE: Age Discrimination

I __(a)__ (to receive) a letter from the Equal Employment Opportunity Commission last week. The commission wants to make sure that we are enforcing the 1967 Age Discrimination in Employment Act. Under this law any business that deprives a person of his or her job and pension benefits based on his or her age may be sued. (Do) you __(b)__ (to know) about this?

Please check the personnel files on all our department's employees. Find out how many of them __(c)__ (to be) evaluated since 1993. Also, please find out if any __(d)__ (to receive) written commendations for good work or if any __(e)__ (to be) promoted to a higher position within the past two years.

I would like you to compile a list of employees who __(f)__ (to be) fired last year. Be sure to include the reason for such action. It would also be a good idea to have a list of those who __(g)__ (to retire) already.

Please report your findings within the week. Thanks.

2. Complete the following sentences using *for* or *since*.

a. *I have worked as a counselor to help unemployed white collar workers _____ six years.*
b. *She has been on welfare _____ her husband abandoned her.*
c. *The Age Discrimination in Employment Act has been in effect _____ 1967.*
d. *These employees have been in a training program _____ two months.*
e. *We have kept a dossier on each of our employees _____ the day they were hired.*
f. *He has been preparing the case with his lawyer _____ one whole year.*
g. *I have been working on my resumé _____ ten hours.*

    h. *They have been interviewing candidates _____ nine o'clock this morning.*

    i. *The employee has been waiting outside _____ twenty minutes.*

3. Indicate whether the verb used in the contraction is *to be* or *to have.* Circle your answer.

    a. *It's been nice meeting you.*
      to be   to have

    b. *She's been told that the company has a very successful in-house degree program for employees.*
      to be   to have

    c. *It's definitely a good job offer. Why's he having doubts?*
      to be   to have to be   to have

    d. *How's that report going?*
      to be   to have

    e. *He's been preparing for this interview for months.*
      to be   to have

    f. *My company's sending me abroad for two weeks.*
      to be   to have

    g. *Where's the folder I just gave you?*
      to be   to have

    h. *The employee's going to file a suit against the company.*
      to be   to have

    i. *Where's she been filing these forms?*
      to be   to have

    j. *The file's on top of the cabinet.*
      to be   to have

4. Fill in the blanks with the appropriate word.

suit	lawyer	to let go	to retire	prosecutor

    a. *Due to budget cuts, the company was forced _____ fifty employees.*

    b. *The defendant's _____ wanted to set bail at $300, but the _____ refused.*

    c. *I'd like _____ when I turn fifty.*

    d. *It would be better if you wore a _____ when you stand before the jury next week.*

5. Fill in the blank with the verb in parentheses. Use either the past perfect or the past perfect continuous.

    a. *I _____ (to finish) reading the newspaper when I heard the crash.*

    b. *The woman _____ (to cry) because her son was killed in the accident.*

c. The lawyer _____ (to leave) when I called his office.
d. The employee _____ (to come) late to work during the last few
    weeks because he was ill.
e. By the time the police arrived, the suspect _____ (to escape).

READING I

ONLINE ETIQUETTE FOR NEWBIES

It is common nowadays for people all over the world to communicate
via the Internet—rather than by phone—with friends, family, and
business colleagues. They feel that this is a faster and more convenient
way to exchange ideas.

The Internet offers several ways for people to communicate: e-mail,
discussion groups, bulletin boards (also called BBSs or forums), chat
rooms, and instant messaging.

E-mail is the most common form of communication through the
Internet, and it is used by nearly everyone the world who has access to
a computer. It has quickly overcome written letters in popularity as a
means of communication. *Discussion groups* are normally formed
around a specific theme of interest to certain individuals, and
everybody who joins the group takes turns in the conversation. *Forums,*
or *BBSs,* are electronic bulletin boards where people can post
messages on specific subjects. *Chat rooms* enable users to
communicate in real time by interactive conversation. The experience is
similar to having a conference call on the phone. The difference is that
the parties are typing messages on the computer rather than speaking
on the phone. *Instant messaging* is similar to a chat room, but it is a
private conversation between two users. You will often see someone
write "IM me later and we'll talk about it." Some businesses encourage
their employees to use instant messaging as a means to communicate;
seeing information relayed back and forth on a screen makes for a
clearer channel of communication.

Just like in any other type of communication, be it by phone, fax, or mail,
Internet users follow certain rules of etiquette. One of the most basic
rules of online etiquette is to be brief and to the point. By doing so, you
get your point across and save time and money. In the interests of being
brief and quick, Internet users have developed an online shorthand. A
number of acronyms replace commonly used expressions, but they are
unfamiliar to a person who is just beginning to use e-mail, chat rooms,
forums, or instant messaging. Some of the most common are:

AFAIK	*As Far As I Know*
AFK	*Away From Keyboard*

AKA	*Also Known As*
ASAP	*As Soon As Possible*
BBIAB	*Be Back In A Bit*
BBIAF	*Be Back In A Few*
BBL	*Be Back Later*
BBN	*Bye Bye Now*
BFN	*Bye For Now*
BRB	*Be Right Back*
BTW	*By The Way*
CID	*Consider It Done*
EOL	*End Of Lecture*
F2F	*Face To Face*
FWIW	*For What It's Worth*
GG	*Good Game*
GL	*Good Luck*
GTG	*Got To Go*
GTGB	*Got To Go, Bye*
IAC	*In Any Case*
IAE	*In Any Event*
IMHO	*In My Humble Opinion*
L8R	*Later*
LOL	*Laughing Out Loud*
MOTD	*Message Of The Day*
NP	*No Problem*
NRN	*No Reply Necessary*
OTOH	*On The Other Hand*
PLS	*Please*
POV	*Point Of View*
ROTFL	*Roll On The Floor Laughing*
TTFN	*Ta Ta For Now*
TTYL	*Talk To You Later*
THX	*Thanks*
TYVM	*Thank You Very Much*
WB	*Welcome Back*
WE	*Whatever*
WTG	*Way To Go*

When you join a discussion group for the first time, it is advisable to *lurk,* or observe what's going on, for a while before actually jumping in to participate in the conversation. Eventually you should participate actively, because lurking without participating is considered rude. It is also considered rude to place offensive or inappropriate messages. This behavior is known as *flaming* and may make some members of the group quite angry. Another inappropriate behavior is to place the same message several times on different areas of a board. This practice is known as *spamming,* and it wastes the time and money of people who want to retrieve messages.

There are also several typing rules to follow. Using all uppercase letters is known as *shouting,* and it is considered rude if used inappropriately. On the other hand, using all lowercase is known as *mumbling.*

E-mail users personalize their messages by adding written clues, which are known as *Smileys* or *emoticons,* to express their mood and emotions. Smileys are formed by using different characters on the keyboard to create a sideways smiley face. Some you might see are:

:) or :-)	*Smiling*	:(or :-(	*Frowning*
;)	*Winking*	:\	*Undecided*
:'(	*Crying*	:c	*Bummed out*
:|	*Indifferent*	:o	*Surprised*
:>	*Sarcastic*	:@	*Screaming*

Many emoticons have been updated with small artistic, colorful smiley faces, but everyone will understand what mood you're in if you type ":)" at the end of a sentence. ;)

VOCABULARY

bulletin board	*to lurk*
character	*e-mail*
to chat	*mood*
chat room	*to mumble*
emoticons	*online*
to flame	*to retrieve*
flaming	*shorthand*
forum	*to spam*
to instant message (IM)	*spamming*
instant messenger	*to type*
keyboard	*uppercase*
lowercase	

LESSON 6
Business Expansion

A. DIALOGUE

A NEW STORE

*Paul and Mary-Hope Adams own a small clothing boutique in the cen-
ter of Winston-Salem, North Carolina.[1] Over the last couple of years
business has been booming,[2] so they're thinking about expanding.*

PAUL: You know the brand-new[3] mall[4] that is under construction on
the other side of town?

MARY-HOPE: Yes. What about it?

PAUL: I spoke to the building contractors yesterday. They told me it
is designed to feature about forty upscale shops.

MARY-HOPE: What kind of shops?

PAUL: I've heard there will be a few department stores, several
clothing boutiques, and a few jewelry stores. The mall is going to
have one floor for fast-food restaurants and another for
entertainment, with three theaters and a bowling alley. Wouldn't it
be perfect for us to open a second store there?

MARY-HOPE: That's an interesting idea. But, what I had in mind[5]
was to expand by selling our products to other stores in the area.

PAUL: Let's discuss[6] this a little bit. Your idea is certainly less risky.

MARY-HOPE: If we distribute our products to other stores, we will
be able to reach customers who don't frequently shop in the
downtown malls.

PAUL: I disagree. Malls are becoming more and more popular each
day. People don't go there just to shop, but also to escape weather
conditions, to socialize, to go window shopping,[7] or simply because
they're bored.

MARY-HOPE: That's precisely what concerns me: window shoppers
don't exactly go on shopping sprees.[8]

PAUL: You're being too negative. Think about it . . . we won't have
to rely on advertising to gain sales. The big stores will do the
advertising, and we'll take advantage of the traffic that flows
through the mall.

MARY-HOPE: That's a good point.[9]

PAUL: Also, think of how our image will be affected. People will associate all those other upscale stores with ours.

MARY-HOPE: True, too. But, what about rent? It's going to be expensive, don't you think?

PAUL: Well, rent will be high. But think about your idea and how much it would cost to either purchase or rent trucks to deliver our merchandise, and to hire a few sales representatives and a truck driver. Not to mention the cost of advertising . . .

MARY-HOPE: We're going to have to hire new staff anyway if we open a second store.

PAUL: Definitely! But it wouldn't cost as much to hire a few sales clerks as it would to hire all those other employees.

MARY-HOPE: Are you aware that we'll have to work nights and weekends?

PAUL: Yes. But if we focused on selling and distributing our clothes to other stores, we would have to work extra hours anyway. So, do you like my idea?

MARY-HOPE: I think it's a bit more risky, but I guess there are more advantages than disadvantages to it.

PAUL: Great! I knew you'd agree with me. I'd better call the real estate people. They're waiting for our decision.

MARY-HOPE: So, you had this set up already!

PAUL: Come on, don't get upset. You know I'd never do anything without asking you first.

MARY-HOPE: You can say that again! Before you speak with the contractors, why don't we call your friend Robert? He knows a lot about retail. It would be good to get his input[10] on this, don't you think?

B. NOTES

1. The state of North Carolina is in the southeastern United States. The state capital is Raleigh and its biggest city is Charlotte, home of the famous Discovery Place museum. Winston-Salem is to the west of Raleigh. In Winston-Salem, one can visit Old Salem, an old town founded in 1766 by Moravian Protestants. North Carolina is the state

with the highest number of golf courses in the country. Home to the tobacco industry and a thriving real estate market, North Carolina has become one of the most desirable states in which to live.

2. In English there are many verbs that resemble the sound made by the action. These verbs, called *onomatopoeic verbs,* are common. In this case, the verb *to boom* does not refer to the sound of an explosion but to a period of political, cultural, or economic expansion.

3. The expression *brand-new* is used as an adjective to place emphasis on the quality of an item. It means "as new as possible." The word *brand* is used as a noun that refers to the make of a manufactured item. The verb *to brand* means "to label" or "to record."

4. The noun *mall* was originally used to describe a pedestrian path or road. Then the meaning was expanded to refer to pedestrian street with roads on both sides. It is now used to refer to the very popular shopping centers with stores, movie theaters, and restaurants. The United States has both indoor and outdoor malls; the largest mall in the world is the Mall of America in Minnesota.

5. The expression *to have in mind* means "to be thinking about." People say that they have something in mind when they are about to propose an idea, often one that contradicts the idea someone may have already proposed. Other popular expressions with the noun *mind* are:

to be in one's right mind	=	to be sane
to be on one's mind	=	to be thought about frequently by someone else
to bear in mind	=	to think about while making a decision, to consider
to change one's mind	=	to change a previously made decision
to bring to mind	=	to suggest
to come to mind	=	to be remembered
to lose one's mind	=	to be insane, to be overly stressed or harried
to speak one's mind	=	to say exactly what one thinks

6. In the context of the dialogue, the verb *to discuss* means "to have a dialogue," "to reason," or "to object." In other words, it is used to refer to an objective and civilized exchange of ideas. In some languages, the verb *to discuss* refers to a heated discussion between two or more people. The English equivalent is *to argue,* which refers to a discussion in which at least one person disagrees and feels some kind of anger.

7. The English expression *to window shop* describes the action of going to the store to look at the merchandise in the window displays without

actually buying anything. There are also two noun forms: *window shopping* and *window shopper* (a person who frequently goes to the store for entertainment without buying anything).

8. The expression *to go on a shopping spree* means to buy many things on one day, usually without paying attention to the money being spent.

9. The popular expression *to make a point* describes someone expressing an opinion and clearly establishing his point of view. Other similar expressions are:

    to be beside the point
    that's just the point
    the point is that . . .
    to carry one's point
    to get the point
    to miss the point
    to get to the point

10. In this context, the noun *input* refers to opinion or advice. This term is also widely used in technology to refer to the action of programming data into a computer system.

C. GRAMMAR AND USAGE

1. THE FUTURE WITH *TO BE GOING*

AFFIRMATIVE

> subject + *to be* + *going* + main verb in its infinitive form

I am (I'm) going to hire a new assistant.
He is (he's) going to buy more merchandise for the store.
We are (we're) going to open a new store in the mall.

NEGATIVE

> subject + *to be* + *not* + *going* + main verb in its infinitive form

He is not (he's not/he isn't) going to open a new store.
We are not (we're not/we aren't) going to find a bigger space in the other mall.
They are not (they're not/they aren't) going to fire any employees.

INTERROGATIVE FORM WITH SHORT ANSWER

> *To be* + subject + *going* + main verb in its infinitive form . . . ?

Is he going to get a loan to open the new store?
Are they going to buy some computers?

INTERROGATIVE FORM WITH COMPLETE ANSWER

> *What/When/Where/Why/Whom/How* + *to be* + subject + *going* +
> main verb in its infinitive form . . . ?

How are we going to deliver the merchandise?
When is the new store going to open?
How many trucks are they going to need?

2. THE FUTURE WITH *WILL*

AFFIRMATIVE

> subject + *will* + main verb in its simple form

He will (he'll) reach more customers by advertising in the paper.
We will (we'll) put our old merchandise on sale every month.

NEGATIVE

> subject + *will* + *not* + main verb in its simple form

I will not (I won't) work after five o'clock for nothing. ·
They will not (they won't) buy more supplies.

INTERROGATIVE CASE WITH SHORT ANSWER

> *Will* + subject + main verb in its simple form . . . ?

Will you deliver the order on time?
Will they be here when the store opens?

INTERROGATIVE CASE WITH COMPLETE ANSWER

> *What/When/Where/Why/Whom/How* + *will* + subject +
> main verb in its simple form . . . ?

What time will the store open tomorrow?
How will she decorate the new store?

A NOTE ON *WHO*
Remember that *who* acts as a subject in the interrogative form, so no additional subject is necessary:

Who is going to deliver the merchandise?
Who will manage the sales staff?

3. THE USAGE OF THE FUTURE TENSE
The future with *to be going to* is used to express the definite intention of carrying out a premeditated action in the future.

I'm glad you agree because I'm going to call the contractors this afternoon.
I've been thinking about expanding our business. I'm going to find out more about how to do it.

To express that a particular event in the future is done voluntarily or the person is willing to do it, you use the verb *will*.

If you'd like, I'll train the new employees.

When making a prediction about something, or when you think that something might happen in the future, you can use either *will* or *to be going to*.

He believes the new mall will be a big success.
He believes the new mall is going to be a big success.
Renting a space there will be expensive, don't you think?
Renting a space there is going to be expensive, don't you think?

4. THE FUTURE WITH TIME EXPRESSIONS
In sentences that use an adverbial phrase of time, the adverb must be followed by a verb conjugated in the present simple.

When I see the contractors tomorrow, I'll ask them.
After I interview the person who applied for the sales position, I'll call you.

The most common adverbs of time are:

after	*as soon as*
always	*before*
as	*by the time*
as long as	*every time*

the first time	*until*
the last time	*when*
once	*whenever*
since	*while*

5. THE USAGE OF THE PRESENT TENSE TO EXPRESS THE FUTURE

In English you may use the present continuous (see Lesson 2) with expressions of time to indicate a future action when it is certain that the event has been planned and is certain to occur.

He's signing the contract tomorrow at six.
We're opening a new store in the mall in June.

When the action isn't certain, the present continuous cannot be used. For example, the verb *to rain* may not be used in the present continuous to express a future action because it is impossible for a person to plan rain.

It's raining (now). The weather report indicates that it'll rain tomorrow.

The present simple is also used to express events that have been planned in the future.

My plane leaves at 6 A.M. tomorrow.
The meeting starts at 9 A.M. next Wednesday.

D. IDIOMATIC STUDY

EXPRESSING AGREEMENT

The verb *to agree* is an intransitive verb that does not require a direct object. Here are some useful phrases for expressing agreement with someone:

I agree (with you).
You're right.
That's right/true.
Absolutely!
Definitely!
No doubt about it!
I feel the same way.
I couldn't agree with you more.
That's just what I was thinking.
You can say that again!
You took the words right out of my mouth!

I suppose/guess you're right.
You might be right.

EXPRESSING DISAGREEMENT
I disagree.
I don't agree.
I don't think so.
I'm not so sure about that.
I wouldn't be so sure about that.
I hate to disagree, but . . .
I don't mean to disagree, but . . .
I don't want to get into an argument, but . . .
I wouldn't say that.

E. STRICTLY BUSINESS

1. THE LATEST IN RETAIL SALES

A revolution has taken place in the United States, and it has changed the way sales are made. The world of telecommunications has altered the way that people buy retail goods. There are many reasons for this. Statistics show that more women (the largest consumer group) are working full-time, and that number continues to increase. Therefore, this group has less free time to go shopping. Consumers in general have also become more demanding and less flexible with their free time. American consumers are making more of their purchases using less traditional channels, such as telephone sales, specialized mail-order catalog, television, and the Internet. The popularity of online book retailers and the shopping sections of AOL and Yahoo has only increased Internet sales.

This type of retail sales has expanded because of advances in telecommunications. Modern consumers can evaluate different products and compare prices, all this without leaving their homes. Buyers can place orders over the phone, enter them into the Internet, or send them via mail or fax. As the merchants receive the orders, they can verify the inventory and prepare to ship in a very short time. The transaction takes place in a matter of seconds. Simultaneously and electronically, credit cards can be charged and funds can be transferred from one bank to another. When the order is made by mail, the merchant generally accepts only checks or money orders. In most other cases, only credit cards are accepted. Buying from a remote location usually entails a charge for shipping and handling, but it is normally a reasonable amount proportional to the amount of money spent on the order. Also, in some states it is mandatory to add sales tax to the final price of the order. Consumers have found these services to be very beneficial to their busy schedules. That is why many department stores, including Macy's, Sears, Gap, Bloomingdale's, and J.C. Penney, offer clients the option to purchase online. When ordering online, buyers may select express delivery for an extra fee. In addition, gift items not only can be sent directly to the recipient, but they can also be gift-wrapped. Finally, in addition to accepting major credit cards such as American Express, MasterCard or Visa, some merchants offer their own lines of credit with special benefits.

2. VOCABULARY

advantage	mall
to argue	merchandise
to be on sale	method of payment
to boom	order
bowling alley	outlet
to brand	purchase
brand-new	retail
to charge	sales
clothing boutiques	sales clerk
deferred billing	sales representative
department store	to sell
disadvantage	shipment
to discuss	shipping and handling
fast-food restaurants	shopping spree
gift wrap	to socialize
to go on a shopping spree	subscription
to have in mind	warehouse
input	to window shop
item	window shopper
to make a point	window shopping

EXERCISES

---

1. Decide if the events described in the following sentences take place in the present or the future.

   a. *As soon as we sign the rental contract, we're having a party.*
   _____ Present   _____ Future
   b. *I'm reading the terms of the contract.*
   _____ Present   _____ Future

c. *He's interviewing potential candidates for the store manager position.*

_____ Present   _____ Future

d. *After the meeting, we're taking a tour of the new facilities.*

_____ Present   _____ Future

e. *She's calling tomorrow to let us know if she got the job.*

_____ Present   _____ Future

f. *We're going to need at least two trucks to be able to distribute our products around town.*

_____ Present   _____ Future

g. *The mall is opening next week.*

_____ Present   _____ Future

2. Complete the following memorandum using either *will/to be going to* or the present continuous of the verb in parentheses.

MEMORANDUM

TO: Henry Holt
FROM: Mary-Hope Adams
DATE: January 22, 1996
SUBJECT: Telecommunications in retailing

Henry, as you know Paul and I ___(a)___ (to think) about expanding our business. We ___(b)___ (to consider) different options. What I had in mind was to expand by direct distribution. I believe that if we were to distribute our products to other stores, we would be able to reach more customers. Paul, on the other hand, believes that we would do better by renting a space at the mall.

We know that in the near future more people ___(c)___ (to shop) at home with a video display catalog provided by participating retailers. We are also aware that presently more and more consumers ___(d)___ (to buy) through catalogs instead of going directly to retail stores.

I ___(e)___ (to spend) the next two weeks researching this. I'd like to know if you have some information on the use of telecommunications in the retailing business.

We'd like to have your feedback on this and some information on operating costs. Thanks.

3. Use the following expressions to complete each sentence. Remember to conjugate the verb according to its subject.

to speak one's mind	*to bear in mind*
to change one's mind	*to bring to mind*
to have in mind	*to lose one's mind*

a. That picture _____ the old store we used to have on Maple Street.
b. When you look at me in that way I know you're planning something. What do you _____ now?
c. I think one salesperson will be enough for the new store. However, if you give me a good reason to hire two people, I will _____.
d. We asked him to give us his opinion about expanding our business because he's very honest and _____.
e. If this client doesn't stop calling every hour, I'm going to _____.
f. _____ that opening a store in the mall is going to increase our costs by 30 percent.

4. Combine the following sentences using the adverb given.

a. (after)
You'll see the mall tomorrow.
You'll want to open another store there.
b. (as soon as)
I'll finish signing the contract.
I'll call you.
c. (When)
We'll hire new employees.
We'll open a new store.
d. (before)
You'll interview her.
She'll take the typing test.
e. (whenever)
You'll be ready.
You'll sign the contract.

LESSON 7
Banking in the United States

A. DIALOGUE

A NEW BANK ACCOUNT

Robert Gremly recently arrived in Chicago[1] where he will be living for about two years. The company he works for, Big Ben Securities in England, is currently opening a branch in Chicago, and Mr. Gremly is in charge[2] of the operations. He has decided to open a checking account at a local bank in order to handle his personal transactions.

TELLER: Good morning. How may I help you?

MR. GREMLY: Good morning. I'd like[3] to open a checking account.

TELLER: You need to speak to one of our customer service representatives. Take the stairs to the second floor. They'll be able to assist[4] you there.

Mr. Gremly goes to the second floor. After a few minutes, a customer service representative comes to greet him.

MS. GREEN: Good morning. My name is Elizabeth Green. How may I help you today?

MR. GREMLY: Hello. My name is Robert Gremly. I'd like to open a checking account.

MS. GREEN: Are you interested in an individual or a joint account?

MR. GREMLY: An individual account, please.

MS. GREEN: Let me explain our service charges. For basic checking accounts there's a nine dollar and fifty cent monthly service fee and a seventy-five cent activity charge per check and ATM[5] withdrawal. Now if you have a monthly balance of more than one thousand dollars, all service charges and transaction fees will be waived.

MR. GREMLY: That sounds reasonable.

MS. GREEN: Would you like to go ahead[6] and open a basic account, or would you like to hear about our interest-bearing accounts?

MR. GREMLY: I think the basic service will be fine.

MS. GREEN: All right. Just fill out this form and sign it on the back. How much do you wish to deposit?

MR. GREMLY: Fifteen hundred dollars.[7]

MS. GREEN: Will this transaction be in cash, money order, or check?

MR. GREMLY: Cash.

MS. GREEN: Very well. Do you have any questions?

MR. GREMLY: Yes, actually. When will I get my checks?

MS. GREEN: We'll give you temporary checks and a bank card right now. You should[8] receive your personalized checks and your permanent bank card in the mail in about a week.

MR. GREMLY: That's fine.

MS. GREEN: What color would you like for your checks—blue, green, or beige?

MR. GREMLY: Green, please. And I'd like my address printed on the checks as well.

MS. GREEN: Okay. How about your phone number?

MR. GREMLY: No, thanks.

MS. GREEN: I almost forgot to tell you! There is a 13-dollar charge for every two hundred checks. This charge will be automatically deducted from your account.

MR. GREMLY: No problem.

MS. GREEN: Along with our checking account we offer an overdraft[9] protection plan which lets you write checks without worrying if they will bounce.

MR. GREMLY: Are there any additional fees involved?

MS. GREEN: You will only pay a fee if you overdraw on your account, and then you'll only pay a finance charge on the amount you borrow.[10] Would you like to sign up for this option?

MR. GREMLY: Well, why not? I don't think I'll ever use it, but one never knows. If it's free, I might as well[11] get it.

MS. GREEN: Good. All you need to do is fill out this additional form. Now, I'll take you downstairs where one of our tellers will deposit your money and give you your temporary checks.

MR. GREMLY: Great. Thanks for all your help.

MS. GREEN: Certainly.

B. NOTES

1. Chicago is located in the state of Illinois, in the north middle section of the country, near Lake Michigan. The city's financial center is famous for its skyscrapers. The Sears Tower is one of the tallest and most well-known buildings in the world. Chicago's second tallest building is the John Hancock Tower. Chicago is known as the Windy City because of its harsh climate, especially during the winter months. The city offers many forms of cultural activities and entertainment such as theater, opera, classical music, comedy clubs, bars, restaurants, and parks.

2. The expression *to be in charge of* means "to be responsible for."

3. Notice the use of the word *would* (contracted with *I* to form *I'd*). It is a polite form of asking for a favor. The use of the word softens the meaning of the sentence.

4. The verb *to assist* means "to take care of or to help." The word *assistant,* meaning "someone who helps someone else," comes from this verb.

   His secretary assists him by handing out copies of the reports and taking notes.
   Her assistant brings her coffee every morning while she catches up on paperwork.

5. ATM is the abbreviation for Automated Teller Machine, a machine that dispenses cash from bank branches or other remote locations.

6. The English expression *to go ahead* is used to give approval and encourage the other person to do something.

7. It is common in English to express numbers in the thousands according to how many hundreds the number contains. For example, the number 2,300 is commonly referred to as "twenty-three hundred" instead of "two thousand three hundred."

8. In this case the word *should* is used to express "I have good reasons to believe, expect, or assume that you will receive your checks in a week." The word is also used to give advice or to express a belief.

   You should always put some money away for savings.
   In many countries, people believe that women should not leave their parents' home until they get married.

9. An overdraft refers to money taken from a bank account beyond the amount of funds that exist for the account. If someone writes a check for more money than is available, the account is said to be *overdrawn*.

You wrote a check for $250, but you have only $200 in your account. Your account is overdrawn by $50.

You can also say that a person is overdrawn, meaning that person's account is overextended. Most banks in the United States offer some kind of overdraft protection plan that allows the account owner to write checks without having to worry about the amount of money in their checking account. Overdraft protection works like a credit line drawn against the person's own funds; the account holder is charged interest on the amount by which he or she is overdrawn.

10. There are two similar verbs in English that have very distinct meanings. The verb *to lend* describes the action of giving money to someone as a loan with the intention of receiving the money back. The verb *to borrow* describes the action of getting money from someone as a loan with the intention of repaying the person.

Last week Mary borrowed $500 from John and now she wants me to lend her $300.

11. *Might as well* is a popular colloquial expression. In this context it means "Given the circumstances, it is better if I get it" or "Since it is free, why not get it?"

It's already 3 A.M. I might as well stay up and finish this banking report.

C. GRAMMAR AND USAGE

1. THE CONDITIONAL

Conditional sentences usually have two parts: One phrase expresses the condition and is preceded by the word *if;* the second phrase states the result of the condition. The order of the phrases is not important, but the two parts of the phrase should be separated by a comma when the phrase that begins with *if* comes first.

You can't transfer money between the two accounts if they're not linked.
If they're not linked, you can't transfer money between the two accounts.

condition: *If they're not linked, . . .*
result: *. . . you can't transfer money between the two accounts.*

There are four types of conditions:

a. Factual
These are sentences that indicate a fact or a habit. Both the condition and the result are expressed using the simple present.

If you don't endorse the check, you can't cash it.
If you hear a beep, it means you have to take your card from the ATM.

b. Future Possibility

These are sentences that express the possibility that something might occur in the future. In this case, the conditional phrase uses the simple present and the phrase that indicates the result uses *will*, *to be going to*, *can*, or *might* followed by the simple form of the verb:

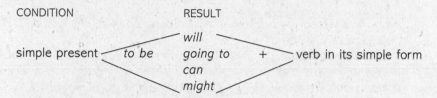

CONDITION   RESULT

simple present — *to be*   *will* / *going to* / *can* / *might* + verb in its simple form

If I get promoted, I'll buy a new house.
If he gets the loan, he can open a new store.
You might be able to cash the check if you get to the bank before three.

c. Speculative

These are phrases that express speculation about an event in the present or in the future. The conditional phrase that states the speculation uses the past tense and the phrase that gives the result uses *would* or *could*.

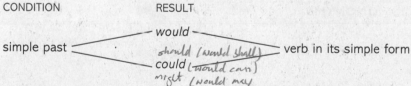

CONDITION   RESULT

simple past — *would* / should (would shall) / *could* (would can) / might (would may) — verb in its simple form

If I won the lottery, I could travel around Europe. (But I haven't won, so I can't.)
If someone tried to blackmail me, I would notify the police. (But no one has, so I don't need to call the police.)

With the verb *to be*, you use the form *were* for both singular or plural subjects. The use of *was* is incorrect in this case.

If I were you, I would invest my money in mutual funds.
She would know what to do if she were here.

d. Contrary to Fact Conditions

Some sentences express conditions that are contrary to fact or reality. In other words, these sentences are used to express what could have happened if a situation had occurred. In this case, the phrase that gives the condition uses the past perfect while the phrase that states the result uses *would have, could have,* or *should have.*

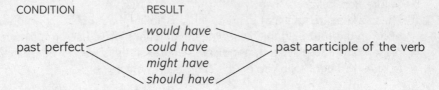

CONDITION   RESULT

                   would have

past perfect   *could have*   past participle of the verb
                   might have
                   should have

If she had signed up for the overdraft protection plan, she wouldn't have paid any overdraft fees.
If we had known that the price of the shares would go down, we would have sold them.
If she hadn't saved her money, she might have gone bankrupt.

The following graph summarizes the four possibilities and the different forms for each case:

TYPE	CONDITION	RESULT
fact/habit	simple present	simple present
future possibility	simple present	*will/going to/can/might*
speculative	past simple	*would/could might/should*
contrary to fact	past perfect	*would have/could have might have/should have*

2. HOMONYMS

Homonyms are words that are pronounced the same way but have different spelling and meaning. The most common homonyms in English are:

a. *brake, to break*
He couldn't come to a stop because he had no brakes.
Be careful with that vase. Glass breaks easily.

b. *to hear, here*
The teller couldn't hear me.
I work in this office right here.

c. *hole, whole*
The road to my house is full of holes.
The employees were on strike for a whole week.

d. *its* (possessive pronoun), *it's* (contraction of *it is*)
I took the overdraft protection plan because of its convenience.
It's a good idea to invest some money in the stock market.

e. *knew, new*
   He knew we were coming, but he didn't wait for us.
   She opened a new account for her daughter.

f. *know, no*
   I know that man, but I can't remember his name.
   No, I don't have ten thousand dollars to lend you.

g. *passed, past*
   I passed by the bank this morning, and I bumped into my former boss.
   In the past, one couldn't do all of these banking transactions over the phone.

h. *peace, piece*
   The peace treaty was signed yesterday morning.
   I'd like another piece of that chocolate cake, please.

i. *plain, plane*
   I'd like to visit the Great Plains some day.
   She wore a plain black dress to the dance.
   The plane crashed just after take off.

j. *right, to write*
   You're right. I should write my phone number on the checks as well.
   My office is on the right.
   Please write down everything we need from the supermarket so we don't forget anything.

k. *two, too, to*
   I have two thousand shares for sale.
   I would like to open a checking account, please. And I need to get a money order, too.
   The interest rate is too high. I can't afford it.

The preposition *to* indicates direction. It cannot be accompanied by any other preposition.

I will be going to the Caribbean next month.
I talked to the bank about getting a loan.

To can also be used to indicate the infinitive form of the verb.

I want to invest in mutual funds.
I would like to be able to save more money.

The preposition *for* is never used with the infinitive form:

Please call the airline to find out at what time the plane arrives.

l. *threw, through*
He threw the keys out the window so I could get in.
I'm afraid my neighbors can peek through my window.

m. *wear, where*
What did you wear to the party last night?
Where did you park your car?

n. *whether* (conditional, *if*), *weather*
I'll have to decide whether to invest my money in bonds or stocks.
The weather in Florida is too humid for my taste.

o. *whose, who's* (contraction of *who is*)
Whose signature is this?
Who's the tall man with the hat?

p. *there, they're, their*
Put the flowers over there.
They're coming to dinner at seven.
Is their daughter coming as well?

D. IDIOMATIC STUDY

ASKING FOR A FAVOR

Use the following phrases when you need to ask for something. It is important to remember the importance of using the word *please* as well as *could* and *would* to soften the expression and make it more polite. Otherwise, the other person might misunderstand you and think that you are giving an impolite order instead of making a kind request.

The following phrases are organized according to how courteous they sound, the last form being the most polite.

Could you please . . . ?
Would you please . . . ?
Would you mind . . . ?
Might I trouble you to . . . ?
Would you be so kind as to . . . ?

These are some possible answers:

FORMAL
Certainly.
I'd be glad to.
It would be my pleasure.

INFORMAL

Sure.
Of course.
Here you go.
No problem.

The following is a common response to the question *Would you mind . . . ?*:

Not at all.

E. STRICTLY BUSINESS

1. BANKS IN THE UNITED STATES

In the United States, banks offer their services to both individuals and businesses. The services offered to individuals include many financial products, such as loans, money transfers, and investment services. Among the most popular services offered to businesses are loans, lines of credit, and investment banking. Before opening an account and depositing your money in an American bank, you should visit several of them to compare the services and fees and find the one that best suits your needs. You can also seek out this information online. The types of accounts offered are similar in all banks, but the fees charged for services vary greatly from one bank to another.

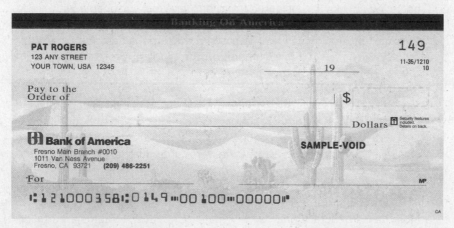

CHECKING ACCOUNT

A checking account is useful and has high liquidity. Most banks will offer you a basic checkbook with one hundred checks when you first open a checking account. You will then have the option to have checks printed with your name, address, and phone number. Keep in mind that most businesses will not accept a personal check that does not have your official information printed on the check. When you pay by check you must show two kinds of identification, normally your driver's license and another type of document. Your job identification card, your passport, or a credit card should suffice. If you elect to use a driver's license, it must be an American license or an international permit; licenses from other countries are not considered sufficient forms of identification. The Department of Motor Vehicles in your state may also issue a non-driver identification card to any individual who does not drive. In some large cities, personal checks are not accepted. Some businesses do not accept checks that are issued from a bank in another state. Therefore, it is always a better idea to have a credit card or enough cash.

OVERDRAFT

If you write a check for an amount that is more than the funds available in your checking account, the bank will charge you between $20 and $30 for each bounced check. The bank normally returns the check to the person who deposited it or tried to cash it. If a store or another type of business attempted to deposit a check that was returned to them, the store will charge you at least $10 and will probably never accept a check from you again. Keep in mind that banks also charge the person who makes the deposit a similar charge, which is annoying since it was not the payee's fault. Regularly bouncing checks is considered fraud and may be punishable with high fines. If it occurs very regularly, it may even lead to imprisonment. Overdraft protection can help you avoid these penalties; ask a bank representative for more information on the types of protection plans.

SAVINGS ACCOUNT

Savings accounts offer higher interest rates than checking accounts (unless you have an interest-bearing checking account, although these are rare). With a savings account, you may withdraw cash whenever you wish. If you need to withdraw a very large amount, you should do so with a certified check from the bank.

AUTOMATED TELLER MACHINE

Most banks generally offer twenty-four-hour access to automated teller machines, or ATMs. You gain access to your account by using a bank card programmed to be accepted in the bank's network of machines. You can make deposits or withdrawals, transfer funds between accounts, and obtain account information. The maximum amount of money that you can withdraw varies from bank to bank (it is normally between $200 and $500 per day).

When you open an account, whether it is a checking or savings account, the bank will issue a bank card for you to use. This card, along with a secret personal identification number (or PIN), gives you access to the ATMs. Your bank card allows you to conduct banking transactions in ATMs owned by other banks, but you are likely to be charged a fee for each transaction.

Finally, if you find yourself short of money, you may use your bank card to pay for supermarket purchases and purchases in other stores that take credit cards (not all stores offer this type of service). By using your bank card, the debit is processed automatically against your checking account.

BANK STATEMENTS
You will periodically receive a statement in the mail showing you the activity and balance of your account. Some banks return your checks to you once they have been cashed. You should review these statements carefully; any charges that you don't recognize should be reported to your bank.

SAFE-DEPOSIT BOXES
Banks offer safe-deposit boxes for rent on a monthly or yearly basis. Absolutely no person other than the person who has the key to the box can access the box or its contents. The bank has access to the box only in the event of the death of the person who rented the safe-deposit box. This type of service is useful to protect objects of great value such as passports, jewelry, foreign currency, or other important documents.

OTHER BANK SERVICES
Most banks offer customer service over the phone. This service saves customers a trip to a bank branch if they need questions answered or need to speak with customer service. With your bank card and the phone keypad you will be able to transfer money from one account to another, request account balances, and pay bills. Many banks also offer Internet banking, which allows you online access to your account to pay bills, make transfers, and perform other transactions.

BANKS IN THE UNITED STATES
The five largest banks in the United States are Citibank, JPMorgan Chase, Bank of America, Wachovia, and Wells Fargo. Online banking has also become very popular with the rising popularity of the Internet. A number of virtual banks have no offices or branches and conduct all

their banking on the Internet or over the phone; E*TRADE is a popular example of this type of banking.

2. VOCABULARY

account	to go ahead
to assist	individual account
assistant	interest
automated teller machine (ATM)	interest-bearing
balance	to issue
banker	joint account
bank check	to lend
to be in charge of	online banking
to be overdrawn	overdraft
to borrow	overdrawn
to bounce (a check)	personal identification number (PIN)
branch	safe-deposit box
to cash	savings
cashier's check	savings account
certified check	savings bank
charge	service fee
check	statement
checking account	transaction
customer service	to transfer
Department of Motor Vehicles	to withdraw
deposit	to yield
to endorse	

EXERCISES

1. Complete the following conditional sentences with the correct form of the verb in parentheses.

   a. If you (to remember) _____ to transfer money into your checking account, the check wouldn't have bounced.
   b. If you tell me how much you are willing to invest, I (to help) _____ you decide which stocks to buy.
   c. The money (to be) _____ available the day after tomorrow if you deposit the check in your account today.
   d. I would change the present economic policy if I (to be) _____ the president of the United States.
   e. That sounds like a good job offer. If I (to be) _____ you, I would accept it right away.
   f. If he had someone to help him, he (to finish) _____ the job on time.

g. She might get the new account if she (to convince) _____ the client that her advertising strategy will be successful.
h. If the real estate agent lowers his fee, I (to take) _____ the apartment right away.
i. I (to be) _____ able to pay my son's school if the bank gives me a loan.

2. Complete the following sentences using *two, too,* or *to.*

a. I had _____ cups of coffee yesterday morning.
b. I would like to go to Rome this summer. My sister would like to go there, _____.
c. I have been _____ Europe _____ times.
d. I can't apply for the overdraft protection plan. The fees are _____ high.
e. _____ cash a check at a bank, the bearer must endorse it.
f. I want _____ listen _____ the news broadcast.
g. _____ people were handing fliers _____ customers inside the bank.
h. I can use my bank card _____ buy groceries or dine at my favorite restaurant.
i. These _____ packages are _____ be signed for by the supervisor.
j. It was _____ late _____ go _____ the movies, so we decided _____ rent one instead.

3. Combine the following sentences using the conditional (with *if*).

a. You need to present proper identification.
    You want to cash a traveler's check.
b. You buy a certificate of deposit.
    You won't be able to withdraw the money until it matures.
c. You will receive a yield of 10 percent.
    You invest in these bonds.
d. You don't have your address printed on your checks.
    Your check will not be accepted.
e. You should diversify your investments.
    You want to minimize your risks.

4. Fill in the blanks with the following words.

an overdraft	a deposit
a statement	a joint account
a broker	a canceled check

a. My wife and I have a checking account in both our names. We have _____.

b. Because the amount of withdrawals was greater than the balance in the account, we charged you _____ fee.
c. A record of a person's deposits and withdrawals is called _____.
d. I made _____ of $500 into my account yesterday.
e. You can use _____ as proof of purchase.
f. A person who buys or sells stocks and bonds is called _____.

5. Complete each sentence with the appropriate word.

a. its   it's
   _____ easy to open a bank account.
   The bank opens _____ doors at 9 A.M.
b. know   no
   All I _____ is that I have _____ money left in my checking account.
c. hear   here
   Could you please come over _____? I can't _____ you because you're too far away.
d. whether weather
   I can't decide _____ I want the overdraft protection plan or not.
   The _____ this week has been dreary.
e. whose   who's
   _____ going to sign for this package?
   _____ briefcase is this?
f. there   they're   their
   I'm unfamiliar with this bank; what is _____ fee for checking accounts?
   Is _____ a fee?
   I think _____ charging a fee.

insuand

driver application form

doto

patient info form   P45

100

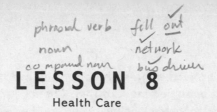
phrasal verb   fell out
noun   network
compound noun   bus driver

LESSON 8
Health Care

A. DIALOGUE

A VISIT TO THE EMERGENCY ROOM

Pia and her eight-year-old son, Johnny, are on vacation with their family. This morning, Pia noticed that a rash[1] covered parts of her son's body. When the rash got worse, she decided to take him to the emergency room at the local hospital in Gardiner, Wyoming.[2]

PIA: Hi. I've brought my son in to see a doctor. He has a pretty bad rash.

NURSE: All right. Has he ever been treated here before?

PIA: No, he hasn't. We're from out of state.[3]

NURSE: Oh, really? Then we'll need you to fill out this patient information form. Now, do you have health insurance that covers[4] out-of-network visits?

PIA: I'm not sure, but I do have insurance. Maybe I should call our provider and check?

NURSE: Good idea. You have no idea how many people get stuck[5] with emergency medical costs. You're welcome to use this phone here.

A little later.

PIA: Well, my insurance said that the closest network physician is all the way in Grant Village. Since that's so far away, they'll let Johnny see a doctor here.

NURSE: Fine. Could I have your insurance card, please? I'll go ahead and get the paperwork started. But if you and Johnny would please take a seat, the doctor will be with you shortly.

Half an hour later, Johnny is called in to see the doctor.

PHYSICIAN: So, what do we have here? Looks like a pretty bad rash. How long has he had it?

PIA: I first noticed it this morning. At the time, I wasn't too concerned. Johnny has always had very sensitive skin. He was

101

scratching his legs a lot, so I thought he had been bitten by mosquitoes or something. But then I noticed that the rash was spreading over the rest of his body, and he seemed to be running a fever.[6] I realized[7] it was some sort of allergic reaction, so I decided to bring him in.

PHYSICIAN: Has Johnny been out in the wilderness lately? Doing any camping, fishing, hiking?

PIA: Yes, actually. Our family went hiking on one of the trails near Mammoth Hot Springs[8] yesterday afternoon. Johnny did wander off[9] the trail for a while . . .

PHYSICIAN: Well, that makes sense, because it looks like poison ivy[10] to me. Let's[11] take a closer look. Does it itch?

JOHNNY: Yes, a lot.

PHYSICIAN: The blisters on his back look pretty bad. Did you apply[12] any lotion?

PIA: I used the calamine[13] lotion from our first aid kit. That seemed to help a little.

PHYSICIAN: It's good you brought him in. Some of the blisters are beginning to ooze and break. I'm going to prescribe a cream to relieve the itching and help the blisters heal.

PIA: How long will that take?

PHYSICIAN: They should clear up[14] within a week. Now, what did you do with the clothes he was wearing?

PIA: I put them aside with the rest of the laundry. Why?

PHYSICIAN: Poison ivy can be contagious, so it's important to wash any clothes or equipment he touched with a strong alkaline soap.

JOHNNY: Mom, I'm thirsty . . .

PHYSICIAN: Being thirsty is normal for someone with poison ivy. Make sure he drinks lots of liquids. And keep an eye on his temperature. It might still be a little high tomorrow, but if it doesn't rise any more, there's nothing to worry about.

PIA: Anything else?

PHYSICIAN: No, that's about it. Here's the prescription for the cream. Just apply it to the affected areas twice a day and cover with a sterile gauze pad. You can get the prescription filled[15] right here at the hospital pharmacy.

PIA: Thank you very much.

PHYSICIAN: You're quite welcome. So, are you going to be in the area much longer?

PIA: Well, we plan to go to South Pass City[16] next. My husband wants the kids to see the gold camp there. Then we'll drive down to the Wyoming Territorial Prison Park.

JOHNNY: That's where Butch Cassidy once did time![17]

PIA: He can't wait to see it! After that, we'll fly home.

PHYSICIAN: Well, enjoy your vacation, and no more walking off the trails through the bushes, young man.

JOHNNY: You bet!

B. NOTES

1. The noun *rash* refers to a skin eruption that can be accompanied by itching and swelling. As an adjective, it refers to something or someone characterized by ill-considered haste or boldness.

   He made a rash decision and lost half his personal fortune.

2. The state of Wyoming is located in the western United States, in the Rocky Mountains region. The state capital is Cheyenne. Yellowstone National Park, founded in 1872, was the first national park in the United States and is perhaps the most famous national park in the country. Many tourists visit the area during all seasons to ski, fish, hike, or camp.

3. *Out of state* is a fixed expression; it does not need an article before *state*. Another similar expression is *out of town.*

4. The verb *to cover* has different meanings that vary according to the context in which it is being used:

   to place something over so as to protect or conceal
   The doctor covered the wound with a bandage.

   to protect or shield from harm; to provide for
   Your insurance plan only covers up to 80 percent of the cost of hospitalization.

to spread over the surface of
The runner covered a distance of 54 miles.

to hide from view or knowledge
The woman was covering her real motives with lies.

5. The phrase *to get stuck* is an example of the passive voice, using the verb *to get* followed by a past participle that functions as an adjective (we'll see more about the passive voice in Lesson 15). Here, the past participle is *stuck,* from the verb *to stick,* meaning "to be fixed, blocked, and unable to move forward." In this dialogue, *to get stuck* means that many people have no choice other than to pay for their medical bills themselves.

6. Note the use of the verb *to run* in the expression *to run a fever.* You may also say *to have a fever.* It is important to remember that in the United States temperature is given in Fahrenheit. The normal body temperature is 98.6°F.

7. The verb *to realize* means "to comprehend completely and correctly."

   When he realized it was poison ivy, it was too late.

   It also has a less common meaning: "to fulfill a dream or goal."

   He had finally realized his dream of becoming a doctor.

8. In the dialogue, the word *spring* describes "a stream of water flowing from underground." Most springs have warm or hot waters. In other cases, the word describes "the season that comes after winter." A spring is also "an elastic device, usually a coil of wire that regains its original form after being expanded or compressed."

   I'm planting these seeds so that I'll have flowers in the spring.
   The springs in that couch are coming out through the fabric.

9. The verb *to wander* means "to move about without a definite destination or purpose." *To wander* should not be confused with the verb *to wonder,* which means "to marvel, to have doubts, or to question oneself."

   I wonder if we should take Johnny to see a doctor.

10. Poison ivy is a poisonous plant that is found in wild areas throughout the eastern and central United States. It has compound leaves with three leaflets, small green flowers, and whitish berries. Most people are allergic to this plant, which causes a rash on contact. In some cases it may even cause blisters, but the allergic reaction is rarely fatal. If you come into contact with poison ivy, wash the affected

areas thoroughly, along with any clothes you were wearing at the time.

11. *Let's* is a contraction of *let us*. This contraction is very popular and has almost completely replaced the expression *let us,* which is considered too formal and outdated. One exception is during Catholic mass when the priest says "Let us pray."

12. The verb *to apply* has several different meanings. In some cases it means "to put on." In other cases it means "to put into action." It can also mean "to request assistance, employment, or admission."

    She applied glue to the paper.
    The driver applied the brakes.
    You have to fill out that form in order to apply for the job.

13. Calamine is a pink, odorless, tasteless powder of zinc oxide dissolved in mineral oils and used in skin lotions. Calamine is regularly used for treating skin rashes or insect bites. Most first aid kits have some kind of cream or ointment with this ingredient.

14. The expression *to clear up* is a phrasal verb. Its meaning varies according to the context in which it is used. In this case, it means "to improve or to disappear." It can also have these other meanings:

    to organize
    I cleared up my desk before I began to write.

    to become bright and sunny
    After the storm, the sky cleared up.

    to fix, rectify, or straighten
    Let's clear up this situation before it gets any worse.

15. The phrase *to fill a prescription* means "to provide the medication specified by a doctor on a prescription form."

    The pharmacy couldn't fill this prescription today; the pills will be in tomorrow.

16. South Pass City is one of the most authentic historic sites in the country. It was one of the first camps on the Oregon Trail, a trail that stretches from the Missouri River to the Columbia River in Oregon. This route was used by most pioneers and people looking for gold between 1840 and 1860.

17. *To do time* is a colloquial phrase that means "to spend time in prison because of a conviction."

C. GRAMMAR AND USAGE

1. THE VERB *TO BE*

a. Form

	SIMPLE PRESENT	SIMPLE PAST	PRESENT PARTICIPLE	PAST PARTICIPLE
I	am	was		
You	are	were		
He/She/It	is	was	being	been
We	are	were		
You	are	were		
They	are	were		

b. Usage

The verb acts as an auxiliary verb to form the present continuous *(to be + verb + -ing)*, as we saw in Lesson 2. But it can also be used as the main verb, as we will see below. The verb *to be* is used with an adjective to describe something:

I'm tall and thin.

It can also be used to identify something or someone:

He's a doctor, and she's a nurse.
The Wyoming Territorial Prison Park is where Butch Cassidy once did time.

The verb *to be* can also be used to describe a physical or mental condition.

They are tired.
She was sick last week.
I was happy when I found out that the insurance would pay for my surgery.

Below are some adjectives that are used with the verb *to be*.

TO BE + ADJECTIVE

cold	*right*
hot	*wrong*
hungry	*sleepy*
thirsty	*awake*

The verb *to be* is also used to indicate the age of a person.

Her son is eight years old.

It can be used to indicate the height and weight of a person or object.

How tall are you?/What is your height?   *I'm 5 feet 4 inches tall.*
How much do you weigh?   *I'm 120 pounds./I weigh*
                                             120 pounds.

It's also used to give the price of something.

How much is your consultation fee?
My fee is $30 per hour.

2. THE VERB *TO HAVE*
a. Form

	SIMPLE PRESENT	SIMPLE PAST	PRESENT PARTICIPLE	PAST PARTICIPLE
I	have	had		
You	have	had		
He/She/It	has	had	having	had
We	have	had		
You	have	had		
They	have	had		

b. Usage

The verb *to have* is used as an auxiliary verb to form the present perfect, the present perfect continuous, and the past perfect continuous, as we saw in Lesson 5. As is the case with the verb *to be*, *to have* can also be used as the main verb. The verb *to have* indicates possession.

He has a new sports car.
She has blue eyes.

It can also be used to indicate that someone is under the influence of an illness or ailment. Compare these two sentences:

The boy has a cold.
The boy is cold.
He has a very high fever, too.

The following are useful expressions that include the verb *to have*:

to have breakfast/lunch/dinner/food/drinks/a class
to have a party/guests
to have trouble/difficulties
to have a good time/weekend
We are having breakfast early tomorrow.
She is having twenty people over for dinner next Monday.
I'm having a wonderful holiday.
Are you having trouble with this math problem, too?

3. THE VERB *TO DO*

a. Form

	SIMPLE PRESENT	SIMPLE PAST	PRESENT PARTICIPLE	PAST PARTICIPLE
I	do	did		
You	do	did		
He/She/It	does	did	doing	done
We	do	did		
You	do	did		
They	do	did		

b. Usage

The verb *to do* serves as an auxiliary verb in questions, in the negative form of the present simple (Lesson 2), and in the simple past (Lesson 4). But as with *to be* and *to have,* it can also be used as the main verb in a sentence.

Its most common meaning is to perform or to execute. There are, however, some other instances in which you will need to use the verb *to do:*

To ask or give information regarding someone's condition:

How's the boy doing? He's doing just fine.

To indicate that something is sufficient or adequate:

I don't have a lantern. Will a candle do?

It can be used colloquially to give the speed of a moving vehicle:

The ambulance did 60 miles per hour.

4. *TO DO* VS. *TO MAKE*

For some speakers of other languages these two verbs appear to have the same meaning. In English there are differences between the two verbs. You must pay attention to the context in order to decide which of the two you need to use.

The verb *to make* means:

to bring into existence by constructing, modifying or shaping
While she waited for the emergency unit to arrive, she made her own tourniquet out of some old sheets.

to prepare
I made dinner for four.

to produce
I made this dress myself.

to deduct, to interpret
What do you make of her reaction?

to be good for something
A clean sheet makes a good tourniquet.

to force
He made me drive to the University Hospital.

to give someone a rank or position
The hospital director made her chief of surgery.

to induce an emotion
The news made me sad.

The verb *to do* means:

to perform or execute
The director of that movie will do a sequel next year.

to arrange, to wash, to clean
Please do the dishes first, then do the floors, and then do the bedrooms.

to work on something
The painters are now doing the hospital's entrance hallway.
What does he do for a living?

to produce something creative
She's doing a book on health-care organizations.

to fulfill a prison sentence
Butch Cassidy did his time in this prison.

to solve in a specific amount of time
I did the math problem in less than five minutes.

D. IDIOMATIC STUDY

GIVING WARNING
There are times when you must act quickly to prevent an accident or a dangerous situation. These phrases are useful in those situations:

> *Don't* + verb in its simple form . . . !

Don't touch that plant! It's poisonous!
(You'd better) get out of the way!

(You'd better) stay away from the edge of that cliff!
You'd better not stay out in the sun too long!
Careful! Look out! Watch out!
Be careful!

In case of an emergency, go to the nearest phone and dial 911, the emergency number used in the United States for emergency assistance. These are some useful emergency phrases:

This is an emergency! Please hurry.
There's a fire! Please hurry!
There's been an accident! Please come quickly.
Help!
I'm bleeding!
Call an ambulance/the police/the fire department!

To express that you are concerned about something, you may use one of these phrases:

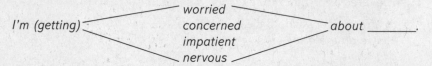

I'm (getting) ⟨ worried / concerned / impatient / nervous ⟩ *about* _____.

I'm getting a little worried about them because it's been twelve hours and they haven't called.

Here are some possible answers:

I wouldn't be concerned.
I wouldn't worry.
You shouldn't worry.
Don't worry.
Don't be concerned.
I'm sure he/she/they'll be fine.

E. STRICTLY BUSINESS

1. MEDICAL SERVICES

HEALTH MAINTENANCE ORGANIZATIONS

Health Maintenance Organizations (HMOs) are privately run programs that offer a network of medical services and hospital care to their members. These organizations combine the functions of an insurance company with the services of doctors and hospitals. HMOs charge an annual fee for membership that is comparable to the fees charged by regular insurance companies. There are two types of HMOs: one that offers group service, and one that offers individual service. The group service HMO works through an association of physicians that operate in conjunction with a hospital or a health center. The individual service HMO works with independent doctors who belong to a network. These doctors agree to limit their private practice to accomodate patients assigned to them by the HMO. Member patients who need to see a doctor are required to select an internist or general practitioner from a list of available physicians. This doctor becomes the person in charge of all tests, checkups, diagnoses, and preventive treatment. Any referral to a specialist must be arranged through the general practioner. Patients cannot select any hospital that they want; they must use only the designated hospital for that doctor or geographical area.

Presently there are more than 650 organizations of this kind in the United States. More than 27 million people in the country get their health care through one of these HMO plans. Seventy percent of physicians have an affiliation with some kind of HMO.

OTHER INSURANCE COMPANIES
Nonprofit health insurance companies, such as Blue Cross/Blue Shield, allow patients to choose their own physician. Each company has its own set of rules and payment schedules. Most companies require patients to fill out forms in order to receive benefits.

MEDICARE
Medicare is a health care social insurance program that offers help to senior citizens over the age of 65. It is funded by employee and employer contributions made according to the employee's salary and income before retirement. Medicare does not cover medical treatment offered abroad.

MEDICAID
Medicaid is a health assistance program offered by the government to those with financial need. In theory, this program should cover all medical expenses, but this can vary from state to state. In some areas, private hospitals do not accept patients who are eligible for Medicaid.

2. EMERGENCY SERVICES
If you have an emergency while you are in the United States, your safest bet is to ask for help from the concierge in the hotel. He or she will probably send you to a doctor or call emergency services. Another option is to seek treatment at the nearest university hospital; these hospitals are known for offering the best treatment in any given area. Once you arrive at the emergency room, you are likely to be treated by one of the internists or resident doctors, who will evaluate the situation

and give you the appropriate treatment. In case of a car accident, an ambulance will take you to the nearest hospital for treatment. In either case, you will be admitted, treated, and held responsible for any medical or hospital fees. Before you travel to the United States, it is important to call your insurance company to find out your plan covers medical expenses incurred in foreign countries. If you are in an accident or an emergency and are unsure what to do, go to the nearest phone and dial 911. This is the emergency number for immediate help throughout the United States.

3. VOCABULARY

to ache	Medicaid
alkaline soap	Medicare
allergic reaction	medication
allergy	medicine
ambulance	on an empty stomach
bandage	pain
benefits	pharmacy
blood test	physician
calamine lotion	poison ivy
cast	prescription
cold	prescribe
contagious	provider
cough	rash
diagnosis	sensitive skin
dose	shot
emergency	side effects
fever	to sneeze
to fill (a prescription)	specialist
general practitioner (GP)	sterile
headache	stretcher
health maintenance	surgery
organization (HMO)	surgeon
immunization	syringe
injection	temperature
insurance	treatment
internist	vaccine
liquids	

EXERCISES

1. Complete the following sentences with one of the following three verbs: *to be, to have, to do.*

112

a. I don't feel well. I _____ a headache, and I _____ very thirsty.
b. She hasn't eaten anything all day, and yet she _____ not hungry.
c. You _____ right. The medicine _____ working.
d. The boy _____ 12 years old, but he _____ very short for his age.
e. How much _____ the antibiotic?
f. What does a chiropractor _____?
g. The dead man _____ about 140 pounds and _____ red hair. The ambulance is taking him to the morgue.
h. He _____ a very high fever. What should we _____?
i. The pharmacist will not give you the medicine unless he _____ a prescription signed by a doctor.
j. _____ you sure this pill doesn't _____ any side effects?

2. Complete the following sentences with the verb *to do* or the verb *to make*.

a. The insurance company _____ me go back to the doctor's office to have him sign the claim form.
b. They _____ a stretcher out of wood and carried the injured man on it.
c. I didn't _____ well on the driver's test.
d. I don't have any pain killers. Will aspirin _____?
e. He didn't _____ what the doctor suggested, and now he's sick again.
f. I'll _____ some chicken soup. I'm sure it will _____ you some good.

3. Complete the following sentences with the verb *to have* or *to be*.

a. I think he _____ a fever because his forehead _____ very warm.
b. I think Tom _____ as tall as Jack.
c. Why don't we get together next week and _____ lunch?
d. You _____ right. Let's take Johnny to the nearest hospital.
e. She _____ thirsty, but she _____ not hungry.
f. I _____ a very important meeting next week.
g. He _____ twenty pounds overweight.

4. Complete the following crossword puzzle by answering the following questions. You may choose the answers from the list of words that appears after the clues.

HORIZONTAL
1. A _____ is used to inject fluids into the body.

2. _____ are responsible for the hereditary characters of each person.
3. When a person suffers an injury such as a cut, doctors generally will cover it with a _____.
4. Spots on the skin produced as a result of an allergic reaction.
5. Opposite of down.
6. The temperature is below 0°F. It is _____.

VERTICAL
1. Another word for operation.
7. Another word for shot.
8. When a person has a temperature of 104°F, it is called a _____.
9. To expel air suddenly and noisely from the lungs as the result of an involuntary muscular spasm in the throat or to clear the air passages.
10. The exact amount of medicine to be taken at one time.

surgery	itch	injection	fever	below	dose
genes	gauze	cold	amount	bandage	temperature
rash	sneezing	cough	operation	up	syringe

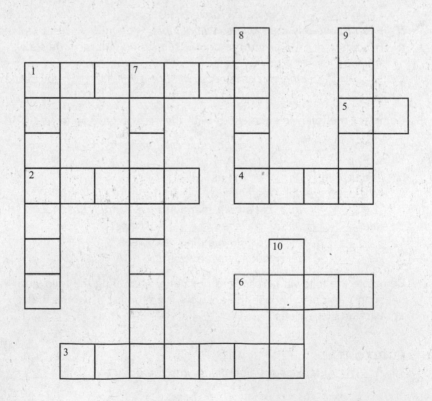

LESSON 9

Social Etiquette

1 contrast
2 new info
3 verb
4 noun
feel
5 strongly

A. DIALOGUE

ARE WE DATING?

Ann Tremba is a quality manager at Electro-cute, a microelectronics manufacturer based in Denver.[1] *Alvaro Jaramillo, who was recently promoted to the same position at Electro-cute's plant in Mexico, has come to Denver for a week-long training session. Yesterday, Ann invited Alvaro to join her for dinner, and tonight they're meeting at a popular Italian restaurant.*

ANN: Hey, there! Glad you could make it! I was a little concerned.[2]

ALVARO: What time is it? Am I late?

ANN: It's almost seven thirty. You're only twenty or so minutes late, so it's no big deal.[3] I went ahead and put my name in.[4] We shouldn't have to wait much longer for a table.

ALVARO: Huh. In Mexico people are usually at least twenty minutes late. If people decide to meet at seven, no one will be there until seven thirty, maybe even eight o'clock.

ANN: You're kidding! Most of the people I know get upset if I'm more than ten or fifteen minutes late. And whenever I'm late, there's usually a pretty good reason. So why are people in Mexico so late all the time?

ALVARO: I don't know exactly. Most Latin Americans are just not as concerned with time.

ANN: I suppose you're right. We are pretty obsessed with it.

HOSTESS: Ann, party[5] of two? Ann, party of two?

ANN: That's us! Let's go.

ALVARO: This whole experience is pretty strange.

ANN: What do you mean?

ALVARO: Well, in my country, women don't invite men to dinner very often.

ANN: Really? I suppose there are a lot of women in the U.S. who won't ask men out[6] either. Many are afraid of rejection. But, there are a lot of women who like doing it, like me. I'd rather be the one in the driver's seat . . .[7]

ALVARO: I'm not sure I understand . . .

ANN: Well, I like to decide who I want to spend my time with and how. Whenever a guy asks me out, that usually means he's the one in charge. I'm not really comfortable with that.

ALVARO: So, are you in charge tonight? You asked me out, you picked the restaurant, you put your name on the table . . .

ANN: Come on! Quit giving me a hard time.[8] I figured you're here by yourself for a week and probably sick[9] of your hotel room. I was just trying to be nice . . .

ALVARO: So this isn't a real date?

ANN: Not at all! No offense, Alvaro, but aren't you engaged?[10]

ALVARO: Yes, I am. I just needed to make sure, you know? People in Mexico don't usually go on, how do I say it, this sort of casual date.

ANN: Huh. People here do it all the time. But believe me, I can understand your confusion. Sometimes even I can't tell what's a casual date and what's a real date. You never really know unless you talk about it.

ALVARO: Well, at home there's nothing to talk about. I would go out with a group of friends if I just wanted to have fun, but going out with just one woman would automatically be considered a date.

ANN: So, what looks good to you?

ALVARO: I don't know what I want. I'm actually not very hungry yet. This is a little early for me.

ANN: What are you talking about? It's almost eight o'clock. I'm starving!

ALVARO: Is this late for you? I usually don't eat dinner until nine or later.

ANN: Well at this rate, it might be nine o'clock before we get some food! Do you want some suggestions? The pasta with the garlic sauce is to die for.[11]

B. NOTES

1. The city of Denver is in the state of Colorado, located in the Rocky Mountains in the western United States. The city is famous as a base for the many great ski resorts that are located nearby. Downtown Denver has several jazz clubs, restaurants, and art galleries. The University of Colorado is located in the nearby city of Boulder. Every summer, Boulder hosts a popular classical music festival.

2. The verb *to concern* means "to be of interest or importance." When it is used as an adjective (*concerned*), as in this case, it means "worried."

3. The expression *It's no big deal* is similar to *It doesn't matter* or *Don't worry.*

4. The expression *to put one's name in* describes adding your name to a waiting list.

5. The noun *party* in this case refers to a group of people. *Party* as a noun can also mean "a celebration." The verb *to party* always means "to celebrate."

6. *To ask someone out* means "to invite someone to go on a date."

7. The expression *to be in the driver's seat* means "to be in control of a situation."

8. *To give someone a hard time* means "to tease someone." Other popular expressions with the verb *to give* are:

to give someone a break	=	to try to be understanding
to give someone five	=	to slap someone's hand in greeting or celebration
to give someone a buzz	=	to call someone on the telephone
to give someone hell	=	to do your absolute best to beat another sports team, impress someone, or berate someone. (This is almost always used as an expression: "Give 'em hell!")

9. In this context, the expression *to get sick of* means "to be fed up and tired of someone or something." It is not to be taken literally. The word *sick* also means "ill," "morbid," or "in bad taste."

   He's been sick for the last two weeks.
   I'm sick of eating pasta every night.
   That was a sick joke.

Other expressions are:

to be sick of it all
to be sick for
to be sick at heart

10. *To be engaged* means that you made a commitment to someone to do something. It is most commonly used to express a commitment to marry. The noun form, *engagement*, refers to the activity that you committed yourself to or the period of time between the time that you accept a proposal of marriage and the actual wedding.

I'm afraid I won't be able to attend the party due to a previous engagement.

11. *To die for* is a colloquial expression that is not to be taken literally. In this case, it means that the pasta with garlic sauce is delicious.

Other expressions with the verb *to die* are:

to die laughing
The clown made the audience die laughing.
to die on someone/something
My car died on me. I couldn't get it started.

There are some other expressions with the adjective *dead:*

to be dead broke	=	to be really poor, destitute
to be dead from the neck up	=	to be not very smart or attentive
to be dead in the water	=	to be over before it got started
to be dead on	=	to be exactly correct

C. GRAMMAR AND USAGE

1. MODAL VERBS: FORM
Modal verbs are auxilary verbs and have only one form, regardless of whether the subject is singular or plural. Most of them are followed by the simple form of the main verb:

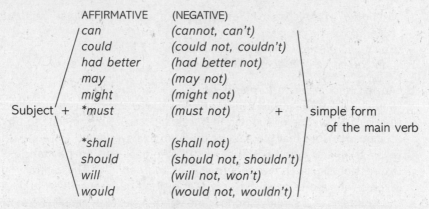

	AFFIRMATIVE	(NEGATIVE)		
	can	*(cannot, can't)*		
	could	*(could not, couldn't)*		
	had better	*(had better not)*		
	may	*(may not)*		
	might	*(might not)*		
Subject +	**must*	*(must not)*	+	simple form of the main verb
	*shall	*(shall not)*		
	should	*(should not, shouldn't)*		
	will	*(will not, won't)*		
	would	*(would not, wouldn't)*		

Some similar expressions are followed by the preposition *to* and the simple form of the main verb:

AFFIRMATIVE

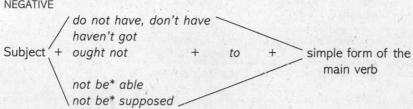

Subject +
have
have got
ought + *to* + simple form of the main verb
be* able
be* supposed

NEGATIVE

Subject +
do not have, don't have
haven't got
ought not + *to* + simple form of the main verb
not be* able
not be* supposed

Notice that some of these verbs do not have a contraction in the negative form.

*NOTE: The verb *to be* must be conjugated to conform to the subject it follows.

2. MODAL VERBS: USAGE

Modal verbs are auxiliary verbs that are used to express a state of being or an attitude. As we will see, some of them may have more than one meaning.

a. Help *(will/would/can/could)*
When asking someone for their help or cooperation, you use *will you, would you, can you,* or *could you.* The expression *can you* is the least formal of these phrases.

Would/will you please ask Susan to give me a call when she gets back from work?
Could you please bring me a glass of water?
Can you come over here for a second?

b. Advice *(should/ought to/had better)*
Should, ought to, and *had better* are used whenever you want to offer advice to someone or suggest that it is important for someone to do something. Note that the past of the verb *to have* is *had*. However, the expression *had better* does not refer to the past. It is an idiomatic expression similar in meaning to *should* and *ought to*. These three expressions are used with the present or the future tense. Of the three, *had better* has a slightly stronger meaning; it generally implies a strong warning or even a threat.

You shouldn't worry so much. Go ahead with your dinner plans.
If it's a formal party, so you ought to wear a cocktail dress.
I think you'd better ask them if they have a special diet.
You'd better eat well or you'll get sick.

c. Deduction *(must)*
Use *must* when you want to express a conclusion reached through logical deduction.

Greg is having his second serving of lasagna.
→He must be hungry.

The Blakes always bring their own food.
→They must be on a special diet.
→They must not like anyone else's cooking.

d. Ability *(can/could)*
The modal *can* is used to express an ability to do something in the present or in the future. The past form of the modal *can* is *could*.

She can cook really well.
We couldn't call you to let you know we'd be late.

e. Need *(have to/have got to/must)*
Use *have to, have got to,* and *must* when you want to express that something is needed or necessary. Notice that *must* is followed only by the simple form of the verb. The modal *must* is stronger in meaning and implies that the action is absolutely necessary (almost obligatory); *must* is, therefore, the least common of the three. It is also considered to be the most formal. *Have got to* is the most informal of the three. This expression is more popular in spoken language than written language. The past tense of this expression is *had to.*

I have to rent a tuxedo for my friend's wedding.
I've got to call all my friends to let them know the party has been canceled.
If you're going to be late, you must/have to let me know.

f. Permission *(may/can/could)*
The modal *may* is generally used to grant permission. If you want to be less formal, use the modals *can* or *could.*

I know you're on a very strict diet, so you may/can bring your own dinner if you'd like.
May/Could I bring a friend to your dinner party?

g. Asking for something *(may/can/could/will/would)*
To ask for something when the subject of the sentence is the first-person singular, use *may* or *could* in a formal question and *can* in an informal question.

May I come in?
Could I borrow your silverware for the dinner party?

Use the modals *will, would,* or *could* when the subject of the sentence is *you.* The modal *would* is the more formal of the three and the most widely used.

Would/could you pass the sugar, please.

You may also use the phrase *would you mind* to ask for something or to ask for permission. The phrase may be followed by a verb in the past tense or by a gerund.

Would you mind if, instead of cooking, I ordered some Chinese food?
Would you mind telling Tom not to be late?

h. Possibility *(may/might/could)*
The modals *may* and *might* are used indistinctively to express that there is a possibility that something will occur in the near present or future. The negative forms are *may not* and *might not.* The negative form does not have contractions. The modal *could* has a similar meaning.

The Blakes may/might call to ask me what I'm serving for dinner.
I may not/might not invite the Blakes to my next party.
I could try to find out what their plans are, but I don't want to call them.

i. Prohibition *(must not)*
When the auxiliary verb *must* is used in a negative sentence, it acquires a stronger meaning. Using this form specifically expresses prohibition of an action.

You must not smoke in areas that are designated for nonsmokers.

j. Suggestion *(could/shall/should)*
Use *could* or *should* when you want to suggest something. When *should* is used, the suggestion is stronger and sounds almost like a command.

You could make several dishes so people who don't eat meat have a choice.

The word *shall* is used in questions with the subjects *I* or *we.* It is used when you are making a suggestion and want to know if the other person agrees with the suggestion or not. The word *shall* is more formal than *should.*

Shall I add more salt to this dish?
Should we bring more wine?

D. IDIOMATIC STUDY

ASKING FOR PERMISSION
When asking for permission it is important to attach a polite expression to your request, such as *is it okay* or *would you mind.* Otherwise, people might interpret some of your phrases to be orders or commands.

Is it okay/all right to smoke?
May/Can I please have some more water?
Would you mind if I brought a friend along?
Would it bother you if I closed the window?
I'd like to bring a friend over, if that's all right with you.

When you want to grant permission, you should use the following phrases:

Certainly.
Of course.
It's all right with me.
I don't see why not.
By all means. Go ahead.
I don't mind at all.
Sure.

To say that you do not give permission, you should use one of these phrases:

I'd prefer/rather you didn't.
I'd rather you wouldn't.
I'm not sure it would be appropriate.

I don't think smoking is allowed in here.
You're not supposed to bring anyone who's not invited.
You may not bring another guest.

E. STRICTLY BUSINESS

1. SOCIAL ETIQUETTE

The United States is such a socially and ethnically diverse country, so it is difficult to be precise about rules of social etiquette. It is possible to be general, however.

Most Americans are generally casual about their professional and social relationships. Therefore, it is not strange to call your colleague, your boss, or a new acquaintance by his or her first name. Americans have a democratic tradition that does not rely heavily on hierarchy, so titles are less important in America than they may be in other countries.

When greeting someone, it is not customary to shake hands unless you are being introduced to someone or in business situations. However, if someone offers you his or her hand, you should shake it. It is also not customary to hug and kiss as a greeting.

Americans are very casual when it comes to the way they dress. Their priority is comfort, which is why they appear to be very informal. When it comes to business attire, there is a somewhat stricter dress code. Women generally wear European-style business suits and men wear suit and tie. It is not uncommon, however, to see men in their shirtsleeves and without their jackets while they are having lunch, especially during the spring and summer months. In many companies, office workers have decided to dress down on Fridays and wear casual, comfortable clothes. This is called "casual Friday." Because comfort is king, women normally take off their high heel shoes when it comes to walking. It is not uncommon to see women wearing fashionable business suits and sneakers as they walk in the city. This trend originated in New York at the beginning of the 1980s during a transit strike, which forced many people to walk for many miles to get to work. During that time many women took to the streets with their sneakers on their feet and their high heel shoes in their bags. Soon enough, this trend became the norm for many working women.

In the United States people give a lot of importance to time. Generally, Americans tend to be very respectful when it comes to schedules, whether it is for business or entertainment. Most people try to stick to their schedules and make every attempt to be punctual. Therefore, if you have a dinner invitation or have arranged to meet someone at a certain time, you are expected to arrive on time and not fifteen minutes late. Most Americans dislike it when people are not punctual. Because time is such an important factor in American life, most Americans are very direct. They generally get straight to the point when they have something important to express.

If you have been invited to go to someone's home for dinner, it is customary to bring something. The gift does not have to be expensive; it is merely a token of appreciation. You may decide to bring flowers, a bottle of wine, or dessert. Remember that roses, especially red ones, have a romantic connotation.

When it comes to personal relations, men or women can invite each other to go out on a date. It is still somewhat customary for men to pay for meals when on a date, though it is not uncommon to split the bill in less formal situations. On certain occasions, women may offer to pay for the entire bill. If you have been invited on a date, you should offer to pay your share of the bill. You can accept you date's invitation to pay if he or she insists repeatedly. Keep in mind that service is generally not included in restaurants. You are expected to pay a tip of 15–20 percent of the total.

2. VOCABULARY

to ask someone out
to be concerned
to be engaged
to be in the driver's seat
to be late
to be on time
boss
casual Friday
colleague
to concern
date
to die for
engagement
etiquette
first name
to get sick of

to give someone a hard time
hierarchy
to hug
to kiss
last name
nickname
obsessed
party
punctual
to put one's name in
schedule
to shake hands
sick
sneakers
suit

EXERCISES

1. Decide whether the preposition *to* is necessary in the following sentences. If it is not necessary, write ∅ in the blank.

   a. When attending a dinner party at someone's house, you might _____ want to bring a bouquet of flowers to the host.
   b. If you're attending a formal dinner, you must _____ be on time.
   c. You ought _____ confirm your attendance if you've been asked to do so on the invitation card.
   d. You'd better not _____ wear casual clothes to a formal dinner.
   e. You don't have _____ bring an expensive gift for the host.

2. Fill in the blanks with one of the auxiliary verbs given in parentheses.

Nicholas:	I _(a)_ (have to, can) make a list of the people I'm going to invite. I _(b)_ (might not, can't) leave anyone out.
Pat:	That _(c)_ (could, shouldn't) be too hard. Have you gone shopping yet?
Nicholas:	No, I haven't. I'm not sure what to cook. Any suggestions?
Pat:	Well, I _(d)_ (could, would) make a vegetarian dish. You _(e)_ (can't, must not) go wrong with that.
Nicholas:	Yes, I _(f)_ (might, must) do that. But I _(g)_ (should, have to) check with Greg first. You know he loves steak.
Pat:	Yes, but he _(h)_ (will, should) know that not everybody is into eating meat. Plus, the dinner is for his colleague. As far as I know, he and his wife are vegetarian, aren't they?
Nicholas:	Yes, you're right. I'll go ahead and make a vegetable lasagna. _(i)_ (could, would) you like to come with me to the supermarket?
Pat:	Sure. I'll meet you there, say, in thirty minutes?
Nicholas:	That's fine. I _(j)_ (had better, have got to) hurry up and put together a shopping list. See you in a little bit.
Pat:	Bye.

3. Change the following sentences to the negative form.

   a. I might have enough time to bake a cake for tonight's party.
   b. People should invite an equal number of men and women to their dinner parties.

c. She can bring a few guests to the graduation ceremony.
d. If I were you, I would ask the host whether she needs any help.
e. You have to bring a gift for the host.

4. From the list below, choose the phrase that best completes the incomplete sentences in the dialogue.

I'd rather you wouldn't	I'm not sure it would be appropriate
would it bother you	certainly
I don't mind at all	is it all right

Debbie:	Hi, Mary. I hope I'm not calling you at a bad time.
Mary:	Not at all. I was just going through the last details of tomorrow's lunch party.
Debbie:	As a matter of fact I was calling you precisely about that. Sally, a friend of mine, will be in town. _(a)_ if I brought her along?
Mary:	Well, _(b)_ .
Debbie:	I'm sorry, but I'm not following you.
Mary:	Tom is also invited, you know?
Debbie:	I still don't understand.
Mary:	Well, she and Tom were dating a few months ago. They had a pretty nasty breakup, and _(c)_ for them to see each other.
Debbie:	Well, _(d)_ with you if we came by after lunch just for a little while?
Mary:	_(e)_ . But, I hate not having you over for lunch.
Debbie:	Don't worry. _(f)_ . Plus, that way Sally and I will be able to catch up on things.

LESSON 10
Real Estate

A. DIALOGUE

LOOKING FOR AN OFFICE SPACE

Mr. David Norton and Ms. Jane Blake are partners in a law firm. They have decided to open a new office in Atlanta.[1] Their real estate agent has already shown them an office in a downtown building. They are now looking at another office on the outskirts[2] of the city.

AGENT: So, here we are. As you can see, this building is more modern than the one we saw before. The office I want to show you is located on the eighteenth floor. Please follow me.

MS. BLAKE: How far did you say we are from downtown?

AGENT: About eight miles, but lots of companies and businesses have offices out here.

They take the elevator to the eighteenth floor and enter the office.

MR. NORTON: Wow! This office is huge, and look at that view! You're right, this is a much bigger space. I like the way it's set up.[3] The other office doesn't have enough space for a reception area.

MS. BLAKE: I like the fact that there are two separate entrances. When we have office supplies delivered, we can do it without inconveniencing the clients sitting in the reception area.

MR. NORTON: Is there a conference room?

AGENT: Yes, right around the corner. It's a bit smaller than the one in the other building, but it has a nicer view.

MS. BLAKE: One thing I definitely like about this office is that it has a lot of built-in bookshelves. It's a shame that the wood has been painted white. I like wood.

AGENT: I'm sure we can take care of that. By the way, I don't know if you noticed, but there are two bathrooms.

MS. BLAKE: So, what do you think?

MR. NORTON: Well, I guess . . .

AGENT: I don't mean to interrupt,[4] but I almost forgot to mention that there's an underground private parking garage.[5] Each office has ten parking spaces.

MR. NORTON: That would be very convenient for our clients. I'd like to go over the rental conditions one more time. How much did you say the rent was?

AGENT: Twelve hundred[6] a month, and there's a security deposit of one month's rent. This money will be returned to you when the lease expires, granted that the office is in good condition. Also, the agency's fee is ten percent of the annual rent.

MS. BLAKE: It's certainly less expensive than the other office.

AGENT: Yes, of course. In downtown Atlanta you're paying a lot more for less space.

MS. BLAKE: But downtown is a prime location. I'm a bit worried that we'll be too far from our clients out here.

AGENT: The proximity of the highway and easy access to public transportation makes this part of town as convenient as downtown. I don't think you need to worry about being too far out. Besides, a lot of people don't want to deal with the traffic downtown.

MS. BLAKE: I guess you're right.

MR. NORTON: Are the utilities[7] included in the rent?

AGENT: You'll only be paying for electricity. Water and heat are included.

MS. BLAKE: You said you'd take care of the bookshelves, am I right?

AGENT: No problem. Let me know if you need anything else repaired or painted. The building's maintenance staff is always available. You can make any changes you wish as long as it doesn't affect the structure.[8]

MR. NORTON: So, Jane, I guess we've pretty[9] much made up[10] our minds, haven't we?

MS. BLAKE: Yes, I think this is a much more functional space. This is by far the best office we've seen.

AGENT: Great! I'll give you a call once I have the lease ready for you to sign.

B. NOTES

1. Atlanta is located in the state of Georgia, in the southeastern United States. The city of Atlanta has grown tremendously during the past few decades. More than three million people currently live in Atlanta. The downtown section is home to the headquarters of the Coca-Cola Company. In the downtown area you will find the Coca-Cola Museum (The World of Coca-Cola), the CNN Center, and the famous shopping area known as The Underground. The Stone Mountain Park, known for its gigantic sculputres of Jefferson Davis, Robert E. Lee, and Stonewall Jackson (Civil War heroes), is located northeast of the city. Atlanta was the home of the 1996 Summer Olympic Games.

2. The word *outskirts* refers to the area or region that lies on the outermost boundary of a city.

3. The verb *to set up* has several different meanings. In this dialogue it refers to the way that the area is organized. It has other meanings as well:

   to start a new business
   He is setting up a new supermarket outside of town.

   to make plans to do something
   I have set up the trip for the first weekend in July.

   to trick someone in order to make them look guilty
   Her sister planted the gun in Tom's car to set him up.

   to assemble something
   Please set up the tent.

4. In America, it is generally considered impolite to interrupt someone while they are speaking. If someone wants to interrupt someone else who is talking, the person should apologize first and then justify the interruption. Most people wait until a person stops talking before interjecting. Generally, Americans get upset if someone interrupts them or makes them stop talking in mid-conversation.

5. The word *garage* has two meanings. In this dialogue, *parking garage* refers to the place where cars are parked. Homeowners also refer to their *garage* as the place they park their car or where they store tools at home. It can also refer to the place where cars are repaired.

6. In English it is common to say large numbers in the amount of hundreds that the number contains. For example, most Americans say "twenty-three hundred" instead of "two thousand three hundred" to speak of the number 2,300.

7. The word *utilities* refers to the combination of water, electricity and heating. Normally, tenants have to pay only for electricity; other utilities (water and heating) are provided by the landlord as part of rent. There are, of course, exceptions to this rule; make sure you investigate which utilities are included before you sign a lease.

8. It is necessary to contact the city's building department before making any changes to the exterior structure of a house or building, as it is sometimes necessary to obtain a permit first.

9. In this case, the word *pretty* does not mean "beautiful." When it is accompanied by another adjective, it means "considerably, very, or rather."

   He was pretty sure that the fee was negotiable.
   He seemed pretty angry to me.

10. The verb *to make up* has several different meanings depending on the context in which it is used. The expression *to make up one's mind* means "to decide or to resolve." Other meanings are:

    to compensate (to repay, to recompense)
    Thank you for lending me your car. I will make it up to you soon.

    to invent in order to deceive
    Her daughter made up a lie in order not to go to school.

    to forgive one another, to resolve an argument
    They had an argument and stopped talking to each other. Last night, they finally made up.

C. GRAMMAR AND USAGE

1. THE COMPARATIVE

The comparative form is used to compare two nouns or actions that have different qualities. It is important to remember that adjectives are used to modify nouns and adverbs are used to modify actions or verbs. The comparative is formed by following this formula:

> adjective/adverb + *-er* + *than*
> or
> *more* + adjective/adverb + *than*

This room is wider than the room in the back.
My rent is more expensive than yours.

In English the comparative element is indicated by -*er* or the word *more*. If the adjective or the adverb has only one syllable, add -*er* to the end of the adjective or adverb.

ADJECTIVES
old → *older*
wise → *wiser*

ADVERBS
fast → *faster*
hard → *harder*

If the adjective has two syllables and it ends in *y,* replace the *y* with an *i* and add -*er.* (This rule does not apply to adverbs.)

busy → *busier*
pretty → *prettier*

If the adjective or the adverb has two or more syllables, use the word *more.*

ADJECTIVES
famous → *more famous*
expensive → *more expensive*

ADVERBS
slowly → *more slowly*
clearly → *more clearly*

Some adjectives and adverbs have irregular forms:

ADJECTIVES
good → *better*
bad → *worse*

ADVERBS
well → *better*
badly → *worse*

Remember that the opposite of *more . . . than* is *less . . . than.*

This month my electric bill was less expensive than last month's.
Tom pays less rent than I do, and he lives in a nicer neighborhood.

2. THE SUPERLATIVE

The superlative is used to compare a noun or action with three or more nouns of different qualities. It is formed by following this formula:

> *the* + adjective/adverb + *-est*
> or
> *the* + *most* + adjective/adverb

This building is the tallest in the city.
My rent is the most expensive in the building.

In English the superlative element is indicated by adding *-est* or by using the word *most*. If the adjective or adverb has only one syllable, add *-est* to the end of the word.

ADJECTIVES
old → oldest
wise → wisest

ADVERBS
fast → fastest
hard → hardest

If the adjective has two syllables and ends in *y*, replace the *y* with a *i* and add *-est*. (This rule does not apply to adverbs.)

busy → busiest
pretty → prettiest

If the adjective or adverb has two or more syllables, use the word *most:*

ADJECTIVES
famous → most famous
expensive → most expensive

ADVERBS
slowly → most slowly
clearly → most clearly

Here are the irregular cases:

ADJECTIVES
good → best
bad → worst

ADVERBS
well → best
badly → worst

Remember that the opposite of *the most* is *the least*.

The northeast part of the city is the least popular section in which to live in because there are many factories.
The office we saw in the downtown area was the least spacious.

3. SENTENCE STRUCTURES OF EQUIVALENCE

To compare two nouns or actions that are equal, we use the following formula:

$$\boxed{as + \text{adjective/adverb} + as}$$

This office is as clean as that one (is).
He gave the real estate agent the check as quickly as he could.

The negative form requires the use of the word *not* before the first *as*. In some cases you may want to qualify the expression by adding *quite* or *nearly*.

Building A is not quite as tall as Building B. = Building A is a little bit shorter than Building B.
The rent in this part of town is not nearly as expensive as the rent in the downtown area. = The rent in this part of town is much cheaper than the rent in the downtown area.

4. *GOOD* VS. *WELL*

The word *well* may serve as an adjective or as an adverb. It is used as an adjective when you want to express that you are in good health. It is used as an adverb when you want to express that an action was executed correctly.

Mary Ann had a cold last week, but now she's well.
Jim plays chess well.

You may use *well* or *good* with the verb *to feel*. When you use *well* you emphasize the state of health of the person, while *good* stresses the physical or emotional condition of the person.

I feel well. (I feel healthy.)
I feel good. (I feel fine emotionally and physically.)

D. IDIOMATIC STUDY

EXPRESSING PREFERENCES

When expressing preferences it is important not to sound too demanding. These are some useful phrases:

a. *I'd Rather . . .*
   I'd rather . . . /I would rather . . . is a common phrase used to express preference. It is used with the simple form of the verb.

   I'd rather rent a place in a more convenient location.
   I'd rather finalize the lease today.

   I'd rather . . . /I would rather . . . can also be used to express your preference about somebody else's actions. In this case, it is used with a subject and a verb conjugated according to the subject.

   I'd rather you finish the report tonight and come in late tomorrow.
   I'd rather you call us when the contract is ready.

b. *I'd Prefer . . .*
   I'd prefer . . . /I would prefer . . . is another common phrase. It is used with the infinitive of the verb or with a noun.

   I'd prefer to lease an office downtown.
   I'd prefer the office with the garden view.

c. *I'd Like . . . /I Like . . .*
   You may also use the verb *to like* to make comparisons.

   I like the suburbs better than the city.

   A: *Would you like to go see the new Woody Allen film tonight?*
   B: *I'd rather go bowling with Mark and Clarissa. How about you?*
   A: *I'd like that, too. Let's call them.*

   A: *I'd like to go on vacation for two weeks in November.*
   B: *I'd prefer you took your vacation in December. November is going to be a very busy month.*

E. STRICTLY BUSINESS

1. REAL ESTATE
One way to find office space, an apartment, or a house is to look in the classifieds section of the newspaper. This section uses many abbreviations, but it is easy to become acquainted with them.

The following abbreviations are commonly used in classified ads:

blk	*block*
BR(s)	*bedroom(s)*
E	*east*
EIK	*eat-in kitchen*
LR	*living room*
lrg wndw	*large window*
renov.	*renovated*
sq. ft.	*square feet*
w/	*with*

Another option is to visit a real estate agency. Generally, in rental situations, the agency will charge you a commission; this commission will vary from place to place. In cities such as New York, where space is very limited, there is strong competition for real estate. The commission in New York can be as high as 15% of the annual rent. In some other states, the real estate broker charges the equivalent of one month's rent.

STUDIOS
Studios are generally the cheapest type of apartment. These one-room apartments with a small kitchen and bathroom are ideal for single occupants.

FURNISHED APARTMENTS

Furnished apartments are usually more expensive than unfurnished ones. By law, most apartments in the United States must have a refrigerator and a stove. Any other furniture or appliances depend on the landlord and the type of contract that you sign. Most buildings have washer and dryer facilities that are generally located in the basement of the building. These are coin-operated machines that can be used by any resident of the building. A furnished apartment generally includes basic furniture, carpeting, lamps, and drapes. Apartments are not normally equipped with kitchen utensils, plates, sheets, towels, or other electrical appliances. Most apartment buildings have wooden floors, so it is often important to have rugs in the apartment to avoid bothering the downstairs neighbors.

2. ROOMMATES

Rent can be extremely high in some places, so many people share apartments or houses to defray costs. Most newspapers maintain a separate section in the classifieds for people looking for roommates. In most cases, once an apartment is rented, each person has a separate bedroom. The living room, dining room, bathroom, and kitchen are usually considered common areas, and all residents divide the price of rent and utilities.

If you decide to reply to one of these ads, you should expect to have an interview with the person who is looking for a roommate. These interviews are a good way to determine whether you are compatible with the person. It is also important to discuss your study and work habits, who will do house cleaning and with what frequency, if the person is a smoker or not, if they host parties frequently, if they have pets, and so forth.

3. THE LEASE

Most lease contracts are written documents. After reading it very carefully, both the tenant and the landlord must sign the lease. Most leases have one-year terms, though in some states it is possible to sign two-year leases. When the lease expires, the tenant or the landlord may decide to cancel the contract or renew it. In some cases, if the tenant decides to break the lease before the end of the term, the landlord may decide to charge the tenant a fee for breaking the lease. It is not uncommon for the landlord to charge rent until he or she finds another tenant for the empty apartment. You may be expected to pay the first and last month's rent at signing. This is done to encourage the tenant to notify the landlord at least thirty days prior to the expected vacancy of an apartment. Some landlords may also demand a separate security deposit. This security deposit is kept to make sure that if there are any damages to the apartment, the landlord has money to pay the repair expenses. The tenant should keep a receipt with the amount of money paid at the time of signing. It is also important to make a list of any damage to the property that you discover when you move in and notify the landlord. That way, the landlord will not make you responsible for any of those damages when you decide to move. Gas and electricity are normally not included in your rent and must be paid directly to the electrical company, normally on a monthly basis. Heating expenses can be very high in some parts of the country. That is why it is important to have an idea of the average monthly payment for the apartment before signing a lease. The gas or oil company can give you that information. In most cases, water is included in the expenses paid by the building.

4. VOCABULARY

block	maintenance
built-in bookshelves	to make up
carpeted	outskirts
classified ads	prime location
cleaning deposit	proximity
commission	real estate
compatible	reception area
conference room	renovated
damages	rent
downtown	rental
eat-in kitchen	roommate
efficiency	rug
electrical appliances	security deposit
fee	to set up
functional	studio
furnished apartments	tenant
garage	unfurnished
heating	utilities
landlord	want ads
lease	

EXERCISES

1. Fill in the blanks using the adjective *good* or the adverb *well*.

   a. How _____ do you know the city?
   b. He's a _____ real estate agent who does his job _____.

c.   Green curtains will definitely go _____ with that couch.
d.   She may not take phone messages very _____, but she's a
     _____ typist.
e.   Pia is a _____ competitor; she performs _____ under
     pressure.

2. Complete the following sentences using the comparative or the
    superlative of the word in parentheses.

    a.   Which of these three highways is the _____ (short, superlative)
         route?
    b.   The apartment will go to the _____ (high, superlative) bidder.
    c.   The office space we saw first was in _____ (good, comparative)
         shape, but this one is definitely _____ (spacious, comparative).
    d.   This lease is _____ (convenient, comparative) for us.
    e.   I liked the _____ (expensive, superlative) apartment, but we
         can't afford it.
    f.   Julia Morgan is one of the _____ (famous, superlative) architects
         in the area. Her _____ (good, superlative) client was William
         Hearst, one of the country's _____ (rich, superlative) newspaper
         publishers.

3. Based on the information provided in the sentences below form new
    sentences using the comparative, the superlative, or the expressions of
    equivalence.

    a.   My apartment is one thousand square feet. Anna's apartment is
         also one thousand square feet. My apartment is _____ (big)
         Anna's.
    b.   The security deposit for an apartment in Atlanta is 8 percent of the
         annual rent. The security deposit in New York City is 12 percent of
         the annual rent. The security deposit in New York City is _____
         (high) the security deposit in Atlanta.
    c.   My lease is for three years. Al's lease is for one year. His lease is
         _____ (short) mine.
    d.   I pay $1,200 for my apartment in New York. Steve pays $1,000
         for his condo in New Jersey. Steve's apartment is _____
         (expensive) mine.
    e.   Our office has two conference rooms. The one on the right is
         comfortable. The one on the left is uncomfortable. The
         conference room on the left is _____ (comfortable) the one
         on the right.
    f.   I live on the tenth floor, my friend Karen lives on the fifteenth floor,
         and Benny lives on the twentieth floor. Benny's apartment is
         _____ (high) of all three.

4. Write the numbers for the following figures and solve the equations.

   a. *Six hundred times two equals?*
   b. *Forty-eight hundred plus twelve hundred equals?*
   c. *Sixteen hundred minus five hundred makes?*
   d. *Fifty-two hundred plus three hundred makes?*
   e. *One hundred thousand minus eight thousand equals?*
   f. *Twelve hundred minus eight hundred equals?*

READING II

"GIVE ME THE SPLENDID SILENT SUN"
FROM *LEAVES OF GRASS*

BY WALT WHITMAN (1819–1892)

1

Give me the splendid silent sun, with all his beams full-dazzling;
Give me juicy autumnal fruit, ripe and red from the orchard;
Give me a field where the unmow'd grass grows;
Give me an arbor, give me the trellis'd grape;
Give me fresh corn and wheat—give me serene-moving animals,
    teaching content;
Give me nights perfectly quiet, as on high plateaus west of the
    Mississippi, and I looking up at the stars;
Give me odorous at sunrise a garden of beautiful flowers, where I can
    walk undisturb'd,
Give me for marriage a sweet-breath'd woman, of whom I should never
    tire;
Give me a perfect child—give me, away, aside from the noise of the
    world, a rural, domestic life;
Give me to warble spontaneous songs, reliev'd, recluse by myself, for
    my own ears only;
Give me solitude—give me Nature—give me again, O Nature, your
    primal sanities!
—These, demanding to have them, (tired with ceaseless excitement,
    and rack'd by the war-strife;)
These to procure, incessantly asking, rising in cries from my heart,
While yet incessantly asking, still I adhere to my city;
Day upon day, and year upon year, O city, walking your streets,
Where you hold me enchain'd a certain time, refusing to give me up;
Yet giving to make me glutted, enrich'd of soul—you give me forever
    faces;
(O I see what I sought to escape, confronting, reversing my cries;
I see my own soul trampling down what it ask'd for.)

Keep your splendid, silent sun;

Keep your woods, O Nature, and the quiet places by the woods;

Keep your fields of clover and timothy, and your corn-fields and
orchards;

Keep the blossoming buckwheat fields, where the Ninth-month bees
hum;

Give me faces and streets! give me these phantoms incessant and
endless along the trottoirs!

Give interminable eyes! give me women! give me comrades and lovers
by the thousand!

Let me see new ones every day! let me hold new ones by the hand
every day!

Give me such shows! give me the streets of Manhattan!

Give me Broadway, with the soldiers marching—give me the sound of
the trumpets and drums!

(The soldiers in companies or regiments—some, starting away, flush'd
and reckless;

Some, their time up, returning with thinn'd ranks—young, yet very old,
worn, marching, noticing nothing;)

—Give me the shores and wharves heavy-fringed with the black ships!

O such for me! O an intense life! O full to repletion, and varied!

The life of the theatre, bar-room, huge hotel, for me!

The saloon of the steamer! the crowded excursion for me! the torch-
light procession!

The dense brigade, bound for the war, with high piled military wagons
following;

People, endless, streaming, with strong voices, passions, pageants;

Manhattan streets, with their powerful throbs, with beating drums, as
now,

The endless and noisy chorus, the rustle and clank of muskets, (even
the sight of the wounded;)

Manhattan crowds, with their turbulent musical chorus—with varied
chorus, and light of the sparkling eyes;

Manhattan faces and eyes forever for me.

VOCABULARY

beam	rack'd (racked)
breath'd (breathed)	reckless
clank	ripe
dazzling	rustle
glutted	sought
grape	throb
orchard	trellis'd

unmow'd
warble
war-strife

wharves
wounded

REVIEW QUIZ 1

A. Use the appropriate tense of the verb in parentheses to fill in the blank. Make sure the verb agrees with its subject.

PRODUCTS AGAINST ANIMAL TESTING

In today's market there __(1)__ (to be) quite a few companies whose main concern __(2)__ (to be) to produce high-quality products without testing them on animals. One such company __(3)__ (to be) the very popular chain of stores known as the Body Shop, which was founded by Anita Roddick, an English housewife and mother in Brighton, England.

Back in 1979, Mrs. Roddick __(4)__ (to borrow) the equivalent of $6,000 from a bank in Brighton and __(5)__ (to use) it to open a store stocked with shampoos, lotions, and creams. All the products in the store __(6)__ (to be) made with natural and exotic ingredients from all over the world. Mrs. Roddick __(7)__ (to have) a very strong passion for traveling and foreign countries. Traditional herbal formulas that __(8)__ (to promote) healthy skin and hair __(9)__ (to have) always fascinated her. One of her great concerns __(10)__ (to be) saving the Earth from environmental pollution and destruction. The store __(11)__ (to give) her the opportunity __(12)__ (to combine) all these passions in one.

Since then, Mrs. Roddick __(13)__ (to use) the Body Shop not only as a place to sell natural cosmetics and cleansers, but also as a clearinghouse for information on environmental concerns. When a customer __(14)__ (to walk) in, he or she __(15)__ (to find) reading material on the plight of inhabitants of the rain forest and of other endangered parts of the world next to the shampoos and facial creams. In addition, the shop __(16)__ (to always take) a strong position against __(17)__ (to use) animals to test the safety of cosmetic products. Mrs. Roddick __(18)__ (to believe) that if cosmetic products __(19)__ (to contain) only natural ingredients and no harmful, artificial ones, such product testing which __(20)__ (to cause) so much suffering to animals, __(21)__ (to not be) necessary anymore.

The packaging of Body Shop products __(22)__ (to be) plain, simple, and recyclable. At the same time, it __(23)__ (to incorporate) written information that __(24)__ (to promote) environmental awareness. The staff of the Body Shop __(25)__ (to go) through a special training program that __(26)__ (to help) them to become experts in the field of herbal cosmetics. In that way, the salespeople __(27)__ (to take) more of an interest in their work and __(28)__ (to serve) customers better.

Today the Body Shop __(29)__ (to grow) from a small shop in an English town to a huge international corporation. The Body Shop now __(30)__ (to operate) in thirty-seven different countries. The United States and Japan __(31)__ (to be) the shop's largest markets.

B. Fill in each blank with either *a, an, the,* or Ø.

1. A: Have you read _____ *New York Times* today?
   B: No, not yet. I haven't had one free minute _____ entire day.
   A: There's _____ article on _____ life on _____ Mars.
   B: Really? Do have _____ newspaper with you?
   A: No, I don't. I left it at _____ home.

2. A: Which is your favorite musical instrument?
   B: That's hard to say. It would have to be _____ piano.
   A: Do you have _____ piano at _____ home?
   B: As a matter of fact, I do. I don't play it, but my sister does.

3. A: I got _____ new job!
   B: Congratulations! Where?
   A: At _____ United Nations!
   B: When do you start?
   A: _____ Tuesday.

4. A: What did you do last night?
   B: I went to _____ movies with Phil.
   A: Me, too! What movie did you see?
   B: The new Tom Cruise film.
   A: Wow! What _____ coincidence I did, too. Which _____ theater did you go to?
   B: _____ one on Broadway and 68th Street.
   A: Oh, we went to _____ one on Broadway and 14th.

C. Join the following words together to form sentences using the comparative.

The Sears Tower/(+) tall/the Empire State Building/
The Sears Tower is taller than the Empire State Building.

1. Jack/play tennis/(+) good/Pete.
2. Some people think that to work for a woman/(+) hard/to work for a man.
3. An athlete/(+) make money/a university professor.

4. The *New York Times*/(+) have readers/the *Boston Globe*.
5. Some people say that people in the South/(+) friendly/people in the North.

D. Join the following words together to form sentences using the superlative.

1. Alaska/(+) large/state/in the United States.
2. English/(+) popular/language in the world.
3. Tom Cruise/one of/(+) famous/actors in the United States.
4. The Lockheed SR-71 Blackbird/(+) fast/airplane.
5. The Nile/(+) long/river in the world.

E. Choose the appropriate modal auxiliary to fill in each blank.

1. When visiting someone in the hospital you _____ (might, will, should) speak in a low tone and talk about things that _____ (can't, won't, shouldn't) agitate the patient. Also, there _____ (shall, should, would) only be two people in the patient's room at one time.
2. I went for my regular checkup yesterday. The doctor said I _____ (will, can, should) walk to work. He said I _____ (have, must, would) to get as much exercise as I _____ (may, will, can) and walking is one of the best ways.
3. This information is top secret and _____ (would, might, must) never be revealed to anyone.
4. I'm not sure yet, but I _____ (might, had better, would) be getting promoted next month.
5. I _____ (wouldn't, shouldn't, couldn't) finish the test because I didn't have enough time.
6. When I first came to the United States, I _____ (should, could, can) hardly speak any English. Now, I _____ (may, will, can) understand everything. It is such a nice feeling.
7. You _____ (had better, have to, could) not drive too fast on this road, or else you _____ (would, should, will) get a ticket.
8. I _____ (can't, shouldn't, wouldn't) invite fifty people because I have a very small apartment.
9. _____ (should, could, would) you like to come over for dinner next Saturday?
10. _____ (shall, may, will) we please adjourn now? We've said everything there is to say at this meeting, haven't we?

LESSON 11

Getting Around

A. DIALOGUE

PIZZA DELIVERY

Andrew is a college student who works at a pizza restaurant in Manhattan delivering takeout food around the Upper West Side.[1] Henry, a reporter for the New York Times,[2] interviews him about the risks of his job.

HENRY: Andrew, why don't you briefly describe what you do?

ANDREW: Well, I'm a deliveryman for an Italian restaurant. Basically, when a delivery[3] order is prepared, I get the customer's address and the telephone number. Then, I get on my bike and deliver it as quickly as possible. Sometimes I'm given two or three orders at a time, so I have to ride[4] even faster. I want to make sure the food is still hot when it gets there.

HENRY: How did you find out about this job?

ANDREW: Well, one of my friends at school was working as a delivery boy. He told me about it. I thought it might be a good way to earn some extra bucks[5] and work out[6] at the same time.

HENRY: Is this your bike or did your employer give it to you?

ANDREW: It's mine. The only thing my boss gave me is this container to keep the food warm. When I'm done for the day, I take the container off and go home.

HENRY: What do you like about your job?

ANDREW: As I said before, it keeps me fit,[7] and I meet lots of interesting people every day. It's really a fun job. It's also nice to be outside.

HENRY: What about during winter? It can't be much fun to be outside when it's cold.

ANDREW: That's true. But, when it rains or snows I make better tips.[8] I guess people feel sorry for me out there in the cold. Besides, there's always the summer to look forward to.[9]

HENRY: So, how many hours a day do you work?

144

ANDREW: It really depends on the season.[10] I like to work in the evenings because that's when most people order food for delivery. During winter, when it's cold and people don't want to be outside, I work about thirty-five hours a week. In the summer, business tends to be a little slower.

HENRY: So what do you consider to be the main hazards you are faced with[11] while you're on the road?

ANDREW: Taxi drivers and anybody else in a four-wheel vehicle!

HENRY: What about pedestrians?

ANDREW: Well, I've had a few close calls[12] with pedestrians. Some people just walk out in the street and don't even bother to look.

HENRY: I guess you learn who's who on the street after a while?

ANDREW: Yeah, you really have to be alert and watch out for the occasional loser who crosses the street without a clue.[13] I sometimes sneak up[14] behind them and shout "Boo" just to watch them jump. Maybe that'll get them to pay attention.

HENRY: What do you think can be done to protect people using bikes from the dangers of the road?

ANDREW: Well, for one thing, the city should have bicycle lanes. I think that would reduce the number of traffic accidents significantly. Other than that, I think we all have to be more alert on the road. I'm always careful, and I always wear my helmet.

HENRY: Is there anything you don't like about your job?

ANDREW: Yeah, sure. I hate having to carry a Kryptonite® lock around. Every time I make a delivery, I have to lock my bike. It's really a drag[15] to have to worry about someone stealing it.

HENRY: Have you ever had a customer complain about your service?

ANDREW: Sometimes people complain that the food isn't hot when it gets there or that it took me too long to deliver it. I'm telling you, it's hard to keep everyone satisfied.

HENRY: How long have you been doing this? Do you have any plans for the future?

ANDREW: I started last winter, and I don't think I'll stick around[16] for too long. It's about time I get a real job, you know?

HENRY: Well, I wish you lots of luck. Thanks for agreeing to do this interview.

ANDREW: You're welcome.

B. NOTES

1. The city of New York is located in the state of New York, in the northeastern United States. The city is divided into five boroughs: Manhattan, Brooklyn, Queens, the Bronx, and Staten Island. Manhattan is the financial and cultural heart of the city. It is known for its skyscrapers (the Empire State Building and the Chrysler Building), its neighborhoods (Greenwich Village, SoHo, Little Italy, Chinatown, Harlem, the Upper East Side, the Upper West Side, and so on), its museums (Metropolitan Museum of Art, Museum of Modern Art or MOMA, Guggenheim Museum), its restaurants, and beautiful Central Park. The city is also the most important center in the country for the arts, fashion, and publishing.

2. The *New York Times* is one of the most important newspapers in the country. Other New York City–based newspapers are the *Wall Street Journal,* the *Daily News,* and the *Post.*

3. In large American cities such as New York, it is common (especially among people who live alone) to have food delivered from restaurants. Most restaurants in New York offer takeout and delivery services. *Takeout* means that you can call the restaurant or go personally and take the food away with you. This is also called *to go.* If the restaurant offers *delivery,* it means that you can call on the phone and have someone from the restaurant bring the food to your house or apartment, normally without any extra charge. It is customary, however, to tip the delivery person.

4. Notice the use of the verb *to ride,* which means "to be carried by a vehicle or animal."

   To ride often indicates that the person using the verb is not in direct control of the vehicle:

   I rode around the block in Steve's new car; he's a good driver.

   Other similar verbs are:

   to drive a car/bus/train
   to sail a boat
   to fly a plane/helicopter
   to ride a bike/horse/bus/train

5. The word *bucks* is a colloquial term used to refer to money. As a singular noun, *one buck* refers to one dollar. The phrase *to earn a buck* means "to earn money."

6. In this context, the verb *to work out* means "to exercise." It can also mean "to turn out well" or "to do a calculation to solve a problem."

   I work out in the gym for an hour every day.
   I hope your plan works out. Otherwise we won't get out of here alive.

7. *To keep fit* means "to keep an athletic, healthy appearance." You may also use the phrase *to be fit*.

8. Tipping is customary in the United States. In most cases you are expected to tip at least 15 percent of the bill, provided that you receive good service. Unlike in other countries, service is not automatically added to the bill.

9. The expression *to look forward to* indicates excitement for an anticipated action. It is normally followed by a verb in its present participle form (ending in *-ing).*

   I look forward to hearing from you soon.
   She's looking forward to meeting him.

10. The word *season* refers to the four metereological divisions of the year: *winter, spring, summer,* and *fall.* Another word for *fall* is *autumn,* although *fall* is used more commonly in the United States.

11. Note the use of the preposition *with* used in the expression *to be faced with.* A similar expression is *to deal with.*

12. *Close call* is a popular colloquial expression. It is used to indicate that a bad situation or an emergency was avoided at the last moment, almost miraculously.

    She was cleaning her windows when she lost her balance and almost fell. It was a close call.

13. The word *clue* refers to something that serves to guide or direct in the solution of a problem or mystery. The expression *to have no clue* means "to have no idea or to not know."

    He didn't have a clue about our plans to surprise him on his birthday.

14. The verb *to sneak* means "to go or move in a quiet manner with the intention of not being noticed." There is also the expression *to sneak out,* which means "to leave without being noticed."

15. *To be a drag* means "to be bothersome, boring, or difficult." It is a very common expression among young people.

16. The expression *to stick around* means "to stay."

C. GRAMMAR AND USAGE

1. NEGATION

The negative form in English is formed by using the word *not* immediately after the auxiliary verb. If the sentence has more than one auxiliary verb, the word *not* is placed immediately after the first auxiliary verb. In the following sentences, the contracted form appears in parentheses.

He will not (won't) deliver the order unless it has been confirmed first.
He could not (couldn't) deliver the order because it hadn't been confirmed first.
He is not (isn't) going to deliver the order unless it has been confirmed first.
He cannot (can't) deliver the order unless it has been confirmed first.
He did not (didn't) deliver the order until it was confirmed.

In English, you cannot use two negative words in the same phrase. The following phrases use correct negative forms:

I didn't see anyone crossing the street.
I saw no one crossing the street.
Carlos never wears his helmet.
Carlos doesn't ever wear his helmet.

Using two negative forms changes the meaning of the phrase, making it a positive sentence. This is unusual and is more commonly heard in a colloquial sense.

I can't not go. (I have to go.) It's too important.

The only exception to the rule is when there are two negative forms in a sentence but each is in a different phrase within the sentence.

A person who doesn't have love can't be truly happy.

The auxiliary verb and the word *not* generally form a contraction. These are some possible contractions:

to be
is not = isn't   *are not = aren't*
was not = wasn't   *were not = weren't*

148

to do
does not = doesn't   *do not = don't*
did not = didn't

to have
has not = hasn't   *have not = haven't*
had not = hadn't

will/would
will not = won't   *would not = wouldn't*

can/could
cannot = can't   *could not = couldn't*

must
must not = mustn't

should
should not = shouldn't

2. ADVERBS OF NEGATION

In addition to the word *not*, there are the following negative adverbs: *never, rarely, seldom*, and *hardly ever*.

I have never been to the coast of Spain.
She rarely drinks beer before dinner.
We seldom order takeout from that restaurant.
They hardly ever come to visit us.

3. THE USAGE OF *NOT* AND *NO*

The word *not* is used to negate a verb.

I didn't sell my stocks because the price was too low.
I decided not to call because it was late.

The word *no* is used as an adjective when placed in front of a noun.

I have no patience today. Please behave.
I have no money left in my wallet.

4. *SOME* VS. *ANY*

The words *some* and *any* indicate quantity. They are used with the plural of countable and noncountable nouns (Lesson 3).

The word *some* is used in affirmative sentences, in questions where the expected answer is affirmative, when offering, or when asking for something.

They drank some wine before dinner.
Did some of you order Indian food?
Would you like some cookies?
Could you get me some milk, please?

The word *any* is used in negative sentences (to avoid the double negative, as discussed above), in questions where the expected answer is unknown, where the expected answer is negative, or with negative adverbs.

I don't have any matches.
Do you have any money?
Is there any way you could work an extra hour tonight?
Did you make any good tips today?
I never see them buy any junk food.

Words that are derived from *some* and *any* are used in the same way:

SOMEONE, SOMEBODY, SOMETHING
Someone/somebody is asking for you at the door.
If you do not want to pay for delivery, you have to send someone/somebody to pick up your order.

ANYONE, ANYBODY, ANYTHING
Anybody/anyone who doesn't obey the law will be fined.
Has anyone/anybody seen my bike?

There is also the absolute negative:

NO ONE, NOBODY, NOTHING
Absolutely nothing about this job bothers me.
Nobody/no one wants to be the first one to eat a piece of the cake.
And the absolute affirmative:

EVERYONE, EVERYBODY, EVERYTHING
In the winter everybody/everyone feels sorry for me, so I make good tips.
Everybody/everyone in New York likes to wear black.

D. IDIOMATIC STUDY

PLACING AN ORDER OVER THE PHONE
If you call a restaurant to place an order for delivery, it is important to have your phone number and address handy. After the restaurant employee answers the phone, he or she will ask you for this information first. If you are going to pay using a credit card, have that information

handy as well. You will have to give them the credit card number over the phone, and sign a receipt when the delivery arrives. The last question will be what you want to order for delivery.

A: Empire Chuang, may I help you?
B: I'd like to order some food to be delivered, please.
A: Your telephone number?
B: 778-9900.
A: Address?
B: 12 Maple Drive.
A: Will you be paying with cash or a credit card?
B: Cash.
A: What would you like to order?
B: I'd like the lunch special, chicken with broccoli on brown rice.
A: Anything else?
B: No, thanks.
A: Thank you. It'll be there in 25 minutes.

These are some useful phrases that you will probably need:

I'd like . . .
What toppings (on the pizza)? Pepperoni, please.
What size?   Small.

E. STRICTLY BUSINESS

1. RELYING ON THE AUTOMOBILE

At the beginning of the twentieth century, most large cities in the United States already had public transportation systems. The first subway line was built in New York after trolleys and cable cars had already become popular modes of public transportation. With the creation of the Ford Motor Company in 1903, a new, private mode of transportation was introduced, seriously affecting Americans and their lifestyle. The first automobile was not built in the United States, but in France.

This new technology from France soon reached other countries, such as Germany and Great Britain. The first car makers in those countries introduced cars as luxury items meant for the wealthy, not for middle classes. The first European cars were sports cars of great luxury and extremely high prices.

In the United States, the new automobile industry took a different approach. The first car makers—Ford and General Motors—designed vehicles that were mass-produced to suit the needs of the general public. These cars were more practical and not as luxurious as their European counterparts. It is estimated that during the 1920s more than fifteen million cars were produced yearly in the United States. As a result, a wide network of roads and highways was built around the country. Some cities replaced roads once used by trolleys and cable cars with paved streets for private cars. As more people began to use private cars to go from one place to another, cities started to neglect public transportation. Maintaining a healthy network of public transportation became very costly after people were relying on their own private cars. Before long, mass transit in many American cities had disappeared or become outdated.

Cars have become an essential part of life in all but a few cities the United States. New York is one of the few cities where cars are not needed because it has always maintained a well-run and efficient public transportation network. In fact, New York is the only major city in the United States where fewer than 50 percent of the city's residents own a car. Outside New York, the distance that some people travel between their home and their job is simply too large for a comprehensive mass transit system. Some cities and their metropolitan areas (such as Los Angeles and Houston) cover thousands of square miles. Many American cities were built over large extensions of land because cars made it possible for the early inhabitants to go from one place to another.

Unfortunately, this dependency on cars has created major traffic and pollution problems for American citizens. Over the past few decades, however, Americans have asked their leaders to address these problems and demanded solutions. Years after eliminating public transportation lines, cities such as Washington, D.C., and San Francisco built new mass transit systems. Unfortunately, these networks are limited, and many people still feel dependent on their cars to carry out their everyday lives. More and more urban planners are taking traffic and road planning into account when planning city structures. Some car makers are building more fuel-efficient cars and some have taken steps to reduce environmental pollution from cars. Many cars now use cleaner fuels. Other alternatives are being planned for the future, such as hydrogen- or electricity-powered vehicles. If urban planners and auto makers work in unison to implement new measures, the negative effects of car dependency may finally be turned around.

2. VOCABULARY

battery	to deal with
to be a drag	to deliver
to be faced with	delivery
bicycle lane	to earn a buck
bucks	fuel
close call	gas station

to have no clue	to sneak out
hazards	to stick around
highway	street
to keep fit	subway
to look forward to	takeout
loser	to tip
means of transportation	tips
pedestrians	"to go"
public transportation	traffic
to ride	traffic accidents
road	traffic jam
season	trolley
service	to work out
to sneak	to yield

EXERCISES

1. Complete the following dialogue using the word *not* and the auxiliary verb in parentheses.

   A: Pizza Express, may I help you?
   B: Yes, thanks. I'm calling to check on my order. I called about an hour ago and it __(a)__ (to have) arrived yet.
   A: What's your telephone number?
   B: 772-9087.
   A: That's a large pepperoni and mushroom, right?
   B: No. I __(b)__ (to do) order pepperoni. I ordered anchovies, tomatoes, and mushrooms.
   A: We __(c)__ (to do) have any more anchovies. Would you like something else?
   B: How about sausage?
   A: Sorry, we __(d)__ (to do) have any sausage either.
   B: Well, what do you have?
   A: Ham, broccoli, and spinach.
   B: OK. I'll have a large pizza with spinach, tomatoes, and mushrooms.
   A: Very well. It will be there in a half hour.
   B: A half hour?
   A: Yes sir. Our delivery boy __(e)__ (to be) here. He's making a delivery right now.

2. Complete the following paragraph using the negative form of the words in parentheses.

   A real estate agent showed Mr. Loo two apartments: a studio in a high-rise and a two-bedroom with a terrace on the third floor. He liked the two-bedroom, but he __(a)__ (can) afford it. Two weeks later he moved into the studio. He thought he had made a good decision. But the real estate agent __(b)__ (tell) him that the apartment had a few problems, and Mr. Loo __(c)__ (notice) anything wrong. Soon Mr. Loo found out that the elevator in the building __(d)__ (will) operate on weekends because there was no one to operate it. The heater __(e)__ (work), and the apartment __(f)__ (have) an air conditioner either. The faucet in the kitchen leaked and only one burner in the stove worked. Mr. Loo tried to call the real estate office to complain, but nobody answered. The office had closed for good, and the real estate agent __(g)__ (have) left a forwarding address or a phone number. Mr. Loo realized that it was all his fault; he __(h)__ (ask) the right questions or carefully inspect the apartment the day the agent showed it to him. Poor Mr. Loo had to start all over again!

3. Fill in the blanks with a word from the following list. You don't have to use all the words, and some words may be used more than once.

some	somebody	someone	something
any	anybody	anyone	anything
no	nobody	no one	nothing
every	everybody	everyone	everything

a. I think _____ is wrong because she hasn't called me yet.

b. Do you think _____ is going to believe us?

c. I don't think _____ in his or her right mind would drive a car after drinking five beers.

d. I didn't see _____ leave after you.

e. Does _____ have the correct time?

f. I just hope _____ comes in on time today.

g. _____ is going to get in the way of this business deal.

h. She had _____ plans for the weekend, so I invited her over.

i. _____ seemed to be interested in the article, so I threw it out.

j. _____ has to know the answer to this question.

LESSON 12

Politics

A. DIALOGUE

I'M AN AMERICAN, TOO!

Marcos is an architect from Chile who's working in New Jersey.[1] He shares an apartment with his fiancée[2], Lisa, who's from Maryland.[3] It's Sunday morning, Marcos is reading the newspaper, and Lisa is watching TV.

MARCOS: I can't believe it!

LISA: What? What's going on?[4]

MARCOS: The title of this article in the *Times*![5] It reads "Native Americans about to Lose Ancestors' Land."

LISA: What's so special about it?

MARCOS: Look at the map!

LISA: Well, it's a map of a region in South America. I still don't understand what your excitement is all about.

MARCOS: It's the first time since I've been living here that the word *American* is used to describe citizens of countries other than the U.S. I think it's great. Finally someone is showing sensitivity toward the implications of leaving most of the continent out when referring to the U.S. as America.

LISA: So you're saying that U.S. citizens shouldn't call themselves Americans?

MARCOS: No, certainly not. U.S. citizens are Americans. But they're not the only ones. Canadians, Colombians, Chileans, Mexicans, and Brazilians are Americans, too. U.S. citizens shouldn't claim the term just for themselves.

LISA: So what do you suggest U.S. citizens call themselves?

MARCOS: Invent a word! Spanish has one: *estadounidense*. Why couldn't English have the same word? Something like United Stadian.

LISA: You're nuts![6]

MARCOS: No. This is a very serious issue.[7]

155

LISA: Come on. Everyone around the globe refers to the United States, when they say *America*. You're never going to change that.

MARCOS: That's not quite true. *America* to the Spaniards is Spanish-speaking America, just as *America* to the Portuguese is Brazil, not the United States.

LISA: OK, so why can't you say that for the non-Spanish-speaking world *America* is the U.S.?

MARCOS: Because it's exclusive. My point is that the term *America* shouldn't be used for the U.S. or any other country exclusively, but for the entire continent inclusively. I was born in Santiago de Chile. And that makes me an American, too, although I'm not a U.S. citizen.

LISA: Why is this so important to you? It's not like all of a sudden it's going to change.

MARCOS: I guess it's a matter of trying to get rid of[8] terminology that is culturally insensitive.

LISA: I don't think U.S. Americans are intentionally insensitive.

MARCOS: Of course not. But in a world that strives for political correctness,[9] I think it's important that we're careful with our words.

LISA: Well, as a United Stadian I couldn't agree with you more.

B. NOTES

1. The state of New Jersey is located in the northeastern United States. The state capital is Trenton. New Jersey is an Atlantic state whose famous coastline, known as the Jersey Shore, extends from the Sandy Hook peninsula in the north to Cape May in the south. The Jersey Shore is very popular during the summer. New Jersey is also home to Atlantic City, a city made popular by its casinos and resorts. The state's main airport is Newark Liberty International Airport, which is can be reached in a few minutes from the city of New York.

2. The word *fiancé* is a French word that describes someone who is engaged to be married. Notice that the masculine form is *fiancé* and the feminine form is *fiancée*.

3. Maryland is located on the eastern seaboard of the United States. Maryland's state capital is Annapolis, and its largest city is Baltimore, home of the world-famous baseball player Babe Ruth. The American writer Edgar Allan Poe lived and died in Baltimore. Baltimore's famous attractions include the National Aquarium, Oriole Park, and the Basilica

156

of the National Shrine of the Assumption, built in 1812 and considered to be the oldest metropolitan church in the nation.

4. The phrase *What's going on?* is popular in colloquial English. It is also commonly used as a greeting when you meet someone in an informal way. Other similar phrases are *What's up?* and *What's happening?*

5. In this case, *Times* is a short way of referring to the *New York Times.* Residents of Los Angeles use the same term as shorthand for their local newspaper, the *Los Angeles Times.*

6. The expression *to be nuts* means "to be crazy or very excited about something or someone."

   He's nuts about opera.

7. The noun *issue* means "point of discussion, debate, or dispute." In different situations it may refer to a copy or edition of a periodical. The verb *to issue* means "to circulate or distribute in an official capacity or to publish."

   This magazine's second issue will come out in the fall.
   The school issued uniforms to all the players.

8. The phrase *to get rid of* means "to free from something undesirable." The transitive verb *to rid* means "to free from."

9. It is common in the United States to hear the phrase *politically correct.* The United States is a diverse country with many cultures, religions, and traditions, and Americans are very sensitive when it comes to the language used to describe other people. There is great concern among some people about using language that does not diminish or disrespect any of the minority groups that live in the United States.

C. GRAMMAR AND USAGE

1. POSSESSIVE NOUNS

To show possession, you need to add an apostrophe followed by an *s* at the end of the noun.

The country has a few social problems.
Politicians are trying to solve some of the country's social problems.

If the singular noun ends in *s*, there are two possible ways of making the possessive form: by adding an apostrophe and an *-s* at the end of the noun, or by adding an apostrophe.

My boss' wife works at the local bank.
My boss's wife only works part-time.

When using a regular plural noun (that is, one that ends in *s)*, you need to add only an apostrophe. If the noun has an irregular plural form, you need to add an apostrophe and an *-s:*

The presidents' families stayed at the Waldorf-Astoria.
The women's rights movement began in the late 1960s.

When the object is implied, there is no need to mention it again.

Mary's dress was light blue. Sally's was green.

2. POSSESSIVE ADJECTIVES

Possessive adjectives are used to modify a noun indicating possession. They are generally placed before the noun and do not need to match their corresponding noun in gender or number. Possessive adjectives are always accompanied by a noun.

my
your
his
her
its
our
your
their

Good morning. My name is Dorothy Parks.
Tom doesn't know where he left his checkbook this morning.
Their new house is on a hill facing a lake.

3. POSSESSIVE PRONOUNS

Possessive pronouns are used to replace a possessive adjective and the noun that it accompanies. They are not followed by a noun and may appear by themselves in a sentence.

mine
yours
his
hers
ours
yours
theirs

Our country is a democracy. Theirs isn't.
Your congressperson seems to be always available. Mine is always too busy to take calls.

158

The following expressions are easily confused because they sound the same: *it's* vs. *its* and *there's* vs. *theirs*.

It's is the contracted form of *it* + *is*.
It's a beautiful day.

Its is a possessive adjective.
The cat has gray hair. Its hair is gray.

There's is the contracted form of *there* + *is*.
There's a new candidate running for president.

Theirs is a possessive pronoun.
Our car is old. Theirs is new.

4. REFLEXIVE PRONOUNS

Reflexive pronouns generally refer to the subject of the sentence and are in agreement with it. Reflexive pronouns are placed after the verb.

myself
yourself
himself
herself
itself
ourselves
yourselves
themselves

Reflexive pronouns are used in the following cases:

a. Reflexive Pronoun as the Object
When the reflexive pronoun is used as direct or indirect object, the subject and object are identical.

I injured myself playing soccer.
She bought herself some flowers.

b. Reflexive Pronouns after Prepositions
When a verb is followed by a preposition and makes reference to the subject of the sentence, the sentence needs a reflexive pronoun.

He's so vain. He's always looking at himself in the mirror.
She lives by herself in that old house.

c. To Place Emphasis
Reflexive pronouns are also used to give emphasis.

She decorated the room for the dance herself.
They built the house themselves.

There are several expressions in English that use reflexive pronouns. The most common are:

to believe in yourself
to blame yourself
to cut yourself
to enjoy yourself
to feel sorry for yourself
to help yourself
to hurt yourself
to introduce yourself
to kill yourself
to be proud of yourself
to talk to yourself
to teach yourself
to work for yourself

5. IMPERSONAL PRONOUNS

Impersonal pronouns are used to refer to any nonspecific person or group of people. There are two impersonal pronouns in English: *one* and *you*. *One* is a bit more formal than *you*.

As a member of this society you have the right to vote.
One should always try to be nice to strangers.

6. WORDS ENDING IN *EVER*

The following is a list of words that end in *ever*.

whoever
whomever
whatever
whichever
whenever
wherever
however

I have enough money to go wherever I want.
Whoever wants to come with me should let me know soon.

7. EXPRESSIONS WITH *OTHER*

Expressions that are formed with the word *other* are used as adjectives or pronouns.

	ADJECTIVE + NOUN	PRONOUN (REPLACES THE NOUN)
SINGULAR	*another* (+ singular noun)	*another*
	the other (+ singular noun)	*the other*
PLURAL	*other* (+ plural noun)	*others*
	the other (+ plural noun)	*the others*

another	=	"one more in addition to the ones mentioned"
other/others	=	"some more in addition to the ones mentioned"
the other(s)	=	"the rest"

There are other expressions that are formed with the word *other:*

each other/one another	=	indicate a reciprocal relationship
every other	=	"alternating" (in numbers: 1, 3, 5, 7, 9 or 2, 4, 6, 8, 10)

I'd like another piece of pie, please.
One of my roommates is from Boston. The other is from San Francisco.
We call each other every week.
I visit my parents every other week.

D. IDIOMATIC STUDY

EXPRESSING INTENTIONS
To ask someone about their plans for the future, you may use one of the following phrases:

What are you going to do tomorrow evening?
Where are you planning to go?
Have you decided where to go?
Have you made up your mind yet?

When you want to say that you have the intention of doing something, you may use one of the following phrases:

I'm going to _____.
I'm planning to _____.
I plan/intend to _____.
I've been thinking about _____.

When you are not sure, or the plans are not final, you may use one of these:

I haven't decided yet.
I haven't made up my mind.
I haven't thought about it yet.
I'm not sure.

E. STRICTLY BUSINESS

1. LAWMAKING IN THE UNITED STATES

After the Declaration of Independence in 1776, the United States fought as a country to create its own government system. The founding fathers saw the need to create a true democracy with which they could write effective and fair laws. After a decade of several failed attempts, Congress finally ratified the Constitution in 1787, and it went into effect in 1789. Since then, the United States has grown to become a nation of fifty states and a population of people from all over the world. But in spite of the changes that have taken place over the past two hundred years, the democratic system delineated by the Constitution has remained pretty much the same. The Constitution divides the government into three independent branches: legislative, executive, and judicial. This system of check and balances, as it is normally known, makes sure that no particular branch has too much power when it comes to dictating the law. Although the process of introducing and approving new laws is long and tedious, those that pass are normally popular with policymakers and the general public.

The creation process of laws begins in the legislative branch of the government. To ensure clean and balanced results, this branch is divided into two chambers: the House of Representatives and the Senate. The House of Representatives and the Senate are known collectively as *Congress*. Each state elects a number of members to the House of Representatives, the number depending on the size of the state's population. The larger the population of a state, the more representation that state will have in the House. On the other hand, each state, regardless of its size or population, sends two representatives to the Senate. The federal legislative process starts when a member of the House of Representatives or the Senate makes a proposal to write a new law. The proposal is discussed, debated, and voted upon. If the majority of that chamber approves it, the proposal goes to the other chamber to be approved. Once the law is approved by both chambers of Congress, it goes to the President of the United States (the Executive Branch). The president normally discusses the new law with members of his cabinet or special counsel before deciding whether to sign it into law or to veto it. If the president approves it, it becomes the law; but if the president decides to veto it, the proposal goes back to the House of Representatives and the Senate for review. Once changes are made, the two chambers vote again. This time, if two-thirds of the members approve the measure, they can overrule the president's veto and turn the measure into law without the president's signature.

Once the proposal turns into law, there is still a third "check" to come: it must pass through the Judicial Branch of the government. The Judicial Branch is made of the Supreme Court and a network of smaller circuit courts that ensure that all laws are constitutional. Even when a law seems to be popular, there is normally a segment of the population that disagrees with the legality of the new measure. These groups normally present their reasons of protest to the Supreme Court, demanding to cancel or change something in the law that they consider to be unconstitutional. The Supreme Court holds discussions and hears arguments to determine whether the law is constitutional or not. If they consider it unconstitutional, they have the right to declare it invalid. If they determine that the law is constitutional, then the law remains in effect.

Some people are critical of the system of check and balances. They argue that the process creates a bureaucratic entanglement that hinders effective legislation. Some old court decisions, such as *Roe vs. Wade,* which legalized abortion in 1973, are still being argued in the Supreme Court. In recent years, there have been several major proposals (health-care reform, gun control, welfare reform) that were never signed into law. Although the process is extremely long, it guarantees that many arguments are heard and that democracy is shared by several groups of people. For more information about the Supreme Court and its projects, visit their Web site at www.supremecourtus.gov.

2. VOCABULARY

to be nuts	insensitive
bill	issue
branch	judicial
cabinet	law
chamber	legislative
checks and balances	political correctness
circuit court	politically correct
citizen	proposal
Congress	to protest
debate	to rid
executive	Senate
fiancé(e)	sensitivity
to get rid of	Supreme Court
gun control	unconstitutional
health-care reform	to veto
hearing	to vote
House	welfare reform
House of Representatives	

1. Complete each sentence with the correct word in parentheses.

   a. The document on top of the file is _____ (my, mine). (Your, Yours) _____ is in the folder over there.

   b. I bought a new car. (It's, Its) _____ a sports car. Although _____ (it's, its) not new, _____ (it's, its) engine runs like a clock. I have a feeling _____ (it's, its) going to last a long time.

   c. (My, Mine) _____ report won't be ready until next week. How about _____ (their, theirs, there's)?

   d. (Their, Theirs, There's) _____ a new restaurant I'd like to try. Someone told me _____ (their, theirs, there's) specialty is lobster.

   e. (He's, His) _____ from New York, but (he's, his) _____ parents are from Seattle.

2. Join the following sentences using possessive nouns. Example: Sally has a husband. Her husband gave her a new car for her birthday. Sally's husband gave her a new car for her birthday.

   a. The children have parents. The parents left for a two-week trip to Hawaii.

   b. The university has a library. The library is closed on Sundays.

   c. This is my friend. Her name is Angela.

   d. I get a check every month. This month the check is late.

   e. That fitting room is for ladies only. The fitting room is not open.

3. Fill in the blanks with the appropriate reflexive pronoun.

   a. I think I hurt _____ this morning when I fell.

   b. Does he ever talk to _____?

   c. I think she should believe in _____ a little more.

   d. I'd like each one of you to introduce _____ to the rest of the group.

   e. I really enjoy living by _____.

   f. They taught _____ how to read and write.

4. Choose a word from the list to complete the following sentences.

another	however	whatever
others	whomever	the others
the other	wherever	whenever

   a. If you are really unhappy with your job, why don't you look for _____ one?

   b. I'll do _____ it takes to not have to take that test again.

c. Some people like to have all their money in a savings account. _____ prefer to invest in the stock market.
d. _____ it rains, I get depressed.
e. This dress looks good on you, but I still prefer _____ one.
f. She'll go _____, with _____, as long as she has enough money to spend.

LESSON 13
Sports and Exercise

A. DIALOGUE

BALLROOM DANCING

Pat is a new employee at a brokerage firm in downtown Cincinnati.1 This is her second week at work, and she's talking to her colleague Margaret.

PAT: I was looking at this flyer that came in interoffice mail about the company's exercise programs. I didn't know there was a gym here for employees to use.

MARGARET: Yeah, it's really convenient. I go there after work almost every day. It's part of the company's wellness program. I guess the company provides this because having healthy employees can mean getting a leg up[2] on the competition.

PAT: No wonder you look so fit.[3]

MARGARET: Thanks. Do you exercise frequently?

PAT: Yes, I have my routine. I normally jog three miles every morning. It all depends on the weather, really.

MARGARET: You should try the gym. There's an indoor track, which is pretty good when it's cold outside. And there's also a pool, and a weight room with brand-new exercise equipment. You can also take aerobics, yoga, or ballroom dancing classes, if you're interested.

PAT: Ballroom dancing? That doesn't sound like much exercise at all!

MARGARET: That's what I used to think. But honestly, it's one of the best workouts[4] I've found. Plus, you get to socialize at the same time.

PAT: Isn't ballroom dancing a little outdated?

MARGARET: No way! It's fun, and you hardly notice you're working out. I've been doing it for quite some time now, and I really feel sorry for joggers like you who are out there in the heat and the cold, with bugs and dogs, breathing in the smog. Instead, I'm in a beautiful temperature-controlled room dancing away to the rhythms of a cha-cha.

PAT: I guess I just prefer jogging because I'm not a good dancer.

MARGARET: See, that's even more reason to join! You'll learn in no time! You really should come one day this week after work. Dancing is such a great way to relieve stress. It's impossible to keep your mind on your problems when you're swirling around the dance floor.

PAT: I don't know . . .

MARGARET: Well just come and watch. It'll do you good. I think you'll be ready to give it a shot[5] once you see how much fun we have. Besides, there's another reason for you to come . . .

PAT: I know, I could stand[6] to lose a few pounds. I'll go on a diet[7] starting tomorrow.

defensive (negatives) go low.

MARGARET: Oh, come on now! That's not it at all. You know the cute guy who works on the fifth floor?

PAT: He's taking ballroom dancing lessons? You must be pulling my leg![8]

MARGARET: Why not come and see for yourself? By the way, about your diet, there's a nutritionist available to give you advice. There's also an exercise specialist who can help you design a complete workout program.

PAT: You've done one hell of a sales job[9]. I don't see how I can say no.

B. NOTES

1. The city of Cincinnati is located in the state of Ohio, in an area known as the Midwest. This area was originally known as the Northwest Territory, and it joined the United States in 1783 after the Treaty of Paris. The state capital of Ohio is Columbus, located in the center of the state. Other big Ohio cities are Cleveland (on Lake Erie), Dayton, and Toledo. Ohio is home to the Rock and Roll Hall of Fame in Cleveland, and the Football Hall of Fame in Canton.

2. The expression *to get a leg up* means "to be in a position of advantage" or "to have a head start." A similar expression is *to have an edge.*

3. The expression *to be fit* or *to look fit* describe an athletic and slim appearance. A similar expression is *to be in shape* or *to get in shape. Fitness* refers to the state or condition of being in good health and physical condition.

Physical fitness is an important part of being healthy.

The verb *to fit* means "to be of the right size and shape or to provide a place and a time."

I've gained so much weight that my clothes don't fit anymore.

The nutritionist had a very busy schedule, but she fit me in at two o'clock anyway.

4. The noun *workout* is used to refer to the act of exercising. It can also refer to any difficult task that requires a lot of effort.

Debugging a computer program is a workout in itself.

The verb *to work out* means "to exercise." However, this verb has several other meanings:

to exercise
I work out every morning at the local gym.

to find the solution to a problem
I managed to work out the problems with my schedule, and now I can take the yoga class.

to formulate
The nutritionist is going to work out a plan to improve my eating habits.

to give results
You've lost a lot of weight. It looks like your diet worked out.

5. The expression *to give something/someone a shot* means "to give something/someone an opportunity or to give something/someone a try." A similar expression is *to give something/someone a chance.* Here are other popular expressions with the verb *to give:*

to give someone a buzz/call	=	to call someone
to give someone an earful	=	to yell at someone
to give someone hell	=	to work hard to impress someone, to berate someone
to give someone the cold shoulder	=	to ignore someone purposely
to give someone the boot	=	to fire someone

6. In this context, the verb *to stand* means "to tolerate." *To stand* also means "to rise to an upright position, to stay on one's feet, or to remain stable. Here are other popular expressions with the verb:

to stand a chance	=	to have a hope
to stand one's ground	=	to not waver in one's decision
to stand someone up	=	to not go to an arranged meeting or date without informing the other person

to stand out	=	to separate oneself from a crowd
to stand tall	=	to be proud
to stand in for	=	to take someone's place
to stand up to someone	=	to confront someone

7. Notice the use of the preposition *to go on a diet* and the use of the verb *to go.* Here are some similar expressions:

   to go on a trip
   to go on vacation
   to go on a holiday
   to go on a shopping spree
   to go on a binge

8. The expression *to pull someone's leg* means "to fool someone." Other similar expressions are *to tease someone* or to kid someone. Here are other popular expressions with the verb *to pull:*

   to pull a fast one
   to pull something off
   to pull the plug on someone/something

9. The expression *one hell of a sales job* means "a really great sales job." *One hell of a* (or *one heck of a* if you are in a situation where you want to avoid offending anyone with the word *hell)* can be used with different nouns following it to mean either "really great" or "really big":

   That's one heck of a snowstorm they're having up in Canada.

   Another similar expression is *a hell/heck of a lot of,* meaning "very many." This expression is more common in Southern regions.

   It takes a heck of a lot of money to look as good as she does.

C. GRAMMAR AND USAGE

1. THE GERUND

a. Definition
   In English the gerund is identified by its *-ing* ending. As we have already discussed, the *-ing* form of the verb is used as the participle in the present and past continuous or as an adjective.

PRESENT CONTINUOUS	*I'm leaving right now to go to work.*
PAST CONTINUOUS	*I was taking vitamin C every day, but I stopped.*
ADJECTIVE	*This is an entertaining way of getting exercise.*

The gerund may also be used as a noun; in other words, it may act as a subject or as the object of the main verb.

Lifting weights can be dangerous without supervision.

In this example, the gerund *lifting* is the subject of the sentence.

She enjoys listening to music while she runs.

In the previous example, the gerund *listening* is the direct object of the verb *to enjoy.*

b. Verbs Followed by a Gerund
    There is a set of verbs in English that, when followed by another verb, dictate that the second verb must be in gerund form. Generally, all verbs similar in meaning to *to like* or *to hate* are followed by the gerund.

to appreciate	*to hate*
to enjoy	*to dislike*
to like	*to loathe*
to love	*cannot bear*
to prefer	*cannot stand*

Other verbs are:

to avoid	*to consider*
to delay	*to discuss*
to finish	*to mind*
to keep	*to mention*
to postpone	*to talk about*
to put off	*to think about*
to quit	*to suggest*
to stop	

We enjoy playing tennis on Saturday mornings.
I prefer working out early in the morning.
She keeps trying to lose weight, but she refuses to exercise.
I avoid running in the park after dark.

c. The Gerund as Object of the Preposition
    Generally, in English when a verb is the object of the preposition, it will be in gerund form.

The nutritionist is interested in knowing all about my eating habits.
You should take advantage of having the gym right here.
We're used to jogging before breakfast.
He showed me how to get to the gym by drawing a map.

When you want to express a negative sentence, the word *not* is placed between the preposition and the gerund.

I have no excuse for not exercising.
I apologized to Ann for not making it on time to our aerobics class.

d. The Verb *to Go* and the Gerund
The verb *to go* is generally followed by a gerund with expressions indicating recreational activities.

to go dancing
to go jogging
to go running
to go skating
to go skiing
to go shopping
to go swimming

We'll go skiing in Vermont next week.
I'd love to go swimming, but I'm afraid the water is too cold.
Why don't we go dancing tonight?

2. PRESENT AND PAST PARTICIPLES

The present participle (verbs ending in *-ing*) and the past participle (verbs ending in *-ed*) may be used as adjectives to describe nouns. The present participle is used to describe a feeling in an active sense. In other words, the noun causes the feeling.

The Olympic games usually excite people.
The Olympic games are exciting.
The New York marathon was so long, it exhausted the group of runners.
It was an exhausting marathon.

The past participle, on the other hand, is used to describe the way that a person feels. The meaning is normally expressed in the passive voice.

People are usually excited about the Olympic games.
The people are excited (about the Olympic games).
The group of runners was exhausted because the marathon was so long.
The exhausted runners sat on the grass to rest.

D. IDIOMATIC STUDY

COMPLIMENTING

These phrases will be useful when you want to compliment someone or something:

That was a great workout!
That was quite a class!
I really like/love your outfit.

You may use several different adjectives with the following phrases:

I think _____ is + adjective. *I thought _____ was* + adjective.

ADJECTIVES
fabulous
good
great
magnificent
terrific
superb
wonderful

I think the evening class is superb.
I thought the instructor was excellent!

These are good responses to use after you receive a compliment from someone:

Thanks.
Thank you (for saying so).
It's nice of you to say/think so.
I'm glad you like it.

EXPRESSING DISPLEASURE
These are useful phrases when you want to express displeasure for something or someone:

I was a little disappointed.
I wasn't very pleased with the class.
The instructor was a little disappointing.
I'm very disappointed with my own performance.
I don't like the people who attend that class.
I don't enjoy dancing very much.
I don't (particularly) care for vegetables.
I'm not (really) crazy about fishing.

EXPRESSING CONGRATULATIONS

Use the following phrases when you want to congratulate someone:

Congratulations!
That's great! Congratulations!
I'm very happy to hear that.
I'm so happy for you.
That's wonderful! You deserve it!
That's wonderful/excellent/fantastic!

E. STRICTLY BUSINESS

1. THE BUSINESS OF SPORTS AND ATHLETES

Sport events are a very important part of the life of many Americans. In almost every major American city you'll find a professional football, baseball, hockey, or soccer team. Every day thousands of spectators watch their favorite teams play in stadiums across the country, while millions more watch games on television.

With this large following, it is not surprising that the best and most charismatic players become celebrities in the United States. Decades ago, the popularity of an athlete helped the team more than it helped the athlete. Babe Ruth, a great baseball player for the New York Yankees in the 1920s and 1930s, helped to sell millions of tickets for his team. This meant that the team owners made a lot of money from ticket sales. In spite of their popularity, though, star players such as Babe Ruth never made anywhere near as much money as many celebrity players make today.

Nowadays, the situation is completely different. Popular athletes still help fill stadiums and arenas, but their incomes can be in the hundreds of millions of dollars. Believe it or not, the atheletes' salaries don't end there. Almost all famous athletes enter into commercial partnerships with other companies to represent and advertise products. These contracts may represent many millions of dollars in revenue for both the athletes and the companies. The atheletes generally do television commercials as part of their contractual arrangements, although many players get paid for simply displaying a company's logo on their outfits or sneakers during a game. Sometimes players advertise products that have very little to do with sports; it is common to see commercial endorsements for car companies, restaurant chains, and department stores. Marketing studies show that most consumers are willing to pay more for a product or service that is endorsed by the athletes whom they most admire.

The most popular and charismatic American athletes earn more millions of dollars working as sports commentators for the major television networks. Some of them even turn to acting on television and in Hollywood. They may not turn out to be great commentators or actors, but generally that is a secondary issue. The simple fact that a famous person is on television or in a film brings in the audiences that advertisers and major studios want.

2. VOCABULARY

aerobics	gym
athlete	indoor
advertisement	sneakers
audience	soccer
ballroom dancing	sport
basketball	sponsor
to be fit	team
championship	track
charismatic	viewer
commentator	weight room
to endorse	wellness
endorsement	to work out
to fit	workout
fitness	yoga
football	

EXERCISES

1. Complete the following sentences with the gerund and appropriate preposition, if required.

   a. Pat is interested _____ (to know) _____ more about the company's fitness program.

   b. Instead _____ (to exercise) _____, Margaret went _____ (to shop) _____.

   c. I'm used _____ (to run) _____ three miles every morning.

   d. I enjoy _____ (to walk) _____ to work because it's invigorating.

   e. I saw the nutritionist yesterday, and we talked _____ (to supplement) _____ my diet with vitamins.

   f. I look forward _____ (to spend) _____ a week hiking and camping in the Rockies.

2. Complete the following sentences with one of the words given below.

a. It was probably very _____ for you to have to sit around and
    wait until I was done with my jazz class.
    boring   bored

b. The yoga class was _____ because, for the first time in my life, I
    was aware of what each one of my muscles can do.
    fascinated   fascinating

c. Most people are _____ about taking ballroom dancing lessons.
    Many don't know how to dance. At first they feel _____ and
    _____. But, once they've got the steps, they're _____. Some
    of them end up being _____ dancers.
    excited   exciting
    confused   confusing
    frustrated   frustrating
    thrilled   thrilling
    amazed   amazing

d. I find it _____ that there are people who continue to smoke even
    though they are aware of the risks.
    surprised   surprising

3. Fill in the blanks in the following dialogue with the verb in parentheses.
   You must decide whether to use one of the following structures: to go +
   -ing, verb + -ing, or a form of to go

Sandra:	We're _(a)_ (to go) on vacation next week.
Lisa:	Sounds great. Where are you going?
Sandra:	We'd like _(b)_ (to go) upstate, near Lake Oneida.
Lisa:	I'm sure Ted is going _(c)_ (to fish).
Sandra:	Probably not too much. The kids want _(d)_ (to hike).
Lisa:	But, you're not into _(e)_ (to hike), are you?
Sandra:	Not really. I think I'll _(f)_ (to swim) in the lake, if it's not too cold. And I'll most likely _(g)_ (to jog) every once in a while.
Lisa:	It sounds like a lot of fun. Enjoy your trip. I've got to run. Beth and I are _(h)_ (to shop).
Sandra:	I'll call you when I get back. Bye-bye.

175

LESSON 14
The Media

A. DIALOGUE

NOTHING TO WATCH

Laura and Catherine live in Little Rock, Arkansas.[1] They're good friends and share an apartment together. It's been a tough day at work for both of them, and they're trying to unwind[2] in front of the television. Unfortunately, deciding what to watch isn't very simple.

CATHERINE: Could you please stop flipping through the channels[3] like that?

LAURA: I'm just trying to find something decent to watch.[4]

CATHERINE: Wouldn't it be easier if you looked in the *TV Guide* instead of driving me nuts?[5]

LAURA: I'm sorry, I don't mean to get on your nerves,[6] but there's absolutely nothing on.[7] Those trashy news programs are on every channel!

CATHERINE: I think *Primetime Live*[8] is on right now, and it isn't a trashy program at all. It's very informative, and besides I really like Diane Sawyer.[9]

LAURA: Oh, come on! All those news programs are the same.

CATHERINE: No way! They're entirely different. I admit there are a few shows out there that focus more on scandals than on real news. *Hard Copy* and *A Current Affair* for example. But programs like *Primetime Live* do cover important stories.

LAURA: Like what?

CATHERINE: Well, they do stories on political candidates, government corruption, insurance fraud, things like that . . . .

LAURA: The problem is the personalities of the news presenters have become more important than the news they are presenting.

CATHERINE: What do you mean?

LAURA: The networks treat newscasts like any other TV show. Their main goal is high ratings. To gain ratings they give journalists celebrity status. Some anchors[10] become so popular that people are willing to believe anything they say, whether it's accurate or not.

CATHERINE: But I don't see anything wrong with treating anchors like celebrities. After all, they're the ones who make the news interesting and credible because of their personality and charm.

LAURA: Yeah, but that's what makes it so impossible to distinguish fact from fiction. Newscasters don't just tell us what happened or give us some shots of the events. It's ironic to see how we're moving away from the news in an era when technology has finally made it possible to experience events as they really happen.

CATHERINE: We're just moving away from traditional ways of presenting the news, that's all. Let me have the remote. I'll find something we can both watch.

LAURA: How about if we go get a movie instead?

CATHERINE: Terrific.[11] I'm in the mood for something light and fun. How about you?

LAURA: I'd like something romantic. There are no good comedies anymore, everything . . .

CATHERINE: Oh, no. Here we go again.

B. NOTES

1. Little Rock is the capital of the state of Arkansas, which is located in the Mississippi Valley in the south-central region of the United States. The city of Little Rock, located on the Arkansas River, is the political and financial center of the state. The eastern and southern parts of the state have vast extensions of land devoted to agriculture, while the north and west consist mostly of forests.

2. The verb *to unwind* has several meanings. In this case it is used in its most colloquial form, which means "to rest or to relax." *To wind* means "to turn in circular motion," as in winding an old mechanical watch. The opposite, *to unwind,* means "to disentangle or to separate parts." Keep in mind that the verbs *wind* and *unwind* are pronounced differently from the noun *wind.*

3. *To flip through the channels* means to use the remote to go from channel to channel rapidly, without direction.

4. The verb *to watch* means "to look at something with attention or to observe." It is used when referring to activities that demand

concentration such as watching television or watching a movie. It may also mean "to take care of or to be careful with":

Please watch the children while I'm out.
Watch out! The glass on that table is broken.

5. The popular expression *to drive someone nuts* means "to irritate or disturb to a breaking point." Other similar expressions are:

   to drive someone bonkers
   to drive someone insane
   to drive someone crazy
   to drive someone up the wall

6. The expression *to get on someone's nerves* means "to bother, to annoy someone, or to irritate."

7. The preposition *on* is used here with the verb *to be.* In this case it means "to be programmed or to be in progress."

   When I got to my friend's house, the football game was already on.
   There is a good movie on TV tonight.
   Robert Redford was on The Tonight Show *last week.*

   It can also mean "in good form":

   That was a great concert. The band was really on tonight.

8. *Primetime Live* is an investigative news program presented by the ABC network. Other similar programs are: *Dateline, 20/20,* and *Nightline.*

9. Diane Sawyer is a famous television personality. She co-anchors both *Primetime Live* and the morning news program *Good Morning America.* Other famous American news personalities are Barbara Walters, Katie Couric, Dan Rather, and Larry King.

10. The noun *anchor* is not to be used literally in this case. It refers to the main person or host of a radio or television program. They are also referred to as the *anchorperson.*

11. The noun *terrific* means "excellent, great, or fantastic. The verb *to terrify* means "to make someone afraid or to intimidate."

C. GRAMMAR AND USAGE

1. THE INFINITIVE
a. Definition
   In English, the infinitive form corresponds to the simple form of the verb preceded by the preposition *to: to watch, to ask, to buy.* As we

have seen earlier, the object of a verb could be a noun, a pronoun, or a gerund. The object of a verb can also be an infinitive:

I want to watch the news before going to bed.

In the previous example the object of the verb *want* is the infinitive *to watch*.

I'd like to buy a 19-inch color television set, but I'm not sure what brand I want.

b. Verbs Followed by an Infinitive
   Some verbs in English only permit an infinitive as the object of the verb, even when the main verb and second verb are separated by a pronoun or a noun functioning as part of the object. These verbs are:

to agree	to need
to appear	to offer
to ask	to plan
to beg	to pretend
to care	to promise
to claim	to refuse
to consent	to struggle
to decide	to swear
to demand	to threaten
to deserve	to try
to expect	to volunteer
to fail	to wait
to hesitate	to want
to hope	to wish
to intend	
to learn (how)	
to mean	
would like	would love
can't afford	can't wait

I plan to go to the movies tonight.
She asked me to stop flipping through the channels.
The network decided to hire two new anchorwomen.
I'm trying to convince her to get another movie, but she won't listen.

c. Verbs + Infinitive or Gerund
   Some verbs can be followed by an infinitive or a gerund without causing a change in the meaning. These verbs are:

to begin
to continue
to hate

to like
to love
to not stand
to start

I hate watching sitcoms.
I hate to watch sitcoms.
She continued making noise even though I asked her to stop.
She continued to make noise even though I asked her to stop.
He had just started watching the game when the lights went out.
He had just started to watch the game when the lights went out.

There are some verbs that change meaning depending on whether the gerund or the infinitive is used:

to forget + infinitive = to forget to do something
to forget + gerund = to forget that something happened in the past

Laura sometimes forgets to turn off the TV.
I'll never forget going to the movies the first time.

to remember + infinitive = to remember to do something
to remember + gerund = to remember that something happened in the past

Please, remember to rewind the movie when you're finished with it.
I remember watching this movie when I was ten years old.

to regret + infinitive = to feel bad about doing something in the present
to regret + gerund = to regret something that happened in the past

I regret to tell you that tonight's performance has been canceled.
I regret asking Laura out tonight. She's always complaining.

to try + infinitive = to try something
to try + gerund = to experiment with something to see if it works

I'm trying to find something interesting to watch.
I tried cleaning the DVD, but the movie still wouldn't play.

d. Adjectives + Infinitive
   Some adjectives, especially those that are used to describe people's feelings or attitudes, are followed by an infinitive:

ashamed	*glad*
content	*happy*
delighted	*lucky*
disappointed	*pleased*
fortunate	*prepared*

proud	shocked
ready	surprised
relieved	sorry
sad	upset

I'm pleased to meet you.
We're not ready to go back to work next week.
She was relieved to hear that her dentist appointment had been canceled.

e. The Infinitive to Express Purpose
In English, to express purpose, use either *in order* + verb in its infinitive form, or just the verb in its infinitive form. Notice that the preposition *for* is not used.

In order to be a newscaster you have to take speech lessons. — *more official and formal for writing*
To be a newscaster you have to take speech lessons.
In order to attract a large audience, networks hire celebrity anchors.
To attract a large audience, networks hire celebrity anchors.
She needs to get another job in order to pay her rent.
She needs to get another job to pay her rent.

D. IDIOMATIC STUDY

APOLOGIZING
The following are useful phrases when apologizing:

FORMAL
Please accept my apology.
I'd like to apologize for interrupting you.
I hope you'll forgive me.
Please forgive me.
I (do) apologize.

INFORMAL
I'm sorry.
I want/need to apologize for disturbing you.
I'm really/very/awfully sorry.
Sorry.

When accepting an apology you may use one of the following phrases:

Don't worry about it.
That's/It's all right.
That's okay.

No problem.
These things happen.
It's not your fault.
I understand.

E. STRICTLY BUSINESS

1. THE POWER OF THE MASS MEDIA

The American public has always depended on mass media to learn about the world around them. After all, mass media is ideal for efficiently transmitting information to a large number of people in a very short period of time. Until the 1950s, information was disseminated through radio airwaves, newspapers, magazines, and other publications. With the arrival of television, mass media was adapted to a new way of bringing the information to the masses. During the past few decades, television has continually proven to be the most efficient means to bring more information to more Americans. Although this may have positive effects on the American society, there is growing evidence that relying solely on television as the main source of information may also have negative effects. For many Americans, mass media (especially television) is their only source of news and information. Mass media has the ability to shape and form public opinion on reported events. This happens in two ways: first, the media is free to choose which stories to report and which to ignore.

This right to select news stories is protected by the Constitution of the United States. Second, although journalism is supposed to be objective, the media may be subjective in the coverage of the events. The presence of any political or sociological bias may have a tremendous effect on the attitudes and perceptions of Americans. When a news story is biased or reported without fairness, the media is abusing its rights, as well as the rights of the public to make well-informed decisions on event based on facts presented fairly, without bias. One of the best examples of media bias is how the major news organizations reported the Gulf War in 1991. The live broadcast of the war made the American public feel that it was a "clean war" with a minimum amount of destruction and deaths. As the war came to an end, reports from many soldiers and journalists painted a completely different picture. As a result, public support for the war declined tremendously.

Critics say that the ability of the media to limit news stories and control information makes its role similar to propaganda. The people who defend the news organizations say that the only reason the media organizations have so much power is because the American public has granted them that right. Some experts believe that giving the public so much information is not a good thing. If the American public had access to unlimited information, they would be inundated with more than they could remember. This overdose of information makes people anxious. Many news organizations try to fix this problem by summarizing the news in brief reports. Instead of telling the whole story, they offer the public an abbreviated version with sound and images that are easier to process and remember. In addition, news reports are often forms of entertainment. The number of television programs that re-create news stories has grown over the past years. Some news channels mix serious information with light entertainment and gossip. These programs attract a larger audience, and they have become very profitable for the television networks. The amount of time devoted to this type of light news has grown at the expense of traditional news reporting. When news reporting is mixed with entertainment, the news organizations trivialize important topics affecting the American public.

There are ways to avoid biased, limited, and trivial news coverage. Although there is a similar trend among newspapers to offer light news, there are still some world-renowned newspapers that offer fair and complete coverage of national and international events. Foreign newspapers are also widely available in the United States. If you look closely and with patience, you will find that there are still some news organizations that offer balanced and professional reporting.

2. VOCABULARY

anchor	newscaster
bias	newspaper
cable television	objective
channel	propaganda
coverage	public opinion
entertainment	ratings
household	scandals
informative	show
journalism	story
to manipulate	subjective
mass media	to transmit
network	trashy
news	to unwind
news presenter	to watch
newscast	

1. Choose a verb from the following list to complete the paragraph below. Decide whether the verb should be in the infinitive or the gerund form.

buy	feel	sell	believe	
promote	put	make	stay	dream

Celebrities have always been paid __(a)__ products, but recently it has become a booming business. Advertisers have discovered that the best way __(b)__ is to put together a star and a product. Consumers tend __(c)__ a product is worth buying simply because a celebrity is promoting it. "It's all about image," says Peter Setts, co-owner of French Style Perfumes. "I can remember __(d)__ certain products because I had seen them advertised by famous celebrities. The same thing happens whenever I have a star promote one of my perfumes. Women want __(e)__ as glamorous and uninhibited as the star herself. So they buy the fragrance she represents. People enjoy __(f)__ about living a more exciting life. __(g)__ together the product and the star is a way of __(h)__ people's dreams come true. It's also important __(i)__ ahead of the competition. Everybody seems to be using celebrities. So why shouldn't we?"

2. Decide whether the verb in parentheses should be in the infinitive or the gerund form.

   a. She's trying _____ (memorize) her lines for the play.
   b. I can't ever remember _____ (watch) a more depressing movie.
   c. She was fortunate _____ (win) two tickets to the Oscars.
   d. She always forgets _____ (rewind) the video tape before _____ (return) it to the store.
   e. I was sorry _____ (hear) that the show had been canceled.
   f. I regret _____ (buy) a bigger TV set.
   g. Celebrities are not always eager _____ (give) people their autograph.
   h. They tried _____ (sell) their product by asking Cher _____ (promote) it, but she refused.

3. Decide whether to use *for* or *to* to complete each sentence.

   a. We could tell the anchor had gone through a lot of trouble _____ get the story.
   b. Maggie bought a new TV set _____ her daughter's birthday.
   c. We have a surprise _____ Jim.
   d. They went to Dallas _____ a business conference.

e. On her way to the airport, she stopped at the office _____ get her mail.

f. I think that you have to be handsome _____ be an anchor.

4. Decide whether the verb in parentheses should be followed by a gerund or an infinitive.

a. Would you like _____ (watch) the sports channel or the movie channel?

b. I enjoy _____ (play) basketball more than volleyball.

c. She quit _____ (smoke) and decided _____ (exercise) instead.

d. They thought about _____ (move) closer to the park so they could go _____ (jog) every morning.

e. Would you mind _____ (pick) my son up from school this afternoon? I have _____ (go) to my aerobics class.

f. I like _____ (watch) people exercise, but I hate _____ (do) it.

LESSON 15
Social Problems in the United States

A. DIALOGUE

AN ENCOUNTER WITH THE HOMELESS

Mark is a graduate student at the University of Pennsylvania. He's currently doing some research on the homeless in the U.S. for his dissertation. He has interviewed almost 50 people who live on the streets of Philadelphia.[1] He's now talking to Jack, who lives under a bridge in the downtown area.

MARK: Excuse me. Do you have a minute?

JACK: Who wants to know?

MARK: My name is Mark, and I'm a college student doing a study of life on the streets. Would you mind if I asked you a few questions?

JACK: Go ahead, shoot. I have all the time in the world.

MARK: I've been told that you're known as the "Looney Tune."[2] Why's that?

JACK: I suppose it's because I used to hang out[3] at the local jazz joint[4] drawing people's portraits for free. I was always told I was loony[5] for not charging anything. I used to be pretty good at it, you know?

MARK: I know it's none of my business, but how did you end up on the streets?

JACK: Would you like me to do your portrait?

MARK: Okay. Why not?

JACK: Thanks. You got any cigarettes on you?[6]

MARK: Sorry, I don't smoke. So, getting back to your story . . .

JACK: Well, I was working late one night. I used to work as a cartoonist. Freelancing, of course. I guess I just fell asleep for a moment or two. Next thing I knew, the place was in flames. I couldn't breathe, and there was fire everywhere.

MARK: Your apartment was on fire?

JACK: Yup. Afterwards, I was told the fire was caused by the cigarette I was smoking. Fell from the ashtray into the trash can when I dozed off.

MARK: Were you injured?

JACK: It was pretty bad. I had third-degree burns over a third of my body. My right hand was burnt. I was told I'd never be able to draw again.

MARK: Did you have any kind of insurance?

JACK: Hell, no! I worked as a freelancer, remember? I could barely afford to pay the rent.

MARK: What happened when you got out of the hospital?

JACK: I was devastated.[7] I had lost everything, you know? So, I began drinking, and the more I drank, the more depressed I got.

MARK: How do you survive now?

JACK: I'm on welfare,[8] but it's not enough to pay for a decent home. I panhandle sometimes . . . But I'll tell you, I'd much rather live here under the clear blue sky than in one of those low-income housing projects.[9]

MARK: Why?

JACK: Too much crime. And who wants to sleep with a bunch of other guys snoring all night?

MARK: So are you looking for work now?

JACK: Come on! No one would hire me now.

MARK: With your skills, you could probably teach at a community center. Have you tried that?

JACK: I'm no teacher . . .

MARK: What do you do during the winter? It must get cold out here.

JACK: The police try to take us into shelters,[10] but I always hide from them. It's really not so bad. You get used to the cold and the hunger. It's surprising to see just how well human beings can adapt.

MARK: So, you've accepted this kind of lifestyle?

JACK: Well, I don't know. More or less. It's tough to deal with people's cold looks. There's not much understanding for people in my situation. What can I do? It's a vicious circle. Without a job, I can't have a home. And without a home, I can't keep a job.

MARK: So you don't see a way out?

JACK: No. Do you? Here. Your portrait is ready.

MARK: Wow! That's pretty good! Thanks. How much do I owe you?

JACK: Don't worry about it. I've enjoyed talking to you. I don't always get company, you know?

B. NOTES

1. The state of Pennsylvania is located near the east coast of the United States, bordered by New York, New Jersey, West Virginia, Ohio, Maryland, and Delaware. The state capital is Harrisburg, and its biggest city is Philadelphia, which was founded in 1683 by the Quaker William Penn. It was in Philadelphia (the fifth city in the country) that the first government capital was established (Independence Hall). The Constitution Act was signed in Philadelphia in 1787. Many of the city's tourist attractions are related to the rich historical past of the city. Independence Square, where Liberty Bell is exhibited, is one of the most visited places in the city. Other important attractions include the house of Betsy Ross, the woman who made the first American flag.

2. *Looney Tunes* is the name given to the cartoon characters created by Warner Brothers. *Tunes* is a pun on the word *toon,* which is an abbreviated version of the word *cartoon.*

3. In this context, the verb *to hang out* means "to frequent." In other contexts, it may refer to "spending free time doing nothing." When used with the preposition *with* (as in *to hang out with*) it means "to spend time with."

4. In colloquial English, the noun *joint* describes a simple, unpretentious bar. This type of place may also be known as a *dive,* but this is a more negative word than *joint.*

   I don't think I want to spend the whole evening in this dive.

5. The noun *loony* means "insane or demented." Other similar words are *crazy* or *mad.* The word *mad* can also mean "angry" or "liking something very much."

   I was mad at myself for sleeping in too late.
   I'm mad/crazy about jazz.

6. Notice that the question "You got any cigarettes on you?" does not begin with the auxiliary verb *to have.* In colloquial English, people sometimes omit the auxiliary verb. The grammatically correct question

would be: "Have you got any cigarettes on you?" or "Do you have any cigarettes on you?"

7. In informal English you can use the verb *to devastate* to describe "being stunned and overwhelmed with sadness and misfortune."

8. *To be on welfare* means that the person is receiving help and benefits from the government because that person is experiencing a lack of financial resources or poverty.

9. *Low-income housing projects* are blocks of government-subsidized apartments that are very inexpensive to rent. These housing complexes are built specifically for people who receive financial aid from the government. Generally, these *projects* are in a very bad state of disrepair and have a higher incidence of crime.

10. *Shelters* are places where homeless people can find a place to sleep. Some shelters distribute food and clothing to those in need.

C. GRAMMAR AND USAGE

1. THE PASSIVE VOICE
a. Form

When passive voice is used, the object or recipient of the verb becomes the subject, and the agent is mentioned in a different clause, normally beginning with the preposition *by.* In many other cases, the agent is simply omitted.

ACTIVE VOICE

> Agent (subject) + verb + recipient (object).

PASSIVE VOICE

> Recipient (subject) + *to be* + past participle
> of the verb + *by* + agent.

ACTIVE VOICE
The parishioners feed the homeless every Sunday.

PASSIVE VOICE
The homeless are fed by the parishioners every Sunday.
The homeless are fed every Sunday.

The passive voice can only be used with transitive verbs, that is, with verbs followed by an object. When using the passive voice, the tense and conjugation is done with the verb *to be* and the main verb is used in the past participle.

ACTIVE VOICE

PRESENT SIMPLE	Mark *prepares* the interview.
PRESENT CONTINUOUS	Mark *is conducting* the interview.
PRESENT PERFECT	Mark *has interviewed* three homeless people.
SIMPLE PAST	Jack *drew* a portrait of Mark.
PAST CONTINUOUS	Mark *was recording* the interview.
PAST PERFECT	Mark *had conducted* the interview.
FUTURE	Mark *is going* to prepare the report.
	Mark *will prepare* the report.

PASSIVE VOICE

PRESENT SIMPLE	The interview *is prepared* (by Mark).
PRESENT CONTINUOUS	The interview *is being conducted* (by Mark).
PRESENT PERFECT	Three homeless people *have been interviewed* (by Mark).
SIMPLE PAST	A portrait of Mark *was drawn* (by Jack).
PAST CONTINUOUS	The interview *was being recorded* (by Mark).
PAST PERFECT	The interview *had been conducted* (by Mark).
FUTURE	The report *is going to be prepared* (by Mark).
	The report *will be prepared* (by Mark).

b. Usage

You use the passive voice to omit the agent of the action when it is either unknown or unimportant. When it is necessary to identify the agent of the action, use the preposition *by* to introduce the agent.

Notice the following phrase:

They told him he would not be able to draw as he used to.

The previous sentence is in the active voice. Because the sentence is in the active voice, the person who hears the sentence would want to know who told him that information.

They told him he would not be able to draw as he used to.

Who told him?
Since the identity of *they* is not known by the speaker, it would be clearer to say the same sentence in the passive voice:

He was told he would not be able to draw as he used to.

It is also possible to use the impersonal subject *they* if the context implies the person to whom the sentence refers.

After the operation, two doctors came and talked to him. They said he wouldn't be able to draw as he used to.

The passive voice can also be used when the speaker wants to emphasize the recipient of the action and not the agent.

This portrait was drawn by a homeless man I met in Philadelphia.

It is common to use the passive voice with impersonal sentences such as these:

The contract was signed.
A new building was erected.

c. Passive Voice with Auxiliary Verbs
When the sentence has an auxiliary verb *(will, would, can, could, may, might, should, ought to, had better, must)*, the passive voice is constructed as follows:

> subject + auxiliary verb + *be* + past participle

Jack will be taken to a shelter in the winter.
The homeless should not be allowed to live on the streets.

d. Passive Voice Working as an Adjective
Generally, the verb *to be* may be followed by an adjective that describes the subject of the sentence. It may also be followed by a past participle serving as an adjective. In other words, the past participle of the verb is used to describe the subject of the sentence. When the past participle is used to describe a state of being and not an action, it is known as stative passive.

to be made of	*The bottle is made of plastic.*
to be qualified	*Jack was qualified to work as a cartoonist.*
to be drunk	*The man at the bar is drunk.*

There are several expressions that use this construction. The most common are:

to be acquainted with
to be bored with
to be broken
to be closed
to be composed of
to be crowded with
to be devoted to
to be disappointed in
to be done with
to be drunk
to be engaged to
to be excited
to be exhausted
to be finished with
to be frightened by
to be gone

to be hurt
to be interested in
to be involved in
to be lost
to be made of
to be married to
to be opposed to
to be pleased with
to be prepared for
to be qualified for
to be related to
to be satisfied with
to be shut
to be spoiled
to be terrified
to be worried about

D. IDIOMATIC STUDY

TAKING LEAVE

The following phrases are useful when you want to say good-bye to someone or you want to indicate that you want to leave.

Well, it's been nice talking to you.
Well, it's been nice seeing you again.
I've enjoyed talking to you.
I'd love to continue this conversation, but I'd better get going.
Sorry I have to run off like this.
I'm afraid it's getting late.
I think I should be/get going now.
I think I'd better get going.
I've (really) got to go now.
I need to go now.
I have to run.

The following phrases are common when you need to say good-bye:

Let's get together again.
I hope we'll see each other again soon.
Give me a ring sometime soon.
Let's stay in touch.
I'll talk to you later/soon.
I'll see you later/soon.
Take care.
Take it easy.

Good-bye.
Bye-bye.
See you soon.
See you later.

E. STRICTLY BUSINESS

1. SOCIAL RESPONSIBILITIES

Since the first British settlers arrived in the United States at the beginning of the seventeenth century, self-sufficiency has been an integral part of American culture and society. The country had an agricultural economy until the middle of the nineteenth century, and therefore during those centuries most Americans never depended on anyone but themselves. They claimed their own land as theirs, built their own houses, cultivated their fields, and educated themselves. As the country changed into an industrial society, this self-sufficiency evolved. Suddenly, people had to depend on others to get affordable housing, food, and employment. In spite of the interdependency that emerged, the generalized belief in self-sufficiency remained strong. Citizens worked hard to make sure that they were contributing to their society and the well-being of their neighbors.

The Great Depression that took place during the 1930s caused the government to create social programs for citizens who needed economic assistance. Under the new laws, the federal government sponsored employment creation in public companies and offered financial aid to those individuals in need. In 1935 the Social Security Act was approved to help senior citizens and people with disabilities. The law was intended to create a permanent system to help those in need. The country eventually recovered from the Great Depression, but many Americans and their families were not as fortunate. The government therefore decided to continue many of the assistance programs that were initially meant to be temporary. As a result, the number of citizens receiving government help increased in alarming proportions.

From the beginning, politicians and citizens expressed their dislike for this kind of government program. While most Americans agree that children and senior citizens should be protected from poverty, many think that there is no reason why the government should help any healthy citizen who has the ability to work. During the fifties and sixties, the number of people in the welfare system grew at an immense rate. Part of it had to do with the fact that the population was growing very fast during that time. This coincided with a long period of unemployment, a reduction in the creation of jobs, and an increase in single-parent homes. As decades went by, the number of people depending on welfare climbed into the millions. It became evident that the welfare system needed to be reformed.

The demands for reform did not originate only from people who wanted to abolish welfare. Many proponents of welfare were in agreement that the system needed to be changed. It is a general view that the welfare system has a negative impact on work ethics because it seems to discourage people from working. The system is also very costly for the government. Many critics claim, too, that the way the system distributes aid is inefficient and unfair. During the last few years, many politicians initiated reforms that include vocational and job training to counteract the dependency that the system seems to promote in some individuals. Others demanded that access to welfare be limited to those who truly need it, and they suggested setting a time limit after which all benefits would expire. Still other politicians wanted to place control of the welfare system in the hands of the individual states, instead of the federal government.

Some reforms have been implemented, but most have been rejected. The federal government still spends millions of dollars per year on welfare, and reform remains a hot political topic. It is safe to say that nearly everyone agrees that the goal of welfare is to help people to become self-sufficient. The real debate is whether the government should continue helping those who need welfare, or whether to cut benefits and force people to depend on themselves.

2. VOCABULARY

agricultural economy	loony
aid	mad
assistance	plight
to be on welfare	poverty
depression	projects
disability	to reform
debt	self-sufficient
elder	senior citizen
employment	shelters
financial aid	social security
Great Depression	unemployed
to hang out	unemployment
industrial society	welfare
joint	

1. Complete the following paragraph with the correct form (active or passive) of the verb in parentheses.

   A homeless man _____ (to find) yesterday on the deck of a cruise ship that _____ (to anchor) in New York Harbor. The man, authorities (to say), had been severely beaten. He _____ (to take) to Bellevue Hospital, where he is in stable condition. The identity of the man (to not disclose). This is the third case this week of a homeless person (to attack) and left to die near the harbor. What _____ (not to know) yet is the motive of these attacks or how the criminals who committed this crime managed to get on the ship. Authorities have several possible suspects and clues, but they refuse to comment any further.

2. Change the following sentences from active to passive.

   a. *The local supermarket employs homeless people to sweep the sidewalk and to remove snow from the parking lot.*
   b. *When it gets too cold, the police pick up homeless people and take them to shelters.*
   c. *Volunteers at the soup kitchen feed and help people in need.*
   d. *Social workers place homeless children in foster homes.*
   e. *Some people give panhandlers money.*
   f. *Many people ignore and mistreat the homeless.*

3. Complete the following sentences using the expressions on the list.

to be shut	to be exhausted	to be qualified	to be scared
to be drunk	to be excited about	to be interested in	

Mark:	*Wouldn't you like to go back to work?*
Jack:	*Of course. But, I __(a)__ . I don't think I __(b)__ to do a lot of jobs. What would I do?*
Mark:	*Well, let's see. What __(c)__ (you) doing?*
Jack:	*I'd like to be able to draw again.*
Mark:	*Maybe you can't draw the way you used to, but that doesn't mean you can't teach others how to do it.*
Jack:	*I guess you're right. But, I __(d)__ . I wouldn't know where to begin. Plus, I __(e)__ . Who's going to hire a drunk?*
Mark:	*Well, the first step is to get you a hot cup of coffee, a shower, and a change of clothes. Come on, let's go to the nearest church. I'm sure they'll be able to help us there.*

Jack: What if it __(f)__ .
Mark: Let's be a little more optimistic, will you? I __(g)__ this. I'm sure it will work.

4. Change the following sentences to the passive voice. If the information introduced in the clause that begins with the word *by* is not important, you may omit it.

   a. Some employers might not want to hire a homeless person.
   b. Mark must hand in the report by Friday.
   c. We ought to find a place for Jack to live.
   d. The government should provide better shelters for the homeless.
   e. The insurance company will mail Jack a form to declare all his losses.

READING III

HOW YOUNG IS TOO YOUNG FOR CEOs?*

BY MICHAEL BRUSH

A 20-something entrepreneur walks through the door with what seems like a great idea, a knockout business plan and a winning exuberance. The youngster with the flip chart could be the next Bill Gates, who founded the Microsoft Corporation at just such a tender age. More likely, though, his business venture will "blow up," as the money managers say. So, in a stock market enamored of hot new companies . . . how is an investor to separate the rockets from meteorites that will crash to earth?

Chief executives under 35 are more likely to succeed both in attracting capital and in long-term performance if they have some reinforcements on their business team with experience, money managers say. In addition, they have a greater likelihood of success if their youth works to their advantage in some way, by putting them close to the age of their customers, for example. . . . In some cases, management's youth might be an outright advantage. "I would argue that because the biotech area is so cutting edge, someone who is younger is closer to what's happening," said Rachel Leheney, who follows biotechnology companies. . . . Technology is not the only field in which young managers may be a plus. Being "with it" can help in fashion, sports, and the Internet.

VOCABULARY

being "with it"

business venture

CEO (chief executive officer)

cutting edge

enamored

entrepreneur

exuberance

flip chart

knockout

likelihood

20-something

LESSON 16
Import and Export

A. DIALOGUE

A LATE SHIPMENT OF SUGAR

John Hume and Kevin Ricksen work for a company in New Haven, Connecticut[1], that imports goods from South America. They are currently working on a sugar deal with Ms. Karen Klett, the U.S. representative for a small Ecuadorian company.

JOHN: Good afternoon, Ms. Klett. Please come in and have a seat.

MS. KLETT: Thanks, and please call me Karen.

JOHN: Very well, Karen. I'm afraid Kevin won't be able to join us. He called about a half hour ago[2] and left a message on my voice mail.[3] He said he was running late[4] and that he wouldn't be able to make it[5] on time. Why don't we go through the final details of this deal, and I'll bring Kevin up to date[6] when he gets in?

MS. KLETT: That's fine with me. But, first of all, I have to tell you that we won't be able to ship the 30 tons of sugar by the end of this month as we had originally planned.

JOHN: That definitely changes things. Why the delay?

MS. KLETT: I'm afraid one of our suppliers . . .

Two hours later Kevin finally makes it to the office. He's running and gasping for air.

KEVIN: I apologize for missing our meeting with Ms. Klett. You'd never believe what happened! There was an oil spill in the middle of the road. Anyway, I'll spare you the details. So, how did it go? Will she be able to supply us with the 30 tons of sugar by the end of the month?

JOHN: Well, not all of it.

KEVIN: What do you mean? What happened?

JOHN: According to Ms. Klett, one of her suppliers lost all of the merchandise in a flood last week.

KEVIN: You've got to be kidding me! What are we going to tell our clients? Are you aware of how much money we're going to lose?

JOHN: Take it easy. After I threatened to sue the company, she finally agreed to send us everything she has in stock now, and the rest ASAP.[7] She figures she has about ten tons, and that should be enough to cover the orders of our most important clients.

KEVIN: When will we get the other twenty tons?

JOHN: Ms. Klett said she'll be able to find a last-minute supplier in Bolivia to cover the rest. We should have it by the middle of next month.

KEVIN: Well, I hope you didn't agree to pay her initial price . . .

JOHN: No way! I got her to lower her price by 20 percent, and she also agreed to ship everything CIF[8] so we don't have to pay extra freight and insurance.

KEVIN: Wow! That's a huge savings for us!

JOHN: I know. Considering the extra money we'll make once the sugar is sold, I'm beginning to think this isn't a disaster after all.

KEVIN: Well, let's hope Ms. Klett doesn't come up with some other excuse for not delivering the sugar on time. Otherwise, this will be the last time we do business with that company.

B. NOTES

1. The state of Connecticut is located in the northeastern United States. Its capital is Hartford. The largest cities in Connecticut are Stamford, Bridgeport, New Haven, and New London. New Haven is home to Yale University, one of the most prestigious universities in the United States. Yale has one of the largest centers of British art outside the United Kingdom, as well as the Peabody Museum of Natural History, one of the largest in the region.

2. The word *ago* is an adverb that indicates passing of time.

   Two months ago we purchased five tons of wheat.

3. Voice mail is popular across all types of companies and organizations. Most corporations, large or small, depend on it because of its convenience. Each employee has a phone that is connected to an answering system that keeps tracks of the time and the origin of the voice message. Employees may access the messages from any phone at any time of the day. If a caller wants to leave the same phone message for several people, there is no need to call several times; by

pressing one key, the message can be transmitted electronically to several different inboxes.

4. The verb *to run* is used with several expressions:

to run against	=	to compete with in an election
to run after	=	to chase
to run away	=	to leave someplace or someone in a hurry
to run for	=	to compete in an election
to run high	=	to be elevated (used for temperature)
to run into someone	=	to meet someone unexpectedly
to run out/short	=	to lack a specific item

5. The English expression *to make it* means "to achieve a goal," "to be successful," or "to get somewhere."

I didn't think Jack would make it to the end of the race because he's never run a marathon before.
Because he was stuck in traffic, he didn't make it to the meeting on time.
The national team made it all the way to the Olympics.

6. The expression *to bring up* means "to introduce into discussion or to mention." Other expressions with the verb *to bring* are:

to bring suit
to bring to mind
to bring to light
to bring into play

7. *ASAP* is an abbreviation for the expression "as soon as possible." This abbreviation is used colloquially.

8. *CIF* is an abbreviation that stands for "cost, insurance, and freight." In international markets it means that the cost of the product includes insurance and transportation. The abbreviation *FOB* stands for "free on board," which means that the price that is paid for the shipping of a product does not include insurance and freight.

C. GRAMMAR AND USAGE

1. DIRECT VS. INDIRECT SPEECH

In English, direct speech is used to quote the exact words of others. In written form you use quotation marks at the beginning and at the end of the quote.

"Hi John, this is Kevin. It's about a quarter to three. I'm calling to let you know that I'm running late for our meeting."

Indirect speech is used when you want to express the idea of the speaker without giving an exact quote. In this case, there are changes in the verbs and pronouns that are used, and quotations marks are not needed.

Kevin called about a half hour ago. He said he was running late.

It is important to remember that all verbs in the sentence must be accompanied by a subject. In other words, the subject cannot be omitted under any circumstances, as is the case in some other languages.

Also, notice that the relative pronoun *that* is optional in most cases.

He said that he was running late.
He said he was running late.

When using indirect speech, it is important to pay attention to the agreement between the subject and the verb once the change of tense occurs. It is generally necessary to change the verb to the past tense. The most frequent changes appear on the list below:

Direct Speech → Indirect Speech
Present Simple → Simple Past

"I work for a company in Connecticut."
He said (that) he worked for a company in Connecticut.

Present Continuous → Past Continuous

"My secretary is answering all my calls."
She said (that) her secretary was answering all her calls.

Present Perfect → Past Perfect

"I've found a new supplier."
He told us (that) he'd found a new supplier.

Present Perfect Continuous → Past Perfect Continuous

"I've been waiting to close this deal for ages."
She said (that) she'd been waiting to close that deal for ages.

Simple Past → Past Perfect

"We purchased three tons last week."
They told us (that) they'd purchased three tons last week.

Future → Conditional

"I'll call you when the shipment arrives."
He said (that) he'd call me when the shipment arrives.

Conditional → Conditional

"I'd like to have it delivered tomorrow."
She said she'd like to have it delivered tomorrow.

The most common verbs that are used to introduce indirect speech are *to say* and *to tell*. The verb *to say* is followed by the subordinant *that* and the reported phrase.

He said (that) his supplier lost all the merchandise.

The verb *to tell*, however, is followed first by an objective pronoun, the subordinant *that*, then the reported phrase.

I told him (that) we'd like to buy more sugar.

Here are some other verbs that are useful when using indirect speech:

to add	*to object*
to admit	*to observe*
to answer	*to point out*
to argue	*to protest*
to assure	*to remark*
to complain	*to reply*
to deny	*to threaten*
to explain	

You may also use the verbs *to agree, to refuse, to offer,* and *to promise* followed by an infinitive:

John agreed to wait for Kevin to arrive.
The bank refused to give us another loan.
My secretary offered to work overtime.
The supplier promised to have the shipment ready by next Tuesday.

There is another group of verbs that can be used in indirect speech. These verbs are followed by a direct object pronoun and the infinitive of a verb.

to advise	*to permit*
to ask	*to remind*
to encourage	*to tell*
to invite	*to warn*
to order	

The president ordered us to buy 30 more tons of sugar.
I invited him to come to the meeting, but he had a previous
engagement.

In interrogative sentences, you must use the interrogative verbs to
introduce indirect speech. These verbs are followed by the conjunctions
if or *whether*. The conjunction *if* is used in conditional affirmative
sentences, and *whether* is used to express other alternatives or options:

to ask if/whether
to inquire if/whether
to wonder if/whether
to want to know if/whether
I asked him if he could give us a lower price.
We wanted to know whether the price would be the same or higher.

D. IDIOMATIC STUDY

EXPRESSING CERTAINTY/UNCERTAINTY
The following phrases are useful when expressing certainty about
something:

I'm positive/certain/sure.
I'm absolutely positive/certain/sure.
I'm a hundred percent sure.
There's no doubt about it.

You may use one of the following phrases to express doubt or
uncertainty about something:

I don't know for sure.
I'm not (completely) positive/sure.
I'm not a hundred percent sure.
I'm not sure/certain.
I don't know yet.
I don't think so.
Not as far as I know.
I doubt it.

E. STRICTLY BUSINESS

1. IMPORTING PRODUCTS INTO THE UNITED STATES
The U.S. trade laws that regulate international freight and commerce
are very complicated, especially the laws that govern exporting goods

to the United States. When imported goods do not fulfill federal standards and requirements (or when the appropriate trade protocol is not followed), U.S. Customs rejects, confiscates, or destroys the merchandise. However, when the trade requirements and the appropriate paperwork is followed, importing goods to the United States can be a relatively simple process.

The only way to prove that merchandise satisfies U.S. requirements is to have the appropriate documentation ready. International cargo without documentation will not be allowed into the country. Here is a list of the most important documentation you must have to import goods into the country:

1. Commercial invoice—This document is required regardless of the type of cargo. Every time you import a product into the United States you must submit a list with the following information: 1) name and address of the manufacturer and shipper; 2) name and address of the buyer in the United States; 3) quantity and complete description of the product; 4) number of boxes in the shipment; and 5) country of origin of the product (where it was manufactured). Whenever possible, the shipping information should also include a receipt. Failure to include any of the above information may cause long delays.

2. Contract of awareness of original shipment—This contract stipulates the terms of shipment and delivery of the merchandise, from its origin, all the way to its final destination. When transporting a large quantity of goods that don't need to arrive at a certain time, most shippers prefer to use maritime freight. Shipment may take several weeks, but maritime freight is reliable and economical. When using this option, the contract of awareness of original shipment must be endorsed and presented to the cargo company at the point of entry before the merchandise is released to the buyer. Other merchants prefer to use air freight for a shipment of smaller packages or merchandise that needs to arrive by a certain time. Air freight can be expensive, but if it is handled the right way, the merchandise can go through customs and be delivered to the buyer the same day it is shipped.

3. Certificate of Origin—This certificate confirms that the exported product was manufactured in the country from which it was shipped. Many countries have trade agreements with the United States that promote international commerce and growth between those countries and American companies. These agreements allow the import of several types of products into the United States without paying the importing company to pay taxes and fees. The most important treaty is

the Generalized System of Preferences, which includes developing countries in Latin America, Africa, and Asia. There are two trade treaties under the Generalized System of Preferences—the Andean Trade Preference and the NAFTA. The Andean Trade Preference covers many South American countries as well as some Caribbean nations. In 1994 the North American Free Trade Agreement (or NAFTA) went into effect. This treaty guarantees free trade between the United States, Mexico, and Canada.

4. Visa—The United States has laws that limit the amount of goods that can be imported from particular countries. These limitations, or quotas, govern the import of certain types of goods, such as textiles, clothing, and food. If a particular product has an annual quota, the shipper must present a specific visa to complete trade. This visa certifies that the quota for the particular product has not been exceeded. Once the Customs Service is able to determine that the product is below the quota level, the product is allowed into the country.

To ease the process of importing and exporting, many foreign manufacturers use international freight companies to transport their merchandise. The freight companies are convenient because they take charge of the paperwork and the legal requirements of international trade as well as the actual shipping of the merchandise. International merchants find that using these companies is cost-efficient because it relieves the company of maintaining their own international shipping department. As an added bonus, cargo companies keep current on the latest information on laws and shipping regulations.

When merchandise enters the entry port in the United States, the cargo has to pass through customs. If the value of the merchandise is less than $1,250 and it contains articles of personal use, you may pick up the merchandise yourself after filling out the necessary paperwork. If the merchandise is worth more than $1,250 or if it is for commercial use, you will need a customs specialist. These companies are licensed by the government and are familiar with the laws that govern the product that is being imported. They will take care of the documentation you must present at customs. The price for these services is normally reasonable, considering the many headaches these companies can save you.

For more information, as well as the latest changes in trade and customs laws, visit the Department of the Treasury's Web site, www.customs.ustreas.gov.

2. VOCABULARY

ago	import
ASAP (as soon as possible)	invoice
to bring up	limitation
bulk commodities	liner trade
cargo	load
certificate	to make it
CIF (cost, insurance, and freight)	manufactured goods
commerce	manufacturer
commercial	merchandise
consumer goods	NAFTA (North American
cost-efficient	Free Trade Agreement)
customs	origin
delay	quota
delivery	to run
documentation	to ship
to exceed	shipment
export	shipper
free alongside ship (FAS)	trade zone
free on board (FOB)	voice mail
freight	waterway systems

EXERCISES

1. Change the following sentences from direct speech to indirect speech.

    a. Tom is giving an explanation to his partner. He explains, "The shipment will arrive next month because of a delay at the docks."
    b. Mr. Brown is asking his secretary something. He orders, "Bring me a copy of the contract, please."
    c. Beth is telling something to her friend. She tells her, "I've just been offered a job at the bank!"
    d. Mark is answering his colleagues question. He answers, "Well, last week the price was very low, but I'm sure it's gone up."
    e. Carol is telling something to her secretary. She tells her, "I'm sure he's inviting everyone to the dinner party, but I'm not going."
    f. Frank agrees with Stephanie. "All right, wait here until Tom arrives," he agrees.

2. Fill in the blank with the appropriate word.

against	away	after	into	for	high	out

    a. My cousin is running _____ governor. She's running _____ a very popular candidate.
    b. The man ran _____ the thief for two blocks, but finally lost him.

c. I think Sally's daughter ran _____. Sally hasn't heard from her in two days.

d. I ran _____ of paper just as I was about to be done printing.

e. I ran _____ my boss at a club last night. It was a bit uncomfortable.

f. Tempers are running _____ at work these days because we're being audited.

3. Find six words in the puzzle that match the definitions below. Circle each word as you find it. The words can be in any direction.

a. Government agency authorized to collect duties or taxes on imported goods.

b. A detailed list of goods or services with an account of all costs.

c. Articles of trade or commerce that can be transported— agricultural/mining product.

d. Amount of material transported by a vehicle.

e. Person in charge of making goods available to a buyer.

f. The maximum number or quantity of a product imported into a country.

```
Y  N  Q  U  O  T  A  F
T  O  E  S  I  C  J  B
I  R  U  T  N  I  S  C
D  S  P  H  V  M  U  I
O  A  V  B  O  Q  P  N
M  G  O  T  I  R  P  E
M  P  S  X  C  D  L  W
O  U  F  N  E  L  I  D
C  Y  A  Z  M  E  E  T
F  D  A  O  L  K  R  R
```

LESSON 17

Higher Education in the United States

A. DIALOGUE

REGISTERING AT THE LOCAL COLLEGE

Juan Luis is a foreign exchange student from Spain at the University of California at Berkeley.¹ This is his freshman² year in college. Rod, his roommate,³ is helping him register.

ROD: OK, let me tell you what you need to do to register. You can register in person or by phone. If you decide to do it in person, you need to walk over to the admissions building and . . .

JUAN LUIS: Will there be someone who can help me?

ROD: I'm sure there will be some advisors and other students to help you. But the process is really easy. I don't think you'll need any help. When you get there, you'll see a room full of computers. Just sit down and key in⁴ your PIN⁵ number.

JUAN LUIS: What's that?

ROD: It's your Personal Identification Number. You should have received one with your acceptance letter.

JUAN LUIS: I was wondering what that number was for. So, I punch it in, and then I enter the numbers of the courses I want, right?

ROD: You got it. But, you can also register by phone. It's easier. Want to try?

JUAN LUIS: Why not?

ROD: Let's use the speaker phone so I can help you. Let me dial the number: eight, zero, five, thirty-five hundred. It's ringing.

PHONE SERVICE: Welcome to the University of California Touch-Tone⁶ services. If you are calling from a Touch-Tone phone, press one now.

JUAN LUIS: OK. One.

PHONE SERVICE: To register or change your registration, press one now. To hear your grades press two now. To change your PIN, press three now.

JUAN LUIS: One, again.

PHONE SERVICE: One moment please . . . Please enter your nine-digit student ID number[7] now.

JUAN LUIS: Is that the same as my PIN number?

ROD: No, your PIN number is a secret number that you can change at any time and only you know.[8] Your ID is generally the same as your social security number. Since you're an exchange student, the university probably assigned you a number.

PHONE SERVICE: You have exceeded your time limit. Please try again.

JUAN LUIS: I'm not sure I can do this. It's a little confusing, and I'm getting nervous.

ROD: Calm down. You'll get the hang of it.[9] Give me that number. Let's see . . . one, two, one, seven, six, three, five, three, zero. There you go.

PHONE SERVICE: Please enter your five-digit PIN, now.

JUAN LUIS: Let's see . . . three, four, eight, five, six.

PHONE SERVICE: You have ten minutes to complete your registration. Enter the information one course at a time. You will receive a written statement within a week. To add a course, press one. To drop[10] a course, press two.

Fifteen minutes later.

JUAN LUIS: Well, that wasn't so bad after all. I'm glad I'm done with this whole thing.

ROD: Not so quick, man. You still have to get your immunizations.

JUAN LUIS: You mean I have to get some shots?[11] Can I do that over the phone, too?

ROD: Very funny!

B. NOTES

1. The University of California at Berkeley is located in Berkeley, near San Francisco, in the state of California, on the west coast of the United States. The state capital is Sacramento. Los Angeles, San Francisco, and San Diego are the largest cities in California. The state is known for its wine industry, its film and television industry, and for Silicon

Valley, home to some of the most important technological corporations. Napa and Sonoma counties produce some of the best wines in the world. The state also has some spectacular natural wild areas, such as Yosemite National Park.

2. First-year students in college or high school are normally referred to as *freshmen.* Second-year students are *sophomores,* third-year students are *juniors,* and fourth- or fifth-year students who are about to graduate are *seniors.*

3. It is common for students to live in university dormitories during their first years in college. Most students share their rooms or apartments with other fellow students, or *roommates.*

4. The verbs *to key in* or *to punch in* means "to enter data into a computer by means of a keyboard." The verb describes entering data with a computer keyboard, a key pad, or a telephone pad.

5. *PIN* is the acronym for Personal Identification Number. If you open a bank account, you will be given a banking card and asked to select a PIN so you can access information or retrieve cash at the bank's automated teller machines.

6. Most telephones in the United States have keys that produce specific tones, which, in turn, are recognized by a computer as a numerical message. Phones that use this system are called *Touch-Tone phones.* There are also some traditional phones called rotary phones. Rotary phones are increasingly rare; these phones do not allow you to punch in codes that are necessary when trying to reach many customer service departments.

7. *ID* is the acronym for "identification." It is used to refer to any identification card or document, whether it is a driver's license, passport, student or work identification card, or any document that has your name and some other background information. A *photo ID* is identification with your picture on it.

8. The verb *to know* has several meanings. It may mean "to regard as true, to have a practical understanding, to be skilled in, to recognize someone or to possess skill and information."

I know how to register by phone. Let me show you.
I know the woman sitting across the hall, but I can't remember her name.

The verb *to know* is irregular. The past tense of the verb is *knew.* Notice that *know* sounds just like the negative adverb *no* while *knew* sounds like the adjective *new* (the opposite of *old).*

9. The colloquial expression *to get the hang of* means "to understand something" or "to learn how to do or use something."

10. In this case the verb *to drop* means "to withdraw or retire from something." This verb also means "to let something fall."

   She dropped the course because it was too difficult.
   I dropped the glass and it broke.

11. In medicine, the noun *shot* is used to refer to a vaccine or an injection.

C. GRAMMAR AND USAGE

1. PREPOSITIONS

Prepositions are words that precede a noun or pronoun and show the relationship between that noun or pronoun and another word in the sentence. There are no distinct rules in English when it comes to prepositions, and, even where there are rules, there are many exceptions. There are even some prepositions that change meaning depending on the context in which they are used. Here is a summary of the most common prepositions:

a. Prepositions of Place *(at, in, under, on, out, above, below, next to, in front of, behind, between, beneath)*

The preposition *in* is used with places that have borders or limits:

in a country/in a town/in a square/in a street/in a room/in a forest
I was in Paris last summer.
Some of my classmates are studying in a foreign country this semester.

The preposition *at* is used to point out a specific place:

at home/at work/at the office/at school/at an address/at the bridge
I am working at home today.
I'll be at work till seven.

Here are some other prepositions of place:

next to	*out*
in front of	*under*
behind	*below*
between	*on*
beneath	*above*
in	

I was sitting in front of Maria and next to Jane.
My school is next to the library.
The ball is in the box.

space   father   closer
below   ≠ underneath / under
above   on

There is a slight difference between *under* and *below* and between *on* and *above*. In most cases, *under* indicates that there may be contact between the two objects (in other words that the objects may be touching each other). *Below* indicates that there is space between the two objects. The same distinction applies to *on and above*. The preposition *on* indicates that the objects may be touching each other while the preposition *above* indicates that there is space between the objects.

The VCR is under the television set.   *surface*
The lamp is on the nightstand.
Mary hung the painting on the wall above the sofa.
The people who live below me are very noisy.

b. Prepositions of Time *(at, on, by, in, for, since)*
   The preposition *at* is used to refer to a specific time or hour:

   at dawn   *at six*   *at midnight*   *at 4:30*

   The class will begin at seven o'clock.
   The party ended at midnight, but we left at three.

   The preposition *at* is also used to express a moment in a person's life, such as age:

   at 20/at the age of 20
   I plan to start my master's degree at the age of 25.

   The preposition *on* is used for days of the week or to indicate a specific date:

   on Monday   *on the Fourth*   *on Christmas Day*
                         of June

   I registered on Friday.

   The preposition *by* is used as a preposition of time when indicating a deadline.

   Registration ends at five o'clock, so you better be there by 4:30.

   The preposition *in* is used with years, months, or seasons:

   in 1911   *in March*   *in the spring*

   I will register for that course in the fall.
   I graduated from high school in 1983.

   Exceptions: *on the weekend, in the morning/afternoon, in the evening, at night*

   I study at night on the weekends.
   In the evening, I'm too tired to study, so I watch TV instead.

212

The preposition *from* is generally used with *to, till,* or *until* to indicate the beginning and ending of a time period.

Most people work from 9 to 5.
The meeting will last from 2 to 3 P.M.

The preposition *since* indicates the starting time of an action. It is normally used with the present perfect or with the past perfect. *(tense)*

He has been in the country since August. It is still true
They had been waiting for this news since they sent in the first application. They are still waiting.

The preposition *for* is also used with the present perfect and the past perfect. It is only used to express the duration of the time period. *(tense*

for six years   for two months   forever

I have been working here for three years. still working
She hasn't worked here for very long; go easy on her.

c. Prepositions of Movement
(from . . . to, into/out of, toward, away from, to)

To indicate the starting and finishing points of an action or time period, use the prepositions *from* and *to.*

They flew from Paris to Rome.

The prepositions *into* and *out of* are used to indicate movement.

He went into the store to buy a pen.

The preposition *toward* means "in the direction of" while the preposition *away* means "in the direction from."

As we were walking toward the coast, we could start to smell the ocean.
We live away from the downtown area because it's too noisy.   denote   location

The preposition *to* is also used to indicate direction.   to →at

The bookstore is to the left of the cafeteria.   on/onto →on
                      point   in/into — in
Notice that the preposition *to* may not be accompanied by any other preposition.

They will come to the city on Friday.   ← to the left
I gave the books to Peter.   from the cafeteria

In English you may never use a preposition before the infinitive form of the verb. You can only do this if you use the gerund form of the verb (-ing form). In English the infinitive form includes the preposition *to.*

in the cafeteria on the left side.
         is   cafeteria
    (volume (area)

After registering, we went to see a movie.
I bought a separate notebook to do my homework.

When using formal English you may not use a preposition at the very end of a sentence.

I don't know for which course my friend registered.
For which courses have you registered?
From which college did you graduate?
For how long have you been waiting in line?

However, when using informal English, you may end a sentence with a preposition. Remember, this should only be used in informal or colloquial English.

I don't know which course my friend registered for.
Which courses have you registered for?
Which college did you graduate from?
How long have you been waiting in line for?

There are certain verbs in English that change meaning depending on the preposition that follows. These phrasal verbs are described in Lesson 19.

D. IDIOMATIC STUDY

OFFERING HELP
There are many ways to offer help to someone. There are occasions in which you should be more formal than others. The following phrases will be helpful when you find yourself in a formal situation:

Would you like me to help you _____?
I'd be glad/happy to help you _____.
I'd be glad/happy to lend a hand.
Is there anything I can do to help?
Is there anything else I can help you with?
Allow me to _____.
May I help you?

In formal written communication, you may want to use one of these phrases:

Please let me know if I can be of further assistance.
If I can be of any further assistance, please don't hesitate to ask/let me know.

The following phrases are useful in more informal situations:

(Do you) need any help?
(Do you) want a hand?
Let me help you _____.
Let me give you a hand.
What can I do to help?

When responding to an offer, you may want to say:

If you don't mind.
If you wouldn't mind.
If it's no trouble.
That would be great.
I really appreciate it.
I don't want to trouble you.
I don't want to bother you.
I don't want to inconvenience you.
No, thanks. I can manage by myself.

E. STRICTLY BUSINESS

1. HIGHER EDUCATION IN THE UNITED STATES

The education system in the United States is complex. Americans tend to use the words *university* and *college* somewhat interchangably. *College* is often used in a more general sense *(I'm going to college this year . . .),* and may refer to a smaller school or a private school. *University,* on the other hand, is usually used in a more specific sense *(. . . at Ohio State University),* and generally refers to a large school consisting of several colleges, graduate schools, and professional schools. Most universities offer undergraduate studies in the liberal arts and sciences. Students prepare to apply to college during their junior, or third, year of high school. During this year high school students take the nationwide standardized test called the SAT, or Scholastic Aptitude Test. Each university establishes the minimum SAT score for acceptance to the school. In addition to the SAT score, the university's admissions department looks at each candidate's grade point average, or GPA, and the student's talents, skills, or leadership abilities. Undergraduate studies normally last four years. Students enroll in classes that carry a predetermined number of credits. A typical undergraduate course has a value of three to four credits. To graduate, a student must complete a predetermined number of credits, approximately 125 in most colleges. During the first two years as an undergraduate, all students in the college are required to take general courses. Most undergraduate students enroll in courses in the fields of the arts, sciences, foreign languages, and philosophy. Students may also enroll in elective specialized courses, depending on the students' degree and concentration. The objective is to have a basic general interdisciplinary foundation. Students have less flexibility when it comes to the courses that are required for their major or concentration.

At the end of the four years, students earn either a Bachelor of Arts (BA) or a Bachelor of Science (BS), depending on the major or concentration they selected. This degree is not a graduate or professional diploma. Students who want to become lawyers or doctors must continue with graduate studies.

Many universities have graduate schools for those students who want to go beyond their four-year studies. Some universities focus on graduate studies by offering only graduate advanced degrees such as Master of Arts (MA), Master of Sciences (MS), Doctor of Philosophy (PhD), or Doctor of Education (EdD).

Graduate studies follow the same credit system, but the course of study generally does not offer much flexibility in the selection of courses, because the study program is more specialized. Professional schools are institutions that are affiliated with a university and specialize in only one field of study, such as medicine, dentistry, law, or business administration. The time it takes to finish a degree in these fields depends on the major or concentration. In some cases, a student is required to fulfill field study or specific training that prolongs the process of getting the graduate degree.

Universities are located on a *campus.* The campus is comprised of the complex of school buildings, dormitories, administrative offices, libraries, cafeterias, sports facilities, theaters, banks, and park areas that make up the university environment. Some universities are located in cities and therefore do not have a specific campus. Most colleges, however, are somewhat isolated from the rest of the outside world.

The United States also has technical or vocational institutions. These are places of study that specialize in nonacademic preparation for a specific job or occupation. The courses offered by these institutions are usually not transferable to a university. These institutions train students to get jobs as mechanics, computer technicians, or dental hygienists. In most cases it is possible to finish the coursework in a matter of months. Those who finish the courses satisfactorily obtain a certificate that allows them to look for employment in a particular field.

Junior colleges, community colleges, and city colleges are also available. These are schools that offer two-year programs of studies in a combination of technical training and basic academic courses. Most students who attend these schools are not full-time students. Community colleges cater to an adult population that needs to find employment easily. Because the typical student at this type of institution is already working, community colleges do not have student dormitories. After finishing the two-year degree, students earn an Associate of Arts degree, or AA. In order to earn a BA, the student would have to apply to a four-year college and have his or her credits transferred.

Most colleges and universities in the United States work on an honor system of honesty and originality. The rules vary from one school to another, so it is very important to know them and understand them. To cheat or to obtain unauthorized information from another student while taking a test or doing research is considered an act of dishonesty. *Plagiarism* is defined as the theft of someone else's material. Students who are caught in any dishonest act are given a failing grade, and depending on the gravity of the offense, may be expelled from the university. Each university offers its students a variety of financial aid programs, as well as different types of scholarships. Some financial aid packages and scholarships are available to foreign students. Investigate financial aid before leaving your home country because this information varies from year to year, and scholarships have become highly contested. Job opportunities in the United States are limited for foreign students, and they depend on the type of visa the student has been granted. These are the most common types of student visas:

F-1 ACADEMIC STUDENT VISA
This type of visa is given to full-time students, that is, students who attend classes at least twelve hours per week. Students with F-1 visas may stay in the country until they finish their studies. To get this visa, students must prove that all personal and academic expenses are covered; therefore, working is not permitted. The only exception to this rule is made for graduate students, who may work in the university as teaching assistants or research assistants. At the conclusion of their studies, students may spend up to twelve months training or getting on-the-job experience.

M-1 VOCATIONAL STUDENT VISA
M-1 visas are given to full-time students who are accepted to technical or vocational schools. As with F-1 visas, students are not authorized to work. The visa requires proof of financial independence; therefore, working is prohibited.

J-1 EXCHANGE VISITOR VISA

This type of visa is given to foreign students who are entering the United States on an exchange program. The J-1 visa allows students to work inside or outside the university campus. At the end of the study program, the student may take up to eighteen months for training. This visa carries a stipulation that once the visa expires, the student is obligated to return to his country and must wait at least two years before being allowed back into the United States. For more information about student visas and their requirements, visit the Department of Justice's Web site at www.usdoj.gov/immigrationinfo. htm.

2. VOCABULARY

authorized
Bachelor of Arts (BA)
Bachelor of Science (BS)
campus
community college
credit
dishonesty
Doctor of Philosophy (PhD)
Doctor of Medicine (MD)
to drop
exchange student
freshman
to get the hang of something
GPA (Grade Point Average)
grades
graduate school
honor code
ID (identification)
instructor
junior

junior college
to key in
major
Master of Arts (MA)
Master of Science (MS)
PIN (Personal Identification
   Number)
plagiarism
practical training
professor
research
roommate
SAT (Scholastic Aptitude Test)
senior
sophomore
student visa
technical institution
Touch-Tone phone
tuition
vocational institution

EXERCISES

---

1. Complete the following sentences with the following words: *had known, know, knew, no,* and *new.*

   a. He's _____ in town, so he doesn't _____ his way to the college.
   b. If I _____ that this class was so hard, I wouldn't have taken it.
   c. _____ , I don't feel any pain.

d. This is a _____ course, but we don't _____ how many students will enroll in it.

e. The professor _____ that there were _____ more books left. The bookstore had to order some _____ ones.

2. Most prepositions have been left out of the following letter. Fill in the blanks with the preposition that best completes the sentence.

June 29, 2005

Mr. Mark Kern
Foreign Student Advisor
Foreign Student Office, Room 345
University of California at Berkeley
Berkeley, CA 94720

Dear Mr. Kern:

I received your letter dated June 3, 2005. Attached you will find an official copy of my undergraduate work. I still don't understand the reason __(a)__ the immunization form. Should I have it signed by my doctor? __(b)__ when do I have to submit it?

I will be arriving __(c)__ San Francisco International Airport __(d)__ Thursday, the 28th of August, __(e)__ 3 P.M. __(f)__ America West, Flight 335. If it is convenient __(g)__ someone in your office to pick me up, I would appreciate it. Otherwise, I will take a bus __(h)__ the airport __(i)__ Berkeley. I'm sure it will not be very difficult.

Anyway, I will call you as soon as I arrive. Thank you very much for all your help. I look forward to meeting you soon.

Sincerely,

Juan Luis Outeriño

3. Complete the following crossword puzzle.

VERTICAL
a. If you want to study in a quiet place, you should go to the
_____.
d. To register by phone, you need a _____-Tone phone,
e. This is his first year of school. He is a _____.
g. Personal Identification Number.

HORIZONTAL
b. I need to buy some books. I'll go to the _____.
c. I think I'm going to _____ this class. I will take it again next semester.

f.   Another way of saying turn left is "_____ a left."

h.   I think I _____ who you're talking about. I met him last week.

i.   This is her third year of school. She is a _____.

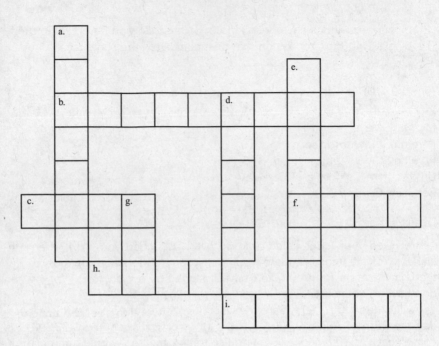

LESSON 18
Marketing and Advertising

A. DIALOGUE

LIKE GOOD WINE

Mary Bailey is the product marketing manager for Kophee, a private company that distributes Colombian coffee around the United States. The company has been studying the possibility of producing its own line of gourmet coffee, and Ms. Bailey is presenting her marketing plan to the CEO,[1] Mr. Ed Smiley.

MS. BAILEY: As you are well aware, there is a growing market for gourmet coffee in the United States. I was surprised to find that the most demanding[2] consumers are not in New York, Boston, or Chicago, but rather on the West Coast. More specifically, in the state of Washington.[3] In fact, not long ago the *Seattle Post* published an article titled "Seattle: Coffee Capital of the World."

MR. SMILEY: Do you have a copy of the article?

MS. BAILEY: As a matter of fact, I do. As you can see, the article summarizes the biggest private exporters and the different U.S. companies that are buying gourmet coffee. In the United States today, coffee is becoming a quality product, just like good wine. Consumers are willing[4] to pay higher prices for better quality and taste. People are looking for new experiences—for products that are unique, special, and trendy.

MR. SMILEY: Let's[5] talk a little about promotion and price. Who exactly are we targeting? What do you anticipate the selling price will be, and will the consumer be willing to pay it?

MS. BAILEY: The price for high quality coffee is not determined by the futures market.[6] This coffee has a specific price depending on two essential factors: exclusiveness and differentiation. In producing this new coffee, we should use trees of the Bourbon variety known for their larger, high-quality beans with a rich, acidic flavor. Since coffee produced from these beans is so rich in flavor and aroma, it will surely meet the standards of even the most selective consumers.

MR. SMILEY: That makes sense to me. But going back to the price . . .

MS. BAILEY: This type of coffee is intended for consumers with a fairly high income. I have the results of a market research survey that shows that the average consumer is willing to pay $8.99[7] for a pound of high-quality coffee, and high-income consumers are willing to pay even more. In order to keep our prices competitive, I figure we should sell our coffee for $10.99 a pound.

MR. SMILEY: Well, we also have to consider that the investment costs of producing such coffee are greater. If I remember correctly, trees of the Bourbon variety, like the ones you suggest we use, produce fewer beans and have to be planted at a greater distance from each other. We would therefore be spending more money for less output. I'm afraid that profits will be low at the price you're suggesting.

MS. BAILEY: I understand, but we're competing with coffees like Blue Mountain from Jamaica, or Kona from Hawaii, which go for[8] two or three dollars more per pound. We're competing in a two-tier market,[9] and evidence suggests that the consumers favor higher quality. But if we can ensure the same quality at a slightly lower price, we will attract more consumers. Our profits would therefore increase relative to the high sales volume that is projected.

MR. SMILEY: This all sounds very interesting, but unfortunately I've got another meeting to go to right now. Would it be possible for you to meet with me again? I'd be interested in hearing some of your ideas on how to entice this market segment to buy our coffee.

MS. BAILEY: Sure, I'd be happy to put some ideas together. Did you have a particular date in mind?

MR. SMILEY: How about next Monday, say, at three in the afternoon?

MS. BAILEY: Sounds great. I'll mark my calendar.

B. NOTES

1. The acronym *CEO* refers to Chief Executive Officer. The CEO is the highest executive or general director of a company.

2. The verb *to demand* means "to claim or to ask for urgently."

3. The state of Washington is located in the northwestern United States. Its capital is Olympia and its biggest city is Seattle. Since 1971,

Seattle has been the coffee capital of the country. Starbucks, the famous coffee company and chain, originated in this city. The state has several national parks, lakes, and mountains. There are also several islands off the coast of Washington that are favorite places among those who enjoy camping and fishing.

4. We have already discussed the use of *will* as an auxiliary verb to express the future. Used as a noun it means "the desire, purpose, or determination of a person or a legal declaration of how a person wishes his or her possessions to be disposed of after death." Some useful expressions with the word *will* are:

   to do something at will
   to make one's will
   Where there's a will, there's a way.

5. *Let's* is the contracted form of *let + us*. It is used to make suggestions.

   I don't want to stay home; let's go to the movies tonight.

6. The *futures market* deals with the buying and selling of merchandise or currency, especially agricultural goods. These negotiations to trade merchandise are not carried out in real time; traders normally speculate the future value of the goods.

7. In English you use a decimal point to express fractional parts in money, and a comma to indicate the place of the thousands.

   For example, the number *five thousand three hundred fifty* is: 5,350 and *twelve dollars and thirteen cents* is: $12.13.

8. In the context of this sentence, the verb *to go for* means "to cost." It has other meanings depending on the situation or context:

   to fetch something or someone
   When does Mary's flight land? If you'd like I'll go for her.

   to attack
   The bull went straight for the man in the red jacket.

   to pass for
   I believe that a classy package can make almost any coffee go for gourmet.

   to approve, to accept
   The board of directors will go for a package that is appealing.

   to choose
   I think I'll go for this design. It's my favorite.

to try
Ms. Bailey proposes that we produce our own gourmet coffee. I say we go for it.

9. The term *two-tier market* describes a market that has two segments for the same type of product: a higher quality and a lower quality version.

C. GRAMMAR AND USAGE

1. RELATIVE PRONOUNS
a. Form
These are the relative pronouns:

	SUBJECT	OBJECT	POSSESSIVE
FOR PEOPLE	*who* *that*	*whom/who* *that*	*whose*
FOR THINGS	*which* *that*	*which* *that*	*whose/of which*

There is a distinction between relative pronouns used with people and those used with things.

b. Usage
A relative pronoun is used to describe the noun that precedes it and to differentiate it from other nouns of the same kind. That is, the relative pronoun is used to introduce something important that adds information about the noun that it modifies.

A relative pronoun can be used to refer to a noun:

People are looking for products that have a history.
I suggest we hire a designer who could take care of the package.

It may also be used to refer to the object of the verb. You should use *whom* when using formal English; however, you may use *who/that* in an informal situation:

The man to whom I spoke told me to come back today.
The man who/that I spoke to told me to come back today.

When referring to the object of a verb, you may use *which, that,* or no relative pronoun at all.

The coffee bean that we planted last year was not good enough to be gourmet.
The coffee bean we planted last year was not good enough to be gourmet.

When the relative pronoun introduces a noun as the object of a preposition, use the following formal construction:

This is the coffee about which I told you.
Did you like the woman to whom we spoke?

It is common in informal speech to place the preposition at the end and use *which, that, who, whom,* or no pronoun at all:

This is the coffee that I told you about.
This is the coffee I told you about.
Did you like the woman who(m) we spoke to?
Did you like the woman we spoke to?

The pronoun *whose* is used to indicate possession. It refers to people or things:

The designer whose sketches I liked lives in San Francisco.
Our supplier has some new beans whose price per pound is very high.

2. COORDINATING CONJUNCTIONS

Conjunctions are words that join two independent phrases. As we have said before, a phrase formed by a subject and a verb is independent when it can stand on its own. The following list shows conjunctions and the punctuation marks that precede them.

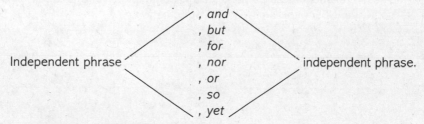

He says he has about ten tons, and that should be enough to cover the orders of our most important clients.
He was running very late, so he called to postpone the meeting.
He didn't have enough sugar in stock, yet he managed to fill our order.

3. COORDINATING ADVERBS

Coordinating adverbs unite two independent phrases and indicate the relationship between the two. These are the most common coordinating adverbs:

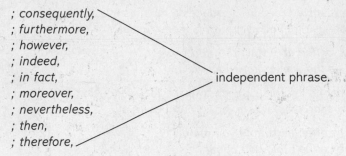

; consequently,
; furthermore,
; however,
; indeed,
; in fact,
; moreover,
; nevertheless,
; then,
; therefore,

independent phrase.

The semicolon can be substituted with a period. In that case, the coordinating adverb should be capitalized because you are dealing with two separate sentences.

I checked with the Department of Commerce, and I was told that the quota won't be filled for another month. Furthermore, the price of sugar is going up and not many people are buying.
Mr. Briz came up with a second excuse for not delivering the coffee on time. Therefore, we canceled our contract with his company.

4. SUBORDINATING CONJUNCTIONS

Subordinating conjunctions are used to link an independent phrase with a dependent clause (that is, a phrase that would not stand on its own). These conjunctions can appear at the beginning or in the middle of a sentence. Notice the difference in punctuation.

		after		
		although		
		as (as if)		
		because		
		before		
		even though		
		if		
Independent phrase	+	*since*	+	dependent clause.
		unless		
		until		
		when(ever)		
		whereas		
		while		

After
Although
As (as if)
Because
Before
Even though
If
Since   +   dependent clause,   +   independent phrase.
Unless
Until
When(ever)
Whereas
While

We had to reduce our order by 40 percent because the price of coffee was too high.
Even though Mr. Briz lowered his price by 30 percent, we decided to cancel our contract with his company.

D. IDIOMATIC STUDY

ASKING FOR AND GIVING ADVICE

You will find these phrases to be useful when asking for advice:

Could you give me some advice?
Would you be able to recommend something/someone?
Do you have any suggestions/recommendations/ideas?
I was wondering if you had any suggestions/ideas.
I'd like your input/opinion (on this).
What do you think about _____?
What are your thoughts/ideas on _____?

To give advice or offer a suggestion, you may use one of the following phrases:

I suggest/recommend _____.
I'd suggest/recommend that you _____.
I advise you to _____.
If I were you, I would _____.
How/What about _____?
Let's _____.
Why don't we _____?
Can I offer you some advice?
Don't you think it might be a good idea to _____?
Have you considered _____?
Have you thought about _____?

Here are some good answers:

That's a good/great idea!
That sounds great!
Why didn't I think of that!
I hadn't thought about that!
That's not a bad idea!

E. STRICTLY BUSINESS

1. MARKETING

Marketing is, in simple terms, how goods and services go from the manufacturer to the consumer in order to fulfill demand. Marketing deals with several issues; one of the most important is the study of how to make a product or service available to the consumers at the time they are most likely to want to acquire it. Market research allows companies to determine a price that is reasonable to the client and profitable to the business. There are four components to marketing: product analysis, pricing, placement, and promotion.

Product analysis is the research a company does about a product the company wants to sell. It generally requires thorough investigations and developments of new products, research about potential markets, testing of the product to assess its quality, and, finally, the product's introduction to the marketplace. In today's economy, consumers have a lot of say in what is being produced and purchased. Once a product is created and manufactured, marketing experts study how to get the product to the general consumer. This is done by making direct market observations and analyzing how potential consumers react to differences in packaging, features, and pricing. Sometimes experts use surveys to determine the needs of different types of consumers.

Once the market for the product has been determined, it is important to present the product in a way that is recognizable for the consumers. This is also known as *branding*. Trademarks for different brands have to be registered with the federal government. Trademarks or registered brands protect the identity of the product at a national or international level.

The company also has to consider the introductory price to be set for the product. They may elect to set a price that is under, above, or at the market level. Most companies choose to set prices that are comparable to the average market price for a similar product. The companies that set prices for other companies in a similar industry are known as *market leaders*. It is important to know that minimum prices (floor prices) should cover production and marketing costs so the company does not lose money on the product. The strategy for selecting the price is simple: If the product is sold at rock-bottom prices, more consumers are likely to purchase it. On the other hand, if the product is sold at a higher price, consumers might think that it is a higher quality product, and therefore a better one, and might buy it instead of a less expensive product. If the product is sold at an average middle price, consumers would expect a product with reasonable quality that is accessible to all. Product placement is the study of how to make sure the product reaches consumers. Experts in marketing determine the best ways to make products are available to the target consumers. The typical channel of distribution operates this way: producers send the products to wholesalers (distributors) and wholesalers sell the products to the stores where consumers will make their purchases. Finally, the success of the product depends on the way that it is promoted. A product or service may be advertised at a local, regional, national, or international level. Most companies use one of several media outlets or rely on special promotions. It is common to see advertising and promotions through television, radio, press, billboards, catalogs, contests, or special offers. Most advertisements include a description of the product and its benefits, followed by a catchy slogan.

2. VOCABULARY

above price	*price leaders*
advertisement	*product*
below price	*product analysis*
billboard	*profit*
branding	*promotion*
catalog	*price*
catchy	*pricing*
ceiling price	*quality*
consumer	*retailer*
distributor	*rock-bottom price*
exporter	*sign*
futures market	*slogan*
manufacturer	*trademark*
market	*two-tier market*
market level	*wholesaler*
marketing	*will*
placement	

1. Complete the following sentences using *who* or *whom*.

   University of Seattle
   Career Services Office
   To __(a)__ It May Concern:
   Please post the following notice:

   We are interested in hiring a graphics designer. Candidates __(b)__ apply for this position should have a Bachelor of Arts degree and credits toward a Master of Arts degree. We are interested in someone __(c)__ has experience with point of purchase design and package design. Anyone __(d)__ is interested should send resumé, portfolio, and salary requirements to:

   Mary Bailey, Manager
   Kophee, Inc.
   345 Lincoln Plaza, Suite 12B
   Miami, FL 00456

2. Fill in the blanks using a coordinating conjunction.

   a. *I'm late because there was an oil spill in the middle of the road, _____ I had a flat tire.*
   b. *We have nothing to worry about, _____ he knows we'll sue him if he doesn't deliver the shipment on time.*
   c. *I tried to call you a couple of times, _____ every time I got a busy signal.*
   d. *I have a meeting at seven tomorrow morning, _____ I'm going to bed early.*
   e. *He didn't have a degree, _____ he got the job anyway.*

3. Join the following sentences using a coordinating adverb.

   a. *I can assure you that we will have the shipment in by the end of the month. _____, you understand that our company is not responsible for delays incurred by customs officials.*
   b. *Each country has its own rules and regulations when it comes to importing and exporting. _____, it's best to use the services of companies that specialize in international trade.*
   c. *You will need an import license along with your government's approval of this shipment. _____, before delivering the coffee, we will need to pass customs inspection and receive a sanitation certificate.*
   d. *Once the goods have cleared customs, it will be your responsibility*

to get them to their final destination. _____, if you'd like, my
company could arrange to deliver the goods for a small fee.

4. Join the following sentences using a subordinating conjunction.

a. _____ we hear from you within the next week, we'll assume the
shipment is ready to be picked up.

b. A nation's trade balance is measured primarily in terms of its
import-export activity. _____ imports are greater than exports, a
negative trade balance is recorded for that year.

c. _____ an import-export deal is signed, the exporter has to make
sure that payment is guaranteed by a bank through a letter of
credit.

d. Domestic trade requires very few intermediaries, _____
international trade requires intermediaries to ensure delivery and
payment to both parties involved.

LESSON 19
The Environment

A. DIALOGUE

THE OZONE LAYER

Professor Sullivan teaches Environmental Science at the University of North Dakota.[1] His recent lectures[2] have focused on global warming and the atmosphere. Today he has invited Dr. Frances Moor, a well-known environmentalist, to be a guest lecturer.

PROFESSOR SULLIVAN: I'd like to introduce a longtime friend and colleague, Dr. Frances Moor, who works for the EPA.[3] She's here today to tell us a little about her efforts to save the ozone layer. Dr. Moor, why don't you give us an idea of exactly what it is you're doing?

DR. FRANCES MOOR: Certainly, Professor Sullivan. But first, I'd like to say that it's a pleasure to be here, and please feel free to ask me questions at any time. As some of you might already know, I spent decades researching the destruction of the ozone layer. Now, however, I've turned my attention toward stopping its destruction. Basically, I do a lot of traveling, mostly to developing countries, and I give lectures on how to eliminate the production and use of chlorofluorocarbons, or CFCs.

STUDENT: What exactly are CFCs?

DR. FRANCES MOOR: These are chemicals commonly used in refrigerators, air conditioners, foam insulation, fast food packaging, cleaning agents, aerosol sprays. These chemicals destroy the shield of ozone gas that protects the Earth's atmosphere from the sun's harmful rays.

STUDENT: What are some of the health problems caused by ozone depletion?

DR. FRANCES MOOR: If there is less ozone in the atmosphere, higher amounts of UV radiation are reaching the Earth. Exposure to this radiation affects the skin, causing premature aging, wrinkling, and several types of skin cancer. It can also affect the eyes, causing cataracts[4] that can eventually lead to blindness. Excessive UV radiation may also affect the immune system, leaving the body too weak to fight off disease.[5]

STUDENT: As I understand it, it can also affect crops and animals.

DR. FRANCES MOOR: That's absolutely correct. UV radiation reduces the yield[6] of certain basic crops, such as wheat and soybeans, and can kill plankton and small fish that serve as food for larger fish.

STUDENT: So why are you targeting the developing world? Aren't the industrialized nations the ones at fault?

DR. FRANCES MOOR: That was the case in the past. But most industrialized countries are aware of the problem and have taken measures to solve it. You see, in 1985 with the discovery of a hole in the ozone layer over Antarctica,[7] industrialized nations were forced to take matters into their own hands. Two years later, more than two dozen countries met in Canada to sign the Montreal Protocol, which provided for a 50 percent phaseout of CFCs over the next ten years. Developing countries, on the other hand, have not yet become aware of the problem or its danger.

STUDENT: I would imagine that since 1985 many non-industrialized countries have already agreed to the Montreal Protocol.

DR. FRANCES MOOR: Certainly. Over the last ten years more than 60 countries have joined in the fight against ozone depletion. However, if this is to work, we need the cooperation of every present and potential user.

STUDENT: What do you think the chances are that these nations will eventually cooperate?

DR. FRANCES MOOR: That's hard to say. There is, in fact, a fund financed by the industrialized nations created to help those countries switch to safer technologies. In all probability, many of these countries will contribute once they realize help is on the way.

PROFESSOR SULLIVAN: Well, I'm sure that you all[8] have lots of interesting questions to ask Dr. Moor. But, unfortunately, we're running out of time. However, she'll be having lunch with me later on in the cafeteria. If any of you are interested, you're welcome to join us.

B. NOTES

1. The state of North Dakota is located in the center of the United States, close to the Canadian border in the north. This area, known as the

Great Plains, includes the states of Missouri, Oklahoma, Kansas, Nebraska, and South Dakota. North Dakota's capital is Bismarck, which serves as an important cultural center along the Missouri River.

2. *Lecture* is a noun that refers to any type of informational speech given by a presenter. It is a term that is very common in academia; most university classes consist of professors giving lectures to students as they listen, participate, and take notes. The verb form— *to lecture*—may also be used informally to refer to reprimanding someone.

   My mother lectured me because I got home late last night.
   Professor Sullivan gave a lecture on endangered species.
   The company's president lectured his employees on the waste of paper in the office.

3. *EPA* is the abbreviation of the Environmental Protection Agency, the federal government agency that deals with the environment.

4. The noun *cataracts* refers to the condition that affects the eyes and can lead to blindness.

5. Note the difference between the noun *disease* and the verb *to decease*. *Disease* refers to an illness while *to decease* means "to die." The two words are pronounced similarly, but be aware of the fact that the *s* sounds in *disease* are more sonorous and marked (similar to a *z* sound) than the softer *s* sounds in *decease*.

6. The verb *to yield* has different meanings depending on the context in which it is found. In this case it means "to produce an outcome after cultivation." It can also be used to express productivity in economic of financial terms. In other contexts, it may be synonymous with "to surrender or to give up."

   We invested our money in funds that yield six percent a year.
   In ancient times, it was customary to yield your land and possessions to your enemy if you were defeated in battle.

7. In 1985, British scientist Joe Forman and his colleagues discovered a giant hole in the ozone layer over the British section of Antarctica. They estimated the size of the hole to be larger than the extension of the United States and compared its depth to Mount Everest's height.

8. In certain areas of the United States (especially in the South), it is very common to use the pronoun *you* followed by the adjective *all* when talking to more than one person. This is colloquially abbreviated to *y'all*. Outside of the South, this expression is much less commonly used.

C. GRAMMAR AND USAGE

1. PHRASAL VERBS

Phrasal verbs are verbs that are used with prepositions. These verbs change meaning depending on the preposition attached to them. Phrasal verbs are also known as two-word verbs or three-word verbs. There are two types: separable and inseparable phrasal verbs.

a. Separable Phrasal Verbs
A phrasal verb is separable when you can place a pronoun or a noun between the verb and its preposition.

At the National Conference on the Environment, scientists handed out brochures.
At the National Conference on the Environment, scientists handed brochures out.

Notice that in the previous example, the noun *brochure* could be placed before or after the preposition *out*.

When a personal pronoun is used with separable verbs, the pronoun should always go between the verb and the preposition.

At the National Conference on the Environment, scientists handed them out.

Here is a list of some common separable phrasal verbs:

to ask out	*to keep out*
to bring about	*to kick out*
to bring up	*to look over*
to call back	*to look up*
to call up	*to make up*
to check out	*to pass out*
to cheer up	*to pick out*
to clean up	*to pick up*
to cross out	*to point out*
to cut out	*to put away*
to drop off	*to put back*
to figure out	*to put off*
to fill out	*to put on*
to find out	*to put out*
to get back	*to shut off*
to give back	*to take off*
to give up	*to take out*
to hand in	*to take over*
to hang up	*to take up*

to tear up	*to turn in*
to think over	*to turn off*
to throw away	*to turn out*
to turn down	*to turn up*

The professor didn't give our reports back until the semester was over.
Don't throw that file away! It contains information I need.
Some nations are passing laws to keep hunters out of certain regions where there are species in danger of extinction.

b. Inseparable Phrasal Verbs

As the name implies, inseparable phrasal verbs must be directly followed by their preposition. You cannot place any word between the verb and the preposition; any pronoun or noun must come after the preposition.

The verb *to fight off* is an inseparable phrasal verb. The verb *to fight* means to have an altercation or battle. When you add the preposition *off*, the meaning of the verb changes to "defend oneself from."

Once the body's immune system is affected, the organism can't fight off disease.

Here is a list of common inseparable phrasal verbs:

to call on	*to get over*
to catch up (with)	*to go over*
to check in	*to grow up*
to come across	*to keep up*
to drop by	*to look after*
to drop out	*to look into*
to get along	*to look out*
to get in	*to pass away*
to get off	*to put up with*
to get out of	*to show up*

Some biologists believe that the worst damage from oil spills in the ocean will not show up until years after the accident.
It's hard for nonindustrialized nations to keep up with the technological advances of industrialized countries.
Many times, I come across people who are so interested in wildlife, that they even adopt and look after wild animals as if they were pets.

2. THE SUBJUNCTIVE

To form the subjunctive in English, you use the simple form of the verb. Unlike some other languages, there are no separate conjugations for each subject. The subjunctive is generally used with certain verbs or clauses that begin with the relative pronoun *that*.

It is very important that the lecturer arrive at the conference on time.

In the example above, the verb *to arrive* is in the subjunctive form. Notice that the verb is in its simple form, and it does not have the *s* that is used for third-person singular subjects. The following verbs generally require the use of the subjunctive:

to demand (that)	*it is important (that)*
to insist (that)	*it is essential (that)*
to request (that)	*it is imperative (that)*
to ask (that)	*it is necessary (that)*
to suggest (that)	*it is vital (that)*
to recommend (that)	

Some environmentalists strongly demand that oil be transported in double-hull tankers to reduce the risk of oil spills in the ocean.
It is important that people around the world become aware of the ozone problem.
It is essential that Congress introduce more bills to tighten restrictions on garbage disposal in the ocean.

D. IDIOMATIC STUDY

EXPRESSING PROBABILITY/IMPROBABILITY
The following phrases are useful when you want to find out how probable something is:

What do you think the chances are of _____?
What's the likelihood/possibility of _____?
Is there a good chance that _____?
In all likelihood _____.
In all probability _____.
The chances are very good.
There's a chance.
It's possible/probable.
It could happen.
You never know!
The chances are not very good.
The chances are pretty slim.
There's not much chance of that happening.
That isn't very likely.
I don't think that will happen.

E. STRICTLY BUSINESS

1. ENVIRONMENTAL PROTECTION

Environmental protection has been one of the biggest concerns of the United States during the past few decades. Although the environmental movement has been around since the nineteenth century when the federal government started protecting forests and parks with national natural park protection, it was not until the 1960s that the general population started paying attention to most environmental concerns. The first reaction at that time was to protest against the chemical pesticides that were being used. Protesters brought to the general public's attention the information that pesticides were contaminating the water supply and had dangerous health effects for those who consumed fruits and vegetables containing pesticides. The general population began to listen and pay attention to other important environmental concerns such as deforestation, the depletion of natural energy sources, environmental pollution, acid rain, and toxic waste. Others thought that these actions were inevitable and of little importance. They argued that any government intervention to protect the environment would come at a significant cost to the American economy. In spite of that, environmental protection became a hot topic in the 1980s, when scientists discovered the disintegration of sections in the ozone layer and identified the devastating effects of the greenhouse effect. From then on, environmental protection was no longer a local problem that affected isolated communities. The whole world faced an enormous environmental challenge that threatened to have a significant effect on the life of the planet.

The United States, along with many other countries, started to implement environmental protection laws to try to reverse the greenhouse effect and stop the depletion of the ozone layer. Initially these laws were severely criticized by some politicians and business leaders who argued that environmental protection carries a negative effect on corporate balance sheets. Any law that required companies to reduce fuel emissions represented an additional expense for the company that would reduce profits. Moreover, the cost of updating machinery and equipment to use cleaner forms of energy such as solar energy or hydroelectricity was so high that it would surely force many companies into bankruptcy.

Over the past few decades, the United States government has introduced several laws intended to protect the environment. However, many critics argue that the government has not done enough to stop the abuse against the planet and the environment. Many experts have said that George W. Bush's administration has reversed earlier progress made regarding environmental protection.

During his last days as president, Bill Clinton tried to pass legislation that would require a significant reduction in the amount of arsenic in drinking water. The next president, George W. Bush, thought that the law asked for an unnecessarily low number and that the implementation of the law would be too costly for companies. After being roundly criticized, he decided to go with Clinton's original legislation.

When it comes to other environmental issues, Bush's administration has been criticized for not doing enough for the environment. Bush wanted to drill for oil in a virgin area in the National Arctic Park in Alaska, but he abandoned this idea after it was strongly criticized. During his tenure, he refused to impose stricter gas emission limits on cars and trucks. He argued that such limits would impose high costs on the automobile industry. Instead he proposed to contribute more money to the research and development of cars that run on hydrogen or other forms of energy. Bush openly rejected some of the objectives of the Clinton administration regarding the greenhouse effect, arguing that changes should not come at the expense of economic prosperity. He wanted to eliminate the complex set of laws that apply to energy plants, stating that they are confusing, promote too many lawsuits and litigation, and do not reach their desired objective. In their place, he proposed a system of fines and fees against production plants that produce the most contamination, allowing the free market to regulate the polluters. There was also much controversy surrounding President Bush's withdrawal from the Kyoto Accords, which sought to limit harmful emissions around the globe. The Kyoto Protocol was signed by President Clinton on behalf of the United States in 1998, but President Bush refused to ratify the protocol.

It is easy to calculate the monetary value of any environmental restriction. However, it is impossible to put a dollar sign to the damage to the planet if these laws are not implemented. Although some of these alternative laws seem to be somewhat effective, the greenhouse effect and the hole in the ozone layer are still environmental threats to the planet. Recent studies have also projected that damage to the Earth's climate could cause irreparable damage to the agricultural systems and economies of many countries, and possibly instigate global warfare. These are factors everyone is forced to weigh when considering their opinions on environmental protection. For more information about government projects and laws to protect the environment, visit the Environmental Protection Agency's Web site at www.epa.gov.

2. VOCABULARY

acid rain	lecture
carbon dioxide	nature
cataracts	ozone layer
chemical pesticide	poison
coal	pollution
to decease	radiation
deforestation	ray
disease	solar energy
environment	toxic
EPA (Environmental Protection Agency)	ultraviolet light
	waste
greenhouse effect	to yield
hydroelectricity	

EXERCISES

1. Choose a phrasal verb to complete each sentence and conjugate each verb to agree with its subject.

   to give up   to wash up   to run across   to cut off   to turn to

   a. Many non-industrialized nations believe that they are being asked _____ the benefits of modern technology.
   b. Many people don't realize that by _____ CFC-free technology, they are improving their quality of life.
   c. It is no longer a surprise _____ garbage on the beaches of almost any country in the world.
   d. As a result of oil spills, many dead sea lions and other animals have _____ on the shores of the Atlantic Ocean.

2. Complete the following sentences using the correct form of the verb in parentheses.

   a. It is vital that people _____ (to become) aware of the importance of recycling garbage.
   b. Dr. Moor _____ (to visit) several factories in each country and _____ (to give) advice on ways to reduce the use of CFCs.
   c. Professor Sullivan asked that each student _____ (to write) a reaction paper to Dr. Moor's lecture.
   d. It's important that developing nations _____ (to realize) that nonpolluting technologies are far better and cost-effective than the existing technologies.
   e. Some industries have _____ (to decide) to follow the EPA's recommendations and have _____ (to switch) to CFC-free technology.

f. A student suggested that the class _____ (to organize) a campaign against air pollution in their neighborhood.

3. Complete the following sentences with the appropriate words. The words can be found in the puzzle below.

a. The less ozone in the _____, the higher the amounts of UV radiation that reaches the Earth.
b. Ozone _____ is caused by chemicals found in aerosol _____.
c. Exposure to UV _____ may affect the _____, causing blindness. It may also affect the skin, causing premature _____.
d. It is important that all nations _____ their technologies to one that is CFC-free.

```
R  I  N  P  T  U  L  A  C  D
A  T  M  O  S  P  H  E  R  E
D  E  S  H  U  G  M  Y  T  P
I  L  P  J  I  R  B  E  S  L
A  M  R  O  R  A  C  S  U  E
T  A  A  Z  I  D  A  N  B  T
I  G  Y  F  O  E  O  P  F  I
O  P  S  Q  N  K  L  S  D  O
N  D  A  G  I  N  G  B  R  N
```

LESSON 20

A Nation of Immigrants

A. DIALOGUE

TOURING ELLIS ISLAND

Lisa and her friend Suzie are from Omaha, Nebraska,[1] and are visiting New York for the first time. After spending a few days sightseeing in Manhattan, they decided to take the ferry across New York Harbor to tour Ellis Island.[2] As the tour group arrives on the island, they are greeted by one of the park rangers.[3]

PARK RANGER: Welcome to Ellis Island National Monument. Before we begin our tour of the main building of the museum, I have to tell you about the Park regulations. No eating, drinking, smoking, or chewing gum is allowed in the museum or exhibit areas. For those of you who would like to tour the park on your own, we have audiotapes available in English, French, German, Italian, and Spanish at the information booth.

LISA: What do you think? Should we tour the island on our own?

SUZIE: No, I'd like to follow the park ranger. It's more fun, don't you think?

LISA: I guess you're right.

PARK RANGER: Ladies, are you with us?

LISA: Yes, wait up! We're coming![4]

PARK RANGER: Ellis Island was originally known to Native Americans[5] as Kioshk, or Gull Island. It was purchased by colonist governors from the Native Americans on[6] July 12th, 1630, in exchange for some goods. During the 1700s, the island was used as a base for oyster fishing and a place to execute state criminals by hanging. About the time of the Revolution,[7] the island was purchased by Samuel Ellis. In the early 1800s, the Ellis family agreed to sell the island to the City of New York for $10,000. As millions of immigrants arrived in New York Harbor throughout the nineteenth century, officials decided they needed a better way to control the immigration process, and the island was designated as an immigration station on April 11th, 1890.[8]

LISA: Someone told me that immigrants were not allowed to get off the arriving ships until they were examined by medical inspectors.

PARK RANGER: That's correct. Ships were anchored in the quarantine area outside the lower bay of New York Harbor. All passengers, except U.S. citizens, were inspected for contagious diseases. Few cabin-class passengers[9] were marked to be sent to Ellis Island for more complete examinations. Steerage passengers,[10] however, were all sent to the island, where a doctor quickly examined their face, hair, neck, and hands. Two out of every ten immigrants were detained for further medical inspection. An *X* was marked on the immigrant's right shoulder if the doctors suspected mental defects, while an *X* was marked on the left shoulder if they perceived a physical deformity or disease. And if a definite symptom was detected, immigrants were marked with an *X* with a circle around it.

SUZIE: That sounds awful! How long did these people have to wait on the island?

PARK RANGER: It all depended on the speed at which they were processed. Sometimes it would take a few days. A marked immigrant would undergo additional examinations and would most certainly be deported. Children who were 12 or older were sent back to Europe alone. Children younger than that had to be accompanied by a parent. Many families were forced to split up and decide who would go back and who would stay. If you take a look at this timetable here, it shows you the number of immigrants arriving on the island each day. It also shows where these immigrants were originally from.

SUZIE: Check this out,[11] Lisa. In 1905, of 100,000 cabin passengers arriving in New York, only 3,000 had to go through the island for additional examinations. In the same year, 800,000 steerage passengers were examined on the island!

LISA: These pictures are so depressing. I can't stop thinking about what it must've been like. How disenchanting it must have been.

PARK RANGER: But you also have to think about the many immigrants who survived and made something of themselves. This chart here shows you a list of Ellis Island immigrants who became famous.

LISA: Kahlil Gibran, the author of *The Prophet,* is on this list. Wow!

PARK RANGER: And on this side, you can look for people related to you. Let's see, who wants to volunteer?

SUZIE: I do.

PARK RANGER: What's your last name?

SUZIE: McKenzie.

PARK RANGER: That's a Scottish name, isn't it?

SUZIE: Sure is.

PARK RANGER: Well, let's look it up on this chart. As you can see, there are several McKenzies who came in at different times.

LISA: Neat![12] Maybe we should try to trace your ancestors!

PARK RANGER: You can if you want. At the end of this visit we'll tell you how to trace your ancestors and find out if any came through the island. In the meantime, let's proceed to the theater. We're going to watch a 30-minute film called *Island of Hopes/Island of Tears,* in which you will hear the accounts[13] of several people who pulled up their roots and came to the United States in search of their dreams.

B. NOTES

1. The state of Nebraska is located in the center of the United States, in the area known as the Great Plains. The Great Plains is a large area of flatlands and prairies to the east of the Rocky Mountains. The capital of Nebraska is Lincoln and its largest city is Omaha, the state's most important center of commerce and industry. Among Omaha's most famous attractions are the Henry Doorly's Zoo, the Western Heritage Museum, and Boys Town, the first town in the United States designed especially for kids.

2. Ellis Island is located in the New York Harbor. It can be visited throughout the year between 9:30 A.M. and 5 P.M; during the summer, hours are extended until dusk. To get to the island, you take a ferry that leaves from Battery Bark in downtown Manhattan. Ellis Island was a famous entry port and detention center from 1892 to 1954, when many immigrants entered the country. For more information about touring the island, visit www.ellisisland.com; for information about the foundation, visit www.ellisisland.org.

3. Most national parks and monuments, including Ellis Island, are patrolled and protected by Nation Park Service rangers.

4. There is a slight difference between the verbs *to come* and *to go*. *To come* means "to advance toward the speaker or to a determined place"; in other words, "to approach someone or something." The verb *to go* means "to move away from a place or to depart."

   We're coming!
   —Suzie, hurry up!—Yes, I'm coming!

5. The term *Native Americans* describes the original inhabitants of North America before Europeans settlers arrived. The term is still used to refer to the descendants of the original Americans.

6. The preposition *on* is used before days and dates:

   I went to Ellis Island on Monday.
   I'm going back to Omaha on March 16.

7. In 1776, the United States proclaimed its independence from the British Empire.

8. Ellis Island officially opened its doors on January 1, 1892. A fire destroyed many of the buildings in 1894; fortunately, there were no victims. After a major restoration, the island's facilities reopened in 1917 as a detention center for foreign enemies and as a deportation center until 1954. The island remained closed until September 10, 1990, when it opened as a national monument.

9. *Cabin passengers* (first- or second-class passengers) generally paid large sums of money for their tickets. These passengers were thoroughly checked onboard by an immigration official before being transferred to New York.

10. *Steerage passengers* (third-class passengers) were taken to the island and subjected to demanding physical examinations and interviewed by an interpreter.

11. The verb *to check out* has several meanings depending on the context in which it is used. In the previous dialogue, it is used informally and colloquially; *check it out* essentially means "look at this." *To check out* is also used to describe "leaving from a hotel or hospital after a stay."

   Mary checked out of the hotel this morning.

   It can also be used when borrowing books from a library:

   My daughter keeps checking out books from the library without remembering to return them.

12. When the adjective *neat* is used colloquially, as in this case, it shows approval and admiration. It is normally used as an adjective that means "orderly, clean, or tidy."

13. The noun *account* is used to refer to a formal banking or brokerage relationship. There are several types of bank accounts, including savings and checking accounts. In other contexts, *account* may refer to "a story, narrative, or record of events." Here are some popular expressions with the word *account:*

on account of
on no account
on one's own account
to give an account of
to make little account of
to settle an account

C. GRAMMAR AND USAGE

1. CAPITALIZATION

Capital letters are always used at the beginning of sentences and for proper names. The English language uses capital letters with more frequency than many other languages.
The personal pronoun for the first-person singular *(I)* is always written with a capital letter regardless of whether it is at the beginning of the sentence or not.

No, I'd like to follow the guide.

You should always capitalize nouns that express the following:

a. Nationality
That's a French name, isn't it?

b. Religion
A great number of the people who live in the northeast are Catholic.

c. Racial or Ethnic Groups
Ellis Island was originally known to Native Americans as Kioshk, or Gull Island.

d. Country/City
Lisa and her friend Suzie, who are from Omaha, Nebraska, are visiting New York for the first time.

e. Month/Day of the Week
It was later bought by the City of New York and designated as an immigration station on April 11, 1890.

f. Holidays
Thanksgiving is a traditional holiday in the United States.

g. Languages
   We have CDs available in English, French, German, Italian, and Spanish.

The following nouns are written with capital letters when they are used as proper names:

Streets: *Main Street*
Buildings: *Chrysler Building*
Organizations: *United Nations*
Historical Events: *World War I*
Titles: *Professor Sullivan*
Family Relationships: *Dad*
Monuments: *Statue of Liberty*

During the Revolution, the island was purchased by Samuel Ellis.
We saw Professor Rodriguez at Silver Hall, where he was delivering a talk on the Spanish Civil War.
I think Aunt Lisa might be able to give us some information on my family's history.
The United Nations is a world organization.

Use capital letters with nouns such as *North, South, East,* or *West* when they are used to refer to a geographical area. When you use them to refer to a cardinal point, write them with lower case.

The tourists went to the South for their winter vacation.
Go south on this road for three miles.

Use capital letters with academic subjects when they refer to the title of a specific course:

Last semester, I took Psychology 101.
Have you ever studied psychology?
I just finished my History of Western Art final exam.

2. PREFIXES

Prefixes are added at the beginning of a word to alter its meaning. The most common English prefixes are:

PREFIX	MEANING	EXAMPLES
bi-	two, twice	*bilateral, biweekly*
co-, com-, con-, col-	together, with	*coexist, commutable, conjunctive, collateral*
ex-, e-, ef-	from, out of	*eccentric, egress, efface*
in-, im-	in	*indoors, immigrate*
in-, il-	negative	*indubitable, illogical*

intro-, intra-	within	*introduce, intravenous*
mis-	badly	*misinterpret,*
		misunderstand
non-	not	*nonviable, nonstop*
over-	too much	*overpay, overproduce*
post-	after	*postpone, postmeridian*
pre-	before	*premeditate, prenatal*
pro-	positive	*proclaim, pronoun*
re-	again	*recapture, recoil*
un-	reversal	*unfold, undo*

3. SUFFIXES

Suffixes are added to the end of a word. There are two types of suffixes: those that have a grammatical purpose but do not change the meaning of the word, such as the endings of conjugated verbs *(-s, -es, -ed, -ing,* etc.) and those that change the meaning of the word. When a suffix changes the meaning of the word, it generally also changes the word's grammatical function. That is why suffixes are also used to classify words.

a. Nouns

The following suffixes indicate rank, condition, process, or quality:

SUFFIX	EXAMPLES
-age	*passage, bondage*
-ance	*alliance, acceptance*
-ate	*delegate, primate*
-ation	*communication, accusation*
-cy	*literacy, accuracy, excellency*
-dom	*kingdom, freedom*
-ence	*evidence, patience*
-ion, -tion	*duration, creation, union*
-ment	*punishment, entertainment*
-ness	*emptiness, fullness*
-tude	*solitude, multitude*
-ty	*novelty, inactivity*
-ure	*culture, signature*
-y	*jealousy, jewelry*

The following suffixes have other meanings:

SUFFIX	MEANING	EXAMPLES
-ee	the person who	*addressee,*
	receives the action	*employee*

| -er/-or | native of, executor of an action | butcher, murderer, foreigner |
| -ess/-ette | feminine suffix | waitress, actress, majorette |

b. Adjectives

SUFFIX	MEANING	EXAMPLES
-able/-ible	capability, probability	probable, audible, capable
-en	made of	wooden, golden
-ful	full of, characterized by	vengeful, beautiful
-ish	like	stylish, foolish
-less	without	tasteless, fearless
-ly	having the quality of	friendly, possibly
-ous	marked by	famous, religious
-some	capable of, showing	fearsome, tiresome, lonesome
-ward	in the direction of	forward, toward, backward

c. Nouns and/or Adjectives

SUFFIX	MEANING	EXAMPLES
-al	executor of an action	rival, animal, autumnal
-an	belonging to	Asian, human
-ant	agent	peasant, servant
-ary	belonging to	penitentiary, primary
-ese	from a place or style	Japanese
-ile	marked by	juvenile, sterile
-ine	pertaining to	genuine
-ory	belonging to	accessory, contributory

d. Verbs

SUFFIX	MEANING	EXAMPLES
-en	to cause	harden, lighten
-ate	to form, to try	cultivate, formulate
-esce	to grow, to continue	convalesce, acquiesce
-fy	to do, to cause	nullify, magnify
-ish	to do, to carry out	punish, finish
-ize	to do, to cause	modernize, capitalize

D. IDIOMATIC STUDY

ASKING SOMEONE TO REPEAT SOMETHING
The following phrases are useful when asking someone to repeat
something that was said.

FORMAL
Would/Could you please repeat that?
Could you say that again, please?
Would you mind saying that again?
Would you mind repeating that?
Could you please repeat the last two instructions/directions?
I'm sorry, could you run that by me again?
I'm afraid I forgot what you just said.

INFORMAL
Sorry, I didn't hear you.
I didn't (quite) catch that.
I didn't get that.
I missed that.
I'm lost.
I'm afraid I'm not following you.
Run that by me again?
What was that?
Excuse me, what did you say?

E. STRICTLY BUSINESS

1. IMMIGRANTS IN THE UNITED STATES
The United States has always been a country of immigrants. Until
1965 most immigrant groups consisted of Europeans. The British,
French, and Germans were the first to arrive; Irish, Italian, and Jewish
immigrants continued to arrive later. Nowadays, Asian immigrants make
up almost half of the 570,000 immigrants who legally enter the
country every year. Latin Americans, mostly Mexicans, make up the
other 40 percent, while only 5 percent are from European origin. It is
estimated that between 300,000 and 500,000 people enter the
country illegally, most of them by crossing the Mexican border along
Rio Grande.

This nation of immigrants is being influenced once again, socially,
culturally, and economically, by this new wave of foreigners. For
example, in the city of Los Angeles there are more than fifty

newspapers that cater to the needs of readers who come from other countries. There are three newspapers in Spanish (the oldest was founded in 1925), six in Chinese, four in Korean, three in Vietnamese, four in English for Filipino readers, and two for the Hindu community. There is a large community of Persians and Farsis that live in an area of Los Angeles known as Irangeles (named for Iran and Los Angeles). Almost half the immigrants who arrive in California settle in the southern part of the state, in an area that has more than 13 million people.

New York City is known as a "melting pot," because a quarter of its eight million inhabitants were born in another country. Each ethnic group establishes its own community and way of life. Many Koreans have opened their own small markets, which are known as Korean delis, and many Hindis operate magazine stands. In Brooklyn, the area of Brighton Beach is home to thousands of Russians, while Queens is home to the largest Latin American community in the city.

Miami, the economic capital of Latin America, is another city of many languages. Approximately 800,000 Cubans live in the area, as well as other Hispanics from all over Latin America. In recent years many people from Brazil and Haiti have made Miami their home.

Many of these new immigrants live in very difficult conditions, working in factories that pay the minimum wage, especially in cities like Los Angeles and New York. They work washing dishes in restaurants, as taxi drivers, in farms, or washing dirty laundry for wealthy families. They work long hours with the hope of achieving the American Dream, occasionally facing the prejudice of others. Many Americans think that immigrants are a burden to society. There have been attempts to pass laws that deny education and health care to any person who has entered the country illegally.

Several states impose fines on companies that hire illegal workers, and there has been discussion of passing laws that prohibit the usage of any language other than English in public places.

Many sociologists think that immigrants are generally very ambitious and hardworking, and in the long run these people offer a positive contribution to society. The variety of customs, beliefs, cultures, and opinions of this country is what keeps the United States in a constant battle for freedom and equality.

Notice the changes in the racial and ethnic makeup of the United States:

	WHITE	BLACK	HISPANIC	ASIAN, PACIFIC ISLANDER	AMERICAN INDIAN, ESKIMO
1995	82.9	12.6	10.2	3.7	0.8
2000	81.9	12.8	11.3	4.4	0.9
2005	80.9	13.1	12.4	5.1	0.9
2010	80.0	13.4	13.5	5.7	0.9
2020	78.2	13.9	15.7	7.0	0.9

2. VOCABULARY

account
census
to check out
community
cross-cultural awareness
to deny
ethnic group
green card

immigrant
illegal alien
intolerance
melting pot
neat
racial
refugee

EXERCISES

1. The following paragraphs have several errors in capitalization. Please correct them:

the statue of liberty

the statue of liberty is located on liberty island in new york harbor. It was designed by frédérique-auguste bartholdi, a french sculptor and painter. The interior framework was designed by famed engineer alexandre-gustave eiffel, who also designed the eiffel tower in paris.

The two designers wanted to present the statue to the united states on july 4, 1876, in honor of the country's centennial. An appeal for funds to underwrite the cost of creating the statue was launched in french newspapers in september 1875. elaborate fund-raising events were organized, including a banquet at the grand hotel de louvre, and a gala benefit performance of a new liberty cantata by french composer charles gounod at the paris opera. Unfortunately, not enough money was collected to complete the statue by the anticipated date. On july 4, 1876, bartholdi visited the site where the statue would be placed. The tiny island was then known as beldoe's island. Eighty years later, in 1956, its name was officially changed to liberty island. In august of that year, the 30-foot arm of the statue arrived in philadelphia, where it was exhibited.

2. Fill in the blank with the appropriate prefix

    a. *Many immigrants who didn't speak English _____ understood what officials said to them.*
       non-   contr-   mis-   un-

    b. *Some immigrants were _____ capable of leaving letting their loved ones go back alone.*
       un-   in-   non-   im-

    c. *Immigrants learned to _____ exist with people from different parts of the world.*
       over-   pro-   contra-   co-

    d. *It seems _____ logical that doctors would examine only steerage passengers.*
       dis-   il-   non-   sub-

    e. *Officials would often _____ spell the last names of immigrants.*
       over-   post-   dis-   mis-

    f. *Although the whole operation was _____ seen by government officials, many _____ legal transactions were happening.*
       inter-   non-   mis-   over-
       il-   post-   non-   pro-

3. Fill in the blank with the appropriate suffix.

    a. *Most immigrants waited for hours in the dark _____ (-ful, -ness, -less, -ment), and damp _____ (-ful, -ness, -less, -ment) of the immigration station.*

    b. *Their disappoint _____ (-ing, -ful, -ment, -ance) began when they realized that it would be days, maybe even weeks, before they would be allowed to leave the island.*

    c. *Many immigrants were thank _____ (-less, -some, -ful, ness) when they saw the island, thinking their trip was final _____ (-ly, -ized, -some, -ment) over.*

    d. *I'm sure many people who came through the island were hope _____ (-less, -some, -ful, ness), but many also felt help _____ (-less, -some, -ful, ness) because they were all alone in a strange country.*

YOU HATE WHEN THEY CALL, BUT THEIR STOCKS LOOK GOOD*

BY SANA SIWOLOP

The phone call always seems to come just as you are sitting down to dinner or turning on your favorite TV show. A relentlessly cheery voice interrupts your evening to doggedly hawk a new credit card, a long distance carrier or, say, T-bone steaks delivered right to your door.

Even if the customer in you recoils from such pitches, the investor in you may want to take note. The telemarketing business is booming, and for the handful of companies that have gone public in the last year, the stocks are soaring. . . .

It doesn't take a marketing wizard to spot what is buoying the stocks. American companies now spend almost $80 billion a year on telemarketing chores—almost triple what they did a decade ago—and the growth continues at 10 percent a year. Most big companies . . . used to handle their own telemarketing. But with corporations shrinking, these chores are increasingly farmed out to . . . independent telemarketing companies, which say they have lower cost and more expertise. The practice, called outsourcing, now accounts for only 5 percent of the telemarketing business, but that segment is growing 50 to 75 percent a year.

. . . Of course, the potential for skyrocketing earnings does not come without risk. These stocks are best suited to investors comfortable with stratospheric price-to-earnings ratios perhaps 50 times estimated 1997 earnings. Aggressive growth stocks with numbers like that could tumble into the cellar if the stock market entered a prolonged slump.

To get a fix on telemarketing stocks, investors may need to discard some of their assumptions about the industry.

People outside the industry, Ms. Pettirossi said, tend to view it as relatively low tech—"a lot of people sitting around in rooms with phones"—as well as "a little shady." In fact, she said, the newly public companies are technology intensive, operating sophisticated information systems that capture data efficiently and limit intrusive calls to consumers.

VOCABULARY

aggressive
assumption
to buoy
to capture
to discard
doggedly
efficient
to farm out
to go public
growth stock
to hawk
intrusive
outsourcing

pitch
price-to-earnings
prolonged
to recoil
relentless
segment
to skyrocket
to soar
sophisticated
stratospheric
to tumble
wizard

REVIEW QUIZ 2

A. Complete the following dialogue with the infinitive or the gerund of the verb in parentheses.

AN INTERVIEW WITH SPIKE LEE

Reporter: Of all the past decade's films yours have been the ones __(1)__ (receive) the most attention. Why is that?

Spike Lee: Well, I try __(2)__ (make) films that are thought-provoking and at the same time entertaining.

Reporter: Your films have put race relations back on the agenda.

Spike Lee: That's right. There are far too many people __(3)__ (walk) around __(4)__ (think) that racism is a thing of the past.

Reporter: How did you get into __(5)__ (direct)?

Spike Lee: I started __(6)__ (make) films a while back. It was a kind of one-man band. You were the one __(7)__ (come up) with the idea in the beginning and in the end you were the one __(8)__ (cut) it as well. I've always had __(9)__ (write), direct, and edit everything myself.

Reporter: Do you like the management side of __(10)__ (direct)?

Spike Lee: I enjoy __(11)__ (do) both. I think you have __(12)__ (know) both in order __(13)__ (make) adjustments, assess priorities, and better execute your ideas.

255

Reporter:	Do you feel under pressure __(14)__ (repeat) the success of say Do the Right Thing or Jungle Fever?
Spike Lee:	I think the key is not __(15)__ (attempt) __(16)__ (duplicate) that success. I'm __(17)__ (go) __(18)__ (continue) to follow my instincts. You can't force lightning __(19)__ (strike) in the same place twice. I'll keep __(20)__ (do) my best. I know that at some point I'll make a better film, but it may take a while.

B. Change the following sentences to the negative form. Use the appropriate frequency adverb when necessary.

1. When she was a child, she was almost always sick.
2. The President has vetoed several bills.
3. Nancy has lived in Paris for ten years.
4. I need some help.
5. Yesterday at the aquarium, we were able to see a few sharks in the water.
6. I see someone coming this way.

C. The following sentences contain separable phrasal verbs. Replace the underlined object nouns with pronouns and place them correctly in each sentence.

1. Kids don't catch colds by taking off _their clothes_.
2. The parents picked up _their children_ after school.
3. The assistant handed in _his report_ two days late.
4. Our boss finally figured out _the problem with the new employee_.
5. She didn't give back _the car_ until after she had it fixed.
6. Please turn off _the lights_.
7. Mary loves to try on _all of my clothes_.
8. He turned down _the volume_, but it was still loud.
9. Immediately after she gave up _smoking_, she gained weight.
10. He tore up her pictures.

D. Rewrite the following sentences. If the sentence is written in the passive voice change to active, and vice versa.

1. Teachers have taught the students special techniques to read faster.
2. English is spoken by a large number of people.
3. Shakespeare wrote Romeo and Juliet.
4. Many people are employed by that company.
5. My next door neighbor bought my old car.
6. I wasn't surprised by the news.
7. Did you write this poem?

E. Decide whether the 's represents *is, has,* or a possessive form.

1. A: Who's that man in the blue suit?
   B: His name's Henry and he's worked at Lloyd's bank for fifteen years.
2. A: She's been there for at least an hour. What's she doing?
   B: She's waiting for my father's sister, who's applying for a driver's license.
3. A: Are all the children's parents coming to the school's fiftieth anniversary celebration?
   B: I don't think so. It's a tough hour for those parents who work the night shift.
4. A: My friend's sister won a free trip to Jamaica. I think she's traveling on her own.
   B: Lucky her! When's she going?
5. A: Excuse me, I ordered today's special, not vegetable lasagna.
   B: I'm afraid there's been a mistake. I'll bring your order right away.

ANSWER KEY

LESSON 1

1. a. I b. they c. them d. you e. I f. you g. I h. you i. it j. them
   k. you l. you m. he n. me o. it
2. a. it b. it c. it d. it e. he/she f. it g. he/she h. him i. she j. he
   k. it l. he
3. a. there are b. there are c. there is/there's d. there is/there's
   e. there are f. there are g. there is/there's h. there is/there's
   i. there are j. there is/there's
4. a. embarrassed b. borrow c. actual d. excited e. lend f. presently
5. a. For most international flights, to arrive at the airport two hours
   prior to departure is required. b. To have to wait for a connecting
   flight is annoying. c. To make flight reservations ahead of time
   during the holiday season is necessary. d. To eat something before
   getting on the plane is important.

LESSON 2

1. a. their b. they're c. there; their d. there; their e. they're; they're
   f. their; there
2. a. loses; loose b. lose c. lose d. loose e. lose; lose
3. a. is writing b. are trying c. begin; talks; want d. are changing; are
   beginning; need e. feel; realize; are getting
4. a. Most of the problems fathers have today aren't due to a lack of
   time. b. The host isn't interviewing several fathers for her show
   today. c. Fathers today don't want to provide financial support.
   d. My husband isn't going through a midlife crisis. e. Many fathers
   don't find it difficult to let go of their children. f. The television crew
   isn't taping two shows today. g. Most fathers don't give their
   children emotional support. h. This show doesn't air everyday at
   4 P.M. i. Some people in the audience don't know Dr. Cassid. j. He
   doesn't want to ask him a question. k. The center doesn't solve all
   of your problems.

LESSON 3

1. a. an b. a c. the d. the e. Ø f. the g. the h. the i. a j. a k. a
   l. an m. Ø n. the o. Ø p. a q. a r. an s. the t. the
2. a. much b. a few c. a lot of d. some e. any f. no g. some
   h. a lot of i. some j. a few

3. a. businesses; technologies b. people; beliefs; customs; languages
   c. feet d. children; computers e. echo; waves f. dentists; tooth
   g. parents h. phenomena i. men; women j. fish
4. innovate = renew delete = erase save = keep return = go back
   withdraw = remove insert = add

LESSON 4

1. a. turned b. decided c. thought d. went e. made f. could not
   g. gave h. seemed i. signed up.
2. a. got used to; used to b. am used to/got used to c. used to d. are
   used to; get used to e. used to f. used to
3. a. were trying b. did not hear; was sleeping c. was climbing;
   tripped; fell, did not hurt d. called; was having e. were recording;
   went

LESSON 5

1. a. received b. Did you know c. have been d. have received e. have
   been f. were g. have retired
2. a. for b. since c. since d. for e. since f. for g. for h. since i. for
3. a. to have b. to have c. to be; to be d. to be e. to have f. to be
   g. to be h. to be i. to have j. to be
4. a. to let go b. lawyer; prosecutor c. to retire d. suit
5. a. had finished b. had been crying c. had left d. had been coming
   e. had escaped

LESSON 6

1. a. future b. present c. present d. future e. future f. future g. future
2. a. are thinking b. are considering c. will shop/are going to shop
   d. are buying e. will spend/am going to spend
3. a. brings to mind b. have in mind c. change my mind d. speaks his
   mind e. lose my mind f. bear in mind
4. a. After you see the mall tomorrow, you'll want to open another store.
   b. As soon as I finish signing the contract, I'll call you. c. We'll hire
   new employees when we open the new store. d. Before you interview
   her, she'll take the typing test. e. Whenever you're ready, we'll sign
   the contract.

LESSON 7

1. a. had remembered b. can help/will help c. will be d. were e. were
   f. might finish/could finish/would finish g. convinces h. will take
   i. might be/will be
2. a. two b. too c. to; two d. too e. to f. to; to g. two; to h. to
   i. two; to j. too; to; to; to
3. a. If you want to cash a traveler's check, you need to present proper
   identification. You need to present proper identification if you want to
   cash a traveler's check. b. If you buy a certificate of deposit, you
   won't be able to withdraw the money until it matures. You won't be
   able to withdraw the money until it matures if you buy a certificate of
   deposit. c. If you invest in these bonds, you will receive a yield of 10
   percent. You will receive a yield of 10 percent if you invest in these
   bonds. d. If you don't have your address printed on your checks,
   your check will not be accepted. Your check will not be accepted if
   you don't have your address printed on your checks. e. If you want
   to minimize your risks, you should diversify your investments. You
   should diversify your investments if you want to minimize your risks.
4. a. a joint account b. an overdraft c. a statement d. a deposit e. a
   canceled check f. a broker
5. a. it's; its b. know; no c. here; hear d. whether; weather e. who's;
   whose f. their, there, they're

LESSON 8

1. a. have; am b. is c. are; is d. is; is e. was/is f. do g. was; had
   h. has; do i. has j. are; have
2. a. made b. made c. do d. do e. do f. make; do
3. a. has; is b. is c. have d. are e. is; is f. have g. is
4. Horizontal: 1. syringe 2. genes 3. bandage 4. rash 5. up 6. cold
   Vertical: 1. surgery 7. injection 8. fever 9. cough 10. dose

LESSON 9

1. a. ø b. ø c. to d. ø e. to
2. a. have to b. can't c. shouldn't d. would e. can't f. might g. have
   to h. should i. would j. had better
3. a. I might not have enough time to bake a cake for tonight's party.
   b. People shouldn't invite an equal number of men and women to
   their dinner parties. c. She can't bring any guests to the graduation

ceremony. d. If I were you, I wouldn't ask the host whether she needs any help. e. You don't have to bring a gift for the host.
4. a. Would it bother you b. I'd rather you wouldn't. c. I'm not sure it would be appropriate d. is it all right e. Certainly f. I don't mind at all

LESSON 10

1. a. well b. good; well c. well d. well; good e. good; well
2. a. shortest b. highest c. better; more spacious d. more convenient e. most expensive f. most famous; best; richest
3. a. as big as b. higher than c. shorter than d. less expensive than e. not as comfortable as/less comfortable f. the highest
4. a. $600 \times 2 = 1,200$ (twelve hundred) b. $4,800 + 1,200 = 6,000$ (six thousand) c. $1,600 - 500 = 1,100$ (eleven hundred) d. $5,200 + 300 = 5,500$ (fifty-five hundred) e. $100,000 - 8,000 = 92,000$ (ninety-two thousand) f. $1,200 - 800 = 400$ (four hundred)

REVIEW QUIZ 1

A. 1. are 2. is 3. is 4. borrowed 5. used 6. were 7. has 8. promote 9. have 10. is 11. gave 12. to combine 13. has been using 14. walks 15. will find 16. has always taken 17. using 18. believes 19. contain 20. causes 21. will not be 22. is 23. incorporates 24. promotes 25. must go 26. helps 27. will take 28. will serve 29. has grown 30. operates 31. are
B. 1. the; the; an; ø; ø; the; ø 2. the; a; ø 3. a; the; ø 4. the; a; ø; the; the
C. 1. Jack plays tennis better than Pete. 2. Some people think it is harder to work for a woman than to work for a man. 3. An athlete makes more money than a university professor. 4. The *New York Times* has more readers than the *Boston Globe*. 5. Some people say that people in the South are friendlier than people in the North.
D. 1. Alaska is the largest state in the United States. 2. English is the most popular language in the world. 3. Tom Cruise is one of the most famous actors in the United States. 4. The Lockheed SR-71 Blackbird is the fastest airplane. 5. The Nile is the longest river in the world.
E. 1. should; won't; should 2. should have; can 3. must 4. might 5. couldn't 6. could; can 7. had better; will 8. can't 9. would 10. may

LESSON 11

1. a. hasn't b. didn't c. don't d. don't e. isn't
2. a. couldn't b. didn't tell c. didn't notice d. wouldn't e. didn't work
   f. didn't have g. hadn't h. didn't ask
3. a. something b. anybody/anyone c. anybody/anyone
   d. anybody/anyone e. anybody/anyone f. somebody/someone
   g. nothing h. no i. nobody/no one j. somebody/someone/everyone

LESSON 12

1. a. mine; yours b. it's; it's; its; it's c. my; theirs d. there's; their
   e. he's; his
2. a. The children's parents left on a two-week trip to Hawaii. b. The
   university's library is closed on Sundays. c. My friend's name is
   Angela. d. This month's check is late. e. The ladies' fitting room is
   not open.
3. a. myself b. himself c. herself d. yourselves e. myself f. themselves
4. a. another b. whatever c. others d. whenever e. the other
   f. wherever; whomever

LESSON 13

1. a. in knowing b. of exercising; shopping c. to running d. Ø; walking
   e. about supplementing f. to spending
2. a. boring b. fascinating c. excited; confused; frustrated; thrilled;
   amazing d. surprising
3. a. going b. to go c. fishing/to go fishing d. to go hiking e. hiking
   f. go swimming g. go jogging h. going shopping

LESSON 14

1. a. to promote b. to sell c. to believe d. buying e. to feel
   f. dreaming g. putting h. making i. to stay
2. a. to memorize b. watching c. to win d. to rewind; returning e. to
   hear f. buying g. to give h. selling/to sell; to promote
3. a. to b. for c. for d. for e. to f. to
4. a. to watch b. playing c. smoking; to exercise d. moving; jogging
   e. picking; to go f. watching; doing

LESSON 15

1. A homeless man was found yesterday on the deck of a cruise ship that was anchored in New York Harbor. The man, authorities said, had been severely beaten. He was taken to Bellevue Hospital where he is in stable condition. The identity of the man was not disclosed. This is the third case this week of a homeless person being attacked and left to die near the harbor. What is not known yet is the motive of these attacks or how the criminals who committed this crime managed to get on the ship. Authorities have several possible suspects and clues, but they refuse to comment any further.

2. a. Homeless people are employed by the local supermarket to sweep the sidewalk and to remove snow from the parking lot. b. When it gets too cold, homeless people are picked up by the police and taken to shelters. c. People in need are fed and helped by volunteers at the soup kitchen. d. Homeless children are placed in foster homes (by social workers). e. Panhandlers are given money (by some people). f. The homeless are ignored and mistreated (by many people).

3. a. am scared b. am qualified c. are you interested in d. am exhausted e. am drunk f. is shut g. am excited about

4. a. A homeless person might not be hired (by some employers). b. The report must be handed in by Friday. c. A place for Jack to live ought to be found. d. Better shelters for the homeless should be provided by the government. e. A form to declare all his losses will be mailed to Jack.

LESSON 16

1. a. Tom explained (that) the shipment would arrive next month because of a delay at the docks. b. Mr. Brown ordered his secretary to bring him a copy of the contract. c. Beth told her friend (that) she had just been offered a job at the bank. d. Mark answered (that) the price last week had been very low, but he was sure it had gone up. e. Carol told her secretary (that) she was sure he was inviting everyone, but (that) she wasn't going. f. Frank agreed to wait there until Tom arrived.

2. a. for; against b. after c. away d. out e. into f. high

3. a. customs b. invoice c. commodity d. load e. supplier f. quota

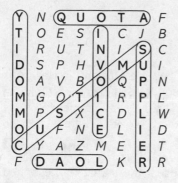

LESSON 17

1. a. new; know b. had known c. no d. new; know e. knew; no; new
2. a. for b. by c. at d. on e. at f. on g. for h. from i. to
3. Vertical: a. library d. touch e. freshman g. PIN Horizontal: b. bookstore c. drop f. hang h. know i. junior

LESSON 18

1. a. whom b. who c. who d. who
2. a. and b. for c. but d. so e. yet
3. a. nevertheless/however b. therefore c. moreover d. however
4. a. unless b. if c. whenever d. whereas

LESSON 19

1. a. to give up b. turning to c. to run across d. washed up
2. a. become b. visits; gives c. write d. realize e. decided; switched
   f. organize
3. a. atmosphere b. depletion; sprays c. radiation; eyes; aging
   d. upgrade

1. The Statue of Liberty

The Statue of Liberty is located on Liberty Island in New York Harbor. It was designed by Frédérique-Auguste Bartholdi, a French sculptor and painter. The interior framework was designed by famed engineer Alexandre-Gustave Eiffel, who also designed the Eiffel Tower in Paris.

The two designers wanted to present the statue to the United States on July 4, 1876, in honor of this country's centennial. An appeal for funds to underwrite the cost of creating the statue was launched in French newspapers in September 1875. Elaborate fund-raising events were organized, including a banquet at the Grand Hotel de Louvre and a gala benefit performance of a new Liberty Cantata by French composer Charles Gounod at the Paris Opera.

Unfortunately, not enough money was collected to complete the statue by the anticipated date. On July 4, 1876, Bartholdi visited the site where the statue would be placed. The tiny island was then known as Beldoe's Island. Eighty years later, in 1956, it's name was officially changed to Liberty Island. In August of that year, the 30-foot arm of the statue arrived in Philadelphia, where it was exhibited.

2. a. mis- b. in- c. co- d. il- e. mis- f. over-; il-
3. a. -ness; -ness b. -ment c. -ful; -ly d. -ful; -less

REVIEW QUIZ 2

A. 1. to receive 2. to make 3. walking 4. thinking 5. directing 6. making 7. to come up 8. to cut 9. to write 10. directing 11. doing 12. to know 13. to make 14. to repeat 15. to attempt 16. to duplicate 17. going 18. to continue 19. to strike 20. doing
B. 1. When she was a child, she was almost never sick. 2. The President hasn't vetoed any bills. 3. Nancy hasn't lived in Paris for ten years. 4. I don't need any help. 5. Yesterday at the aquarium, we weren't able to see any sharks in the water. 6. I don't see anyone (anybody) coming this way.
C. 1. Kids don't catch colds by taking them off. 2. The parents picked them up after school. 3. The assistant handed it in two days late. 4. Our boss finally figured it out. 5. She didn't give it back until after

she had it fixed. 6. Please turn them off. 7. Mary loves to try them on. 8. He turned it down, but it was still loud. 9. Immediately after she gave it up, she gained weight. 10. He tore them up.

D. 1. The students have been taught special techniques (by their teachers) to read faster. 2. A large number of people speak English. 3. *Romeo and Juliet* was written by Shakespeare. 4. That company employs many people. 5. My old car was bought by my next door neighbor. 6. The news didn't surprise me. 7. Was this poem written by you?

E. 1. is; is; has; possessive 2. has; is; is; possessive; is; possessive 3. possessive; possessive; is 4. possessive; is; is 5. possessive; has

APPENDIXES

A. PRONUNCIATION TABLE

Use this pronunciation table as a reference guide.

CONSONANTS
Some letters in English have more than one sound.

LETTER		PHONETIC SYMBOL	EXAMPLE
b		[b]	_b_oy
c	(before *a, o, u*)	[k]	_c_at
	(before *e, i*)	[s]	_c_ereal
d		[d]	_D_avi_d_
f		[f]	_f_ine
g	(before *a, o, u*)	[g]	_g_ame
	(before *e, i*)	[dʒ]	_G_erman
h		[h]	_h_ome
j		[dʒ]	_j_acket
k		[k]	_k_eep
k	(before *n*)	(silent)	_k_nown
l		[l]	_l_ife
m		[m]	_m_onth
n		[n]	_n_ever
p		[p]	sto_p_
qu		[kw]	_qu_ickly
r		[ɹ]	_r_um
s	(at the beginning or end of syllable)	[s]	_s_ame
	(between vowels)	[z]	ro_s_e
	(before *-ure*)	[ʃ]	_s_ure
t	(at the beginning or end of a syllable)	[t]	_t_ip, respec_t_
	(before *-ion*)	[ʃ]	recep_t_ion
	(before *-ure*)	[tʃ]	ma_t_ure
v		[v]	_v_erbal
w		[w]	_w_elcome
y		[j]	_y_ellow
z		[z]	_z_oo

CONSONANT BLENDS

LETTERS		PHONETIC SOUND	EXAMPLE
ch		[tʃ]	check
dge		[dʒ]	knowledge
gh	(at the end of a syllable)	[f]	laugh
		(silent)	dough, eight
	(beginning of a word)	[g]	ghost
ph		[f]	telephone
sh		[ʃ]	shoes
th	(verbs)	[Θ]	thanks
	(articles, pronouns, etc.)	[∂]	the
wh	(before letter o)	[h]	whose
	(before letters a, i, e)	[w]	white, where

VOWELS

There are five vowels in English, and each vowel makes several different sounds.

LETTER		PHONETIC SYMBOL	EXAMPLE
a		[ɑ]	car
		[ɛ]	many
	(before a consonant + final e)	[eɪ]	late
		[æ]	thanks
e		[ɛ]	let
	(end of a monosyllable)	[i]	he, be
	(before letter w)	[ju]	few, new
	(end of a word)	(silent)	fine, live
i		[ɪ]	sister
	(end of a syllable)	[aɪ]	hi
		[i]	marine
o	(between consonants)	[ɑ]	not
	(after letters d, t)	[u]	to, do
		[aʊ]	how
	(end of a word)	[oʊ]	hello
u	(before a consonant + final e)	[ju]	excuse
		[ʊ]	put
		[u]	attitude
		[ʌ]	under
y	(end of a one-syllable word)	[aɪ]	my, by
	(end of multisyllable word)	[i]	prodigy, many
		[ɪ]	rhythm, hysteria
		[aɪ]	tying, rhyme

COMBINATION OF VOWELS

LETTER		PHONETIC SYMBOL	EXAMPLE
ai	(between consonants)	[eɪ]	r*ai*n
au		[ɑ]	c*au*se
ay		[eɪ]	m*ay*be, d*ay*
ea	(before letters *t, d*)	[i]	*ea*t, r*ea*d
		[eɪ]	gr*ea*t
		[ɛ]	sw*ea*ter
ee	(after *a* consonant)	[i]	s*ee*, b*ee*
ei		[i]	n*ei*ther
		[eɪ]	*ei*ght
ey		[eɪ]	h*ey*, ob*ey*
ie		[i]	f*ie*ld
		[aɪ]	p*ie*
oa	(between consonant and final *t*)	[oʊ]	c*oa*t
oo		[u]	f*oo*d
		[ʊ]	g*oo*d
ou		[u]	y*ou*
		[aʊ]	r*ou*nd
ou		[ʌ]	t*ou*gh
oy		[oɪ]	b*oy*

There are some English vowels that are pronounced in a neutral and relaxed way, especially in unstressed syllables. This is known as the *schwa* sound. fr*o*m, t*o*night, *a*bout

B. GRAMMAR SUMMARY

1. THE ARTICLE

In English there is one definite article *(the)* and two indefinite articles *(a* before consonants and *an* before vowel sounds).

The man is eating an apple and a banana.

The definite article is not used as frequently as it is used in other languages. It is not used to refer to days of the week and seasons:

next Tuesday

It is not used in front of general abstract nouns:

Love is blind.

Or in front of colors or substances:

I don't like red.

Or in front of nouns that refer to general species or classifications:

Cats and dogs are faithful.

Or in front of nouns that refer to the arts or sciences in general:

I like music and history.

Or in front of geographical locations:

Alaska is a cold state.

Or in front of names of languages:

Tommy is studying French.

Or in front of names of avenues, streets, or squares:

Mary lives on Main Street.

Or with other common expressions:

last month
all day long
at work

Use a possessive adjective instead of a definite article when talking about body parts and items of clothing:

Take your shoes off.

Never use the definite article to express the time:

It's six o'clock.

Use an indefinite article before the words *hundred* and *thousand:*

a thousand dollars

Use an indefinite article before an occupation, profession, title, or nationality:

He's a student.

2. CONTRACTIONS
Contractions are accepted when using informal speech. Contractions should be avoided in formal or written language.

a. Contractions with personal pronouns:

I am	*I'm*
he is	*he's*

they have	they've
I will	I'll
I would	I'd

b. Contraction with *not:*

is not	isn't
are not	aren't
was not	wasn't
were not	weren't
have not	haven't
has not	hasn't
had not	hadn't
do not	don't
does not	doesn't
did not	didn't
will not	won't
should not	shouldn't
would not	wouldn't
cannot	can't
must not	mustn't

c. Contractions with question words:
How's your father? (How is . . . ?)
Where's . . . ? (Where is . . . ?)
What's . . . ? (What is . . . ?)

3. ADJECTIVES

English adjectives do not have gender (masculine, feminine) or number (singular, plural). They precede the noun that they modify:

a young boy

There are several ways of forming compound adjectives in English:

light blue
hardworking
lightheaded
poorly lit

4. THE POSSESSIVE

The possessive is formed by adding *'s* after the person or thing to which the noun belongs:

a child's toy

Add an apostrophe at the end of plural nouns and proper names of more than one syllable that end in *s.*

the girls' skirts

Sometimes you may use a longer form of expressing the possessive by using the preposition *of*. For example, *a doctors' conference* may also be *a conference of doctors*.

5. THE COMPARATIVE AND THE SUPERLATIVE

REGULAR COMPARATIVES AND SUPERLATIVES:

nice	→	*nicer*	→	*the nicest*
expensive	→	*more expensive*	→	*the most expensive*

Here are some of the most common irregular comparatives and superlatives:

good	→	*better*	→	*best*
bad	→	*worse*	→	*worst*
little	→	*less*	→	*least*
much	→	*more*	→	*most*

6. PERSONAL PRONOUNS
a. Subject Pronouns:

I	*it*
you	*we*
he	*you*
she	*they*

b. Direct and Indirect Object Pronouns

me	*it*
you	*us*
him	*you*
her	*them*

c. Reflexive Pronouns:

myself	*oneself*
yourself	*ourselves*
himself	*yourselves*
herself	*themselves*
itself	

d. Reciprocal Pronouns:
Each other is used to refer to two people:

They love each other.

One another is used to refer to more than two people:

The girls argued with one another.

7. RELATIVE PRONOUNS

	SUBJECT	OBJECT	POSSESSION
PEOPLE	*who, that*	*who(m), that*	*whose*
THINGS	*which, that*	*which, that*	*whose*

8. INTERROGATIVE ADJECTIVES AND PRONOUNS

who?
(to) whom?
whose?
which?
what?
where?
when?

9. DEMONSTRATIVE ADJECTIVES AND PRONOUNS
Demonstrative adjectives and pronouns have no gender:

this
these
that
those
this one
that one

10. POSSESSIVE ADJECTIVES AND PRONOUNS
a. Possessive Adjectives

my
your
his
her
its
our
your
their

b. Possessive Pronouns

> *mine*
> *yours*
> *his*
> *hers*
> *ours*
> *yours*
> *theirs*

11. NEGATION

When the main verb of the sentence is the verb *to be,* the verb does not change in form. The negative is formed by adding *not.*

She is at the beach.
She is not at the beach.

Use the auxiliary verb *to do* (*does, did*) with one-verb sentences that do not use the verb *to be.* Use the infinitive form without the preposition *to* after *does* and *did.*

She studies at night.
She doesn't study.

The negative of a sentence with an auxiliary verb (*to be, to have,* modals) is formed by adding *not* to that verb.

I can work tomorrow.
I can't work tomorrow.
I have eaten.
I haven't eaten.

12. QUESTIONS

To pose a question, the word order of the sentence changes: the subject and the verb are reversed. When the sentence contains the verb *to be* (whether it is the sentence's main verb or a helping verb) or another helping verb, the question is formed by placing the helping verb at the beginning of the question.

They are all hungry.
Are they all hungry?
I have made a mistake.
Have I made a mistake?
You can go.
Can you go?

276

If the sentence does not contain *to be* or another helping verb, use the auxiliary *do* or *did* followed by an infinitive without the preposition *to*.

She eats chicken every day.
Does she eat chicken?
I went to the park.
Did you go to the park?

13. ADVERBS

Words that end with the suffix *-ly* are considered adverbs. These are words that are used to modify a verb, an adjective, or another adverb.

necessarily
quickly
exclusively

14. PREPOSITIONS

Prepositions are difficult to translate from one language to another because their usage depends on the context. Here are some of the most common prepositions:

at, to	*along*
in, into, within, inside	*about*
out, out of, outside	*around*
on, upon	*from*
over, above	*of*
under, below	*through, across*
between, among	*by, for*
before, in front of	*with*
behind, in back of	*without*
up	*except*
down	*for, in order to*
by, near, close to, beside	*in spite of*
against	

15. CONJUNCTIONS

Here are some of the most common conjunctions:

and	*then*
or	*therefore*
but	*while*
that	*as soon as*
as	*unless*
since	*till, until*

if, whether	*since*
why	*before*
because	*provided that, so that*
yet, still, however	*though*

16. VERB TENSES

The infinitive form refers to the simple form of the verb preceded by the preposition *to*: *to walk*.

THE SIMPLE TENSES

a. The present indicative: Add -*s* for the third-person singular.
b. The simple past: Add -*ed* in all cases.
c. The future: Use the modal *will* + simple form of the verb.
d. The conditional: Use the modal *would* + simple form of the verb.

THE COMPOUND TENSES

a. The present perfect: Use the present of *to have* + past participle.
b. The past perfect: Use the past tense of *to have* + past participle.
c. The future perfect: Use *will* + *have* + past participle.
d. The past conditional: Use *would* + *have* + past participle.
e. The present continuous: Use the present form of *to be* + present participle.
f. The past continuous: Use the past form of *to be* + present participle.
g. The future continuous: Use *will* + *be* + present participle.
h. The conditional continuous: Use *would* + *be* + present participle.
i. The present perfect continuous: Use the present of *to have* + *been* + present participle.
j. The past perfect continuous: Use the past of *to have* + *been* + present participle.
k. The future perfect continuous: Use *will* + *have been* + present participle.

The past participle: If it is a regular verb, add -*ed* to the simple form.
The present participle: Add -*ing* to the simple form of the verb.

17. CONJUGATING A REGULAR VERB

INFINITIVE
to work

a. Present

I work
you work

he works
she works
it works
we work
you work
they work

b. Past

I worked
you worked
he/she/it worked, etc.

c. Present Perfect

I have worked
you have worked
he/she/it has worked, etc.

d. Past Perfect

I had worked
you had worked, etc.

e. Future

I will work
you will work, etc.

f. Future Perfect

I will have worked
you will have worked, etc.

g. Present Conditional

I would work
you would work, etc.

h. Past Conditional

I would have worked
you would have worked, etc.

i. Imperative

Work!
Let's work!

j. Infinitive

to work

k. Progressive (continuous) Forms

Present: *I am working*
Past: *I was working*
Present Perfect: *I have been working*
Future: *I will be working*
Conditional: *I would be working*
Past Perfect: *I had been working*
Future Perfect: *I will have been working*
Past Conditional Perfect: *I would have been working*

18. THE IMPERATIVE

For the second person, use the infinitive without the preposition *to* or the personal pronoun.

Go to your room!
Be quiet!

Use the verb *to let* for the first-person plural.

Let's go!
Let's eat!

19. THE PASSIVE VOICE

The passive voice is formed by using the verb *to be* + past participle + (by + agent/subject).

The oven was fixed by the electrician.
The turkey was prepared with a special recipe.

20. MODAL VERBS

MODAL VERB	MEANING
can, could	to be able to
may, might	to be allowed to
must	to have to
will, would	to be going to
shall, should	to have to, to be obliged to
ought to	to be obliged to

21. PHRASAL VERBS

to ask out
to bring about
to bring back
to bring down

to bring forth
to bring up
to bring down the house
to call back
to call on
to call up
to catch up (with)
to check in
to check out
to cheer up
to clean up
to clear up
to come across
to cross out
to cut out
to drop by
to drop off
to drop out
to end up
to figure out
to fill out
to find out
to get along
to get back
to get in
to get off
to get out of
to get over
to get through
to give back
to go over
to grow up
to hand in
to hang out
to hang up
to keep out
to keep up
to key in
to kick out
to look after
to look into
to look out
to look over

to look up
to make up
to pass out
to pick at something
to pick on someone
to pick out
to pick up
to point out
to put away
to put back
to put off
to put on
to put out
to put up with
to run after
to run against
to run away
to run for
to run high
to run into someone
to run out/short
to stand someone up
to stand out
to stand in for
to stand up to someone
to set up
to show up
to shut off
to stick around
to take off
to take out
to take over
to take up
to tear up
to think over
to throw away
to turn down
to turn in
to turn off
to turn out
to turn up
to wind up
to work out

C. IRREGULAR VERBS

INFINITIVE	PAST	PAST PARTICIPLE
to bear	bore	born
to beat	beat	beaten
to become	became	become
to begin	began	begun
to bend	bent	bent
to bet	bet	bet
to bind	bound	bound
to bite	bit	bitten
to bleed	bled	bled
to blow	blew	blown
to bring	brought	brought
to build	built	built
to burst	burst	burst
to buy	bought	bought
to catch	caught	caught
to choose	chose	chosen
to come	came	come
to cost	cost	cost
to cut	cut	cut
to deal	dealt	dealt
to do	did	done
to draw	drew	drawn
to drink	drank	drunk
to drive	drove	driven
to eat	ate	eaten
to fall	fell	fallen
to feed	fed	fed
to feel	felt	felt
to fight	fought	fought
to find	found	found
to fly	flew	flown
to forget	forgot	forgotten
to forgive	forgave	forgiven
to freeze	froze	frozen
to get	got	gotten
to give	gave	given
to go	went	gone
to grow	grew	grown
to hang	hung	hung

to have	had	had
to hear	heard	heard
to hide	hid	hidden
to hit	hit	hit
to hold	held	held
to hurt	hurt	hurt
to keep	kept	kept
to know	knew	known
to lay	laid	laid
to lead	led	led
to leave	left	left
to lend	lent	lent
to let	let	let
to lie	lay	lain
to lose	lost	lost
to make	made	made
to mean	meant	meant
to meet	met	met
to owe	owed	owed
to pay	paid	paid
to quit	quit	quit
to read	read	read
to ring	rang	rung
to rise	rose	risen
to run	ran	run
to see	saw	seen
to shake	shook	shaken
to sell	sold	sold
to send	sent	sent
to set	set	set
to shine	shone	shone
to shoot	shot	shot
to show	showed	shown
to shrink	shrank	shrunk
to shut	shut	shut
to sing	sang	sung
to sink	sank	sunk
to sit	sat	sat
to sleep	slept	slept
to slide	slid	slid
to speak	spoke	spoken
to spend	spent	spent
to split	split	split
to spread	spread	spread

to stand	stood	stood
to steal	stole	stolen
to stick	stuck	stuck
to strike	struck	struck
to swear	swore	sworn
to sweep	swept	swept
to swim	swam	swum
to swing	swung	swung
to take	took	taken
to teach	taught	taught
to tear	tore	torn
to tell	told	told
to think	thought	thought
to throw	threw	thrown
to wear	wore	worn
to weep	wept	wept
to win	won	won
to write	wrote	written

D. WRITING LETTERS

1. FORMAL INVITATIONS AND RESPONSES

a. Invitations

Mr. and Mrs. John Zamora
request the honor of your presence
at the marriage of their daughter
Sandy Angelica
to
Mr. Victor Smith
on Sunday, the third of July
Two thousand and five
at four-thirty in the afternoon
Our Lady of Pilar Church
Main Street and Lincoln Boulevard
Seattle, Washington

Mr. and Mrs. Peter Levenfeller cordially invite you to a reception given for their daughter Annemarie, on Saturday evening, November 26, 2005, at nine o'clock, at the Yacht Club.

b. Responses

Mr. and Mrs. Steve Houston thank Mr. and Mrs. Levenfeller for their kind invitation and regret that they are unable to attend due to a previous engagement.

Mr. and Mrs. Brown thank you for your kind invitation and will attend with pleasure the reception on November 26th.

2. THANK-YOU NOTES

August 3, 2005

Dear Sandy,

I just wanted to say hello and let you know that I received the beautiful picture frame you sent me. I used it for one of my wedding pictures. I've hung it on the wall in the family room, and you can't imagine how nice it looks. I hope to see you at Julie's party tomorrow. I think it's going to be a lot of fun.

I hope your family is well. Everyone here is fine.

Love,

Joyce

3. BUSINESS LETTERS

Sports & Co. • 888 W. 29th Street, Suite 290 • New York, NY 10011
212-555-1999 (tel) • 212-555-1888 (fax)

October 28, 2005

Andrew Tyler
Account Executive
FunAdvertising
777 E. 28th Street
New York, NY 10012

Dear Mr. Tyler:

We have received your drafts for our upcoming print advertisement campaign in Harper's and the New Yorker. We have already discussed your concept with our sales and marketing staff and are quite pleased with your suggestions.

As we discussed on the telephone, we would like to make a few minor changes to the advertisements. Our sales manager, Susan Haywirth, will be in contact with you directly to discuss our suggestions.

We would also like to discuss the proposed budget in more detail. Please give me a call at your earliest convenience to set up a meeting.

We look forward to working with you.

Sincerely,

Barbara Millers
Vice President, Sales and Marketing
Sports & Co.

The Sweet Tooth
123 Main Street
New Haven, CT 23456
215-777-8888
215-777-8889 (fax)

November 3, 2005

Karen Klett
Director
Sugar Exports
Avenida de las Américas No. 23
Quito, Ecuador

Dear Karen:

We are in receipt of your shipment of 9.8 tons of sugar. Thank you very much.

The invoice included does not reflect the 20 percent discount we agreed upon in our meeting on October 24, 2005. As we assume that this was an oversight, we will adjust the bill accordingly and transfer the funds less 20 percent to your account as usual.

We are looking forward to receiving the remaining 20 tons of sugar later this month. Please be so kind and let us know when exactly we can expect this shipment.

Sincerely,
John Hume
Manager, Import

The Sweet Tooth
123 Main Street
New Haven, CT 23456
215-777-8888
215-777-8889 (fax)

November 3, 2005

Karen Klett
Director
Sugar Exports
Avenida de las Américas No. 23
Quito, Ecuador

John Hume
Manager, Import
The Sweet Tooth
123 Main Street
New Haven, CT 23456

Dear John:

We apologize for having failed to adjust our invoice according to our agreement from October 24. Enclosed is an adjusted bill for your files. Please do transfer the funds to our account as usual. The remainder of the shipment will go out to you by November 15, 2005. I will call you personally to confirm this date within the next few days.

We apologize for any inconvenience this delay may have caused you.

> *Best,*
> *Karen Klett*
> *Director, Sales and Marketing*

4. INFORMAL LETTERS

February 23, 2005

Dear Victor,

I was happy to receive your letter. It was good to hear that you're feeling better after your stay in the hospital. I have some good news for you. I have finally decided to make the trip to New Mexico. I will probably spend at least three weeks there, starting on the first of August. Thanks so much for the invitation to stay with you. It'll be wonderful to see you.

Laura is going with me. She is excited about meeting the two of you. We'll finally have a chance to catch up. The business seems to be doing fine. I saw Albert the other day, and he asked me about you.
Write soon. Give my regards to Sandy.

> *Yours,*
> *Michael*

5. GREETINGS AND CLOSINGS IN LETTERS

a. Formal Greetings

Sir:	*Dear Miss McCurdy:*
Madam:	*Dear Ms. Smith,*
Dear Sir:	*Dear Dr. Harris:*
Dear Sir or Madam:	*Dear Professor Kozlowsky:*
Dear Mr. McCurdy:	*Dear Colonel Kent:*
Dear Mrs. McCurdy:	

b. Informal Greetings:

Dear Mr. Gill,	*Dear Victor,*
Dear Mrs. Gill,	*Dearest Robert,*
Dear Sandy,	*My darling Maya,*

c. Formal Closings

Very truly yours,	*Sincerely,*
Yours very truly,	*Cordially,*
Sincerely yours,	*Very cordially,*
Yours sincerely,	

d. Informal Closings

Best (regards),	*Yours,*
With our very best regards,	*Love,*
Affectionately,	*With love,*

6. ADDRESSING AN ENVELOPE

Boxer & Hunter, Inc.
240 Main St., Suite 431
Santa Monica, CA 90404

Mr. Matthew Morfin
456 Franklin Avenue
St. George, UT 84770

Or:

Boxer & Hunter, Inc.
240 Main St., Suite 431
Santa Monica, CA 90404

Mr. Matthew Morfin
456 Franklin Avenue
St. George, UT 84770

VOCABULARY LIST

A
a lot
a mind to
assist (v)*
abdomen
above
above price
abroad
absolutely
accept (v)
accident
account
ache
ache (v)
achieve (v)
acid rain
activity
actor
actually
add (v)
additional
admit (v)
adult
adulthood
adventure
advertisement
advice
advise (v)
affliction
after
after all
afternoon
age
agree (v)
air conditioner
airplane
airport
aisle
algebra
almost
already
also
always
amazing

American dream
an
anchor (news)
and
angry
ankle
annoying
annual
answer (v)
anxious
anymore
anyway
apartment
appear (v)
apple
application
appointment
appreciate (v)
argue (v)
argument
arm
around
arrival
as
as soon as
as long as
as usual
ask (v)
ask out (v)
assistance
assure (v)
at
athlete
attitude
attorney
attorney-at-law
audience
aunt
automated teller machine (ATM)
auto insurance
auto shop
available
avoid (v)

*(v) indicates a verb

B

baby
baby-sitter
Bachelor of Arts (BA)
Bachelor of Science (BS)
bachelor party
back
bad
bag
baggage
baggage carousel
bake (v)
balance
ball
band
bandage
bank
bank check
bank statement
banker
bar
barbecue
bargain (v)
baseball
basketball
bath
bathroom
bathtub
battery
be (v)
be allowed (v)
be careful (v)
be hungry (v)
be in charge (v)
be late (v)
be on one's mind (v)
be on sale (v)
be on time (v)
be proud (v)
be supposed (v)
be worth it (v)
beach
bear in mind (v)
beautiful
because
because of
become (v)
bedroom
beef
beer
beg (v)
behind
believe (v)
belong (v)
below price

bet (v)
better
between
big
bill
billboard
blinker
block
blood test
blouse
board (v)
boat
book
borrow (v)
boss
both
bother (v)
bottle
box
boxing
boy
branch
bread
break (v)
break down (v)
breath
breathe (v)
breakfast
bride
bring (v)
bring about (v)
bring back (v)
bring back memories (v)
bring forth (v)
bring to mind (v)
bring up (v)
broadcast
broadcast (v)
broccoli
broken
brother
brotherhood
brother-in-law
brush
bucks
buddy
build (v)
bulk commodities
bulletin board
bumper
bumper-to-bumper traffic
burn (v)
bus
business
busy

but
buy to
by
by the time
bye

C
cabinet
cable television
call
call (v)
camp
campaign
can
candidate
capacity
capital
car
carjacking
carbon dioxide
card
care (v)
career
carefully
careless
carpeted
carrot
carry (v)
carry out (v)
carve (v)
cash
cash (v)
cash register
cashier's check
casserole
cast
cause
ceiling price
census
certainly
certified check
chair
chairperson
championship
change (v)
change one's mind (v)
channel
character
charge (v)
chat (v)
cheap
checking account
check
check (v)

check in (to a hotel) (v)
check out (of a hotel) (v)
checks and balances
Cheers!
chemical pesticide
chest
chicken
child
childhood
choose (v)
Christmas
Christmas Eve
Christmas card
Christmas tree
cigarette
citizen
civil rights
claim (v)
class
classical
classified ad
clean (v)
climate
clock
closet
clothes
cloudy
clover
coach
coal
coast
coat
coffee
coincidence
cold
colleague
collection
collision
come (v)
come back (v)
come in (v)
come to mind (v)
Come on! Let's go!
comedy
commentator
company
compare (v)
complain (v)
complete
complicated
complimentary (free)
compose (v)
computer
condition
confess (v)

Congratulations!
Congress
consent (v)
consequently
conservative
consider (v)
consist of (v)
consumer
consumer goods
contain (v)
continue (v)
control key
convince (v)
convinced
cookie
cooking
correct (v)
correctly
cost (v)
cough
counter
courses
cousin
cover (v)
cover up (v)
coverage
cream
credit
credit card
crime
critic
cross-cultural awareness
cruise
cultural
cure
customer
customs
cut (v)
cut off (a car) (v)

D
dad
dare (v)
date
daughter
day care
deal
debate
debt
decide (v)
decision
declare (v)
declaration
decoration

deductible
deep
defeat (v)
defeated
deferred billing
deficient
deforestation
delay
delay (v)
delicious
delivery
demand (v)
demanding
Democrat
democratic
den
dentist
deny (v)
Department of Motor Vehicles
departure
deposit
depressed
depression
deserve (v)
desk
dessert
diagnosis
diet
different
dinner
directly
director
disability
disappointed
discount
discrimination
discuss (v)
dish
dislike (v)
divorced
dizzy
Doctor of Philosophy (PhD)
Doctor of Medicine (MD)
documentary
doll
dollar
door
dose
doubt (v)
downtown
drama
dress
drink (v)
driver's license
drop by (v)
drop off (v)

drums
dry (v)
due
due (v)
dust (v)
duty-free
dye (clothes, hair) (v)

E
ear
early
early riser
east
economical
educate (v)
educated
efficiency studio
egg
elbow
elder
elect (v)
electrical appliance
electricity
e-mail
embarrassed
emergency
emotional
employee
encourage (v)
end (up) (v)
endorse (v)
endorsement
endurance
engaged
engineering
enjoy (v)
enough
entertainment
enthusiastic
environment
envy (v)
equipment
escape (v)
essential
essentially
ethnic group
even
evening
event
every
every time
exactly
excited
exciting

executive
excuse
excuse (v)
exercise
exercise (v)
exist (v)
exit
expect (v)
expected
expense
expensive
extra
eye

F
fail (v)
fall (v)
fall down (v)
family
fascinating
fast
father
fatherhood
father-in-law
faucet
fault
favorite
fear
fear (v)
federal
fee
feel (v)
fever
few
field
fill (out) (v)
film
finally
find (v)
finger
finish (v)
first
first name
fish
fitting room
fix (v)
fixed
flexibility
flight attendant
flip (channels) (v)
floppy disk
flu
fluid
fly (v)

foggy
follow (v)
food
foot
football
forbid (v)
force (v)
forecast
forget (v)
form
former
free
free on board
freeway
freight
freshman
friend
friendly
from
frozen
frustrating
fuel
fun
function key
furniture

G

gain (v)
gain weight (v)
game
gang
garage
garage sale
gardening
garlic
gas station
gasoline
gate
gelatin
general
general education
gesture
get (v)
get away (v)
get drunk (v)
get married (v)
get off (v)
get something fixed (v)
get somewhere (v)
get up (v)
ghost
gift
gift exchange

gift wrap
girl
give (v)
glad
glasses
glove compartment
go (v)
go ahead (v)
go away (v)
go back (v)
go by (v)
go down (v)
go in (v)
go out (v)
go up (v)
Good morning
Good evening
gorgeous
grade point average (GPA)
grades
grandfather
grandma
grandmother
grandpa
grandparents
gravy
great
green card
greenhouse effect
groceries
groom
ground transportation
guess (v)
guest
guilty
guitar
gun
gun shot
guys

H

hall
half
ham
handicapped
handsome
handyman
happy
harass (v)
hard disk
hardly
hardware store
hate (v)

have (v)
Have a good trip!
have doubts (v)
have to (v)
head
headache
health
health nut
healthy
hear (v)
hearing
heat
heater
here
hello
help (v)
help oneself (v)
hi
highway
hike (v)
hit (v)
hobby
home
hope
hope (v)
hors d'oeuvre
hot
hotel
hour
house
House (of Representatives)
household
how?
how much?
how many?
how about . . . ?
How are you?
How's it coming along?
however
hug (v)
humid
hurry (v)
hurt (v)
husband

I

ice
ice cream
icon
identification (ID)
illegal alien
illness
imagine (v)

immediately
immigrant
immunization
impossible
improve
in
inadequate
include (v)
inconvenience
individual
individual account
inhibit (v)
injection
insist (v)
instructor
instrument
insurance
insurance policy
intend (v)
intensive care
interested
international
interesting
interrupt (v)
interview
into
intolerance
invite (v)
invoice
Ireland
Irish
ironing board
island
issue (v)
item
itinerary

J

jealous
job
jog (v)
join (v)
joint
joint account
journalism
joy
joyous
judge
judicial
jump
jump (v)
jump start (a car) (v)
junior

jury
just

K

keep (v)
keep up (v)
key
keyboard
kick (v)
kid (v)
kill (v)
kill time (v)
kilo
kiss (v)
kitchen
knee
knife
know (v)

L

lake
land (v)
landlady
landlord
lane
lasagna
laser printer
last
last name
last night
late
lately
laugh (v)
laundry
law
lawyer
lead (actor)
leader
leaf
leak (v)
learn (v)
lease (v)
leave (v)
legislative
lemon
lend (v)
let go (v)
let me
let's go
Let's see.
letter
liberal
library

life insurance
light
light bulb
like (v)
liner trade
liquid
list
little
live
live (v)
living room
load
loathe (v)
lobby
local
lock
lonely
long
look (seem) (v)
look around (v)
look at (v)
look for (v)
look forward to (v)
look into (v)
look over (v)
loose
lose (v)
lose one's mind (v)
love (v)
lovely
lowercase
luggage
lunch
lurk (v)
luxury

M

mad
magazine
mail (v)
maintenance
major
majority
make (v)
make a decision (v)
make a good impression (v)
make an offer (v)
make ends meet (v)
make it (v)
make sure (v)
make up one's mind (v)
mall
manage (v)
manager

mandatory
manufacturer
many
marketing
married
mashed potatoes
mass media
Master of Arts (MA)
Master of Science (MS)
match (sports)
match
match (clothes) (v)
mathematics
mature
may
maybe
mean (v)
means of transportation
meat
mechanic
medication
medicine
meet (v)
meeting
memories
mention (v)
menu
merchandise
Merry Christmas
mess (v)
meter
method of payment
midsize
midnight
might
mileage
milk
mind (v)
minimum
minority
minute
misery
miss (v)
mistake
mister
mom
money
money order
monthly
mood
morning
most
mother
motherhood
mother-in-law
mouse

mouth
move (v)
move up (in the world) (v)
movie
mug (v)
mugging
mumble (v)
muscle
mushroom
music
musician
must
mystery

N
name
nature
near
neck
need (v)
neighbor
neighborhood
nephew
nervous
network
networking
never
nevertheless
new
news
newspaper
next
nice
Nice to meet you.
nickname
niece
nightclub
nobody
noise
noisy
noon
nose
not
not yet
note
note (v)
notify (v)
novel
now
nurse

O
object (v)
observe (v)

obviously
occasion
occasionally
occur (v)
of course
offer
offer (v)
office
often
old
on
on the house (free)
once
operation
opinion
option
orange juice
order
order (v)
ornament
other
our
out of wedlock
outlet
outstanding
oven
overdraft
overdrawn check
over there
overpriced
owe (v)
own (v)
owner
ozone layer

P

package
pain
paint
paint (v)
pale
pants
parade
parenthood
parents
park
parking
party
pass (on) (v)
passport
past
pasta
peaceful
pediatrician

performance
permit (v)
personal
personal identification number (PIN)
personnel
persuade (v)
pharmacy
piano
pick (v)
pick at (something) (v)
pick on (somebody) (v)
pick out (v)
pick up (v)
picnic
picture
pie
pig out (v)
pinch (v)
pineapple
pitiful
pitifully
pity (v)
place
placement
plain
plaintiff
plan (v)
plane
plate
play (v)
plight
plumber
plumbing
pocket
point out (v)
poison
political
political party
poll
pollution
poor
popular
possess (v)
post office
postcard
postpone (v)
potato
pound
poverty
practical training
practice
practice (v)
prairie
prefer (v)
pregnancy
pregnant

premium
preparation
prepare (v)
prescribe (v)
prescription
present
present (v)
presently
presidential
pretend (v)
pretty
preventive care
preview
previous
price
price leaders
pride
print (v)
printer
problem
produce
product
professional
professor
program
programmer
project
promise (v)
promotion
promote (v)
propose (v)
prosecutor
protest (v)
proud
public transportation
publish (v)
pumpkin
purchase
purchase (v)
pursue (v)
put (v)

Q

quarter
question
quickly
quit (v)

R

racial
radiation
rainy
raise children (v)

rarely
rash
ray
ready
real estate
realize (v)
really
Really?
recall (v)
recently
reception
receptionist
recklessly
reclining chair
recognize (v)
refrigerator
refugee
refuse (v)
regular
relatives
relax (v)
reliable
remark (v)
remember (v)
remind (v)
remote control
renovate (v)
renovated
rent (v)
rental agency
repair (v)
reply (v)
Republican
reputation
require (v)
requirement
resign (v)
respected
rest (v)
restaurant
resumé
retail
retailer
retire (v)
retrieve (v)
return (v)
rice
right
right away
right now
rise (v)
road
rob (v)
robbery
rock and roll
rock-bottom price

room
roommate
rose
rug
ruin (v)
rumor
run (v)
run into (v)
rush hour

S
sad
safe
safety deposit
salad
salary
sale
sales
salmon
same
satellite
sauce
savings
savings account
savings bank
saxophone
scandal
scare away (v)
schedule
Scholastic Aptitude Test (SAT)
science
scrub (v)
season
second
section
security deposit
sedan
see (v)
See you later.
seem (v)
seldom
select (v)
self-sufficient
sell (v)
Senate
senator
send (v)
senior
senior citizen
sensationalist
separate
serious
service
set

shake hands (v)
shape
sharp
shift
Shift key
shipment
shipping and handling
shirt
shoe
shop (v)
short
shorthand
shoulder
shout (v)
show
show (v)
shower
siblings
sick
sickness
sigh
sign
sign (v)
signal
signal (v)
signature
silk
since
single
sink
sir
sister
sisterhood
sister-in-law
sit (v)
sitcom
size
skill
skirt
skycap
sleep (v)
slow
small
smile
smile (v)
smoking
sneakers
sneeze (v)
snow
snowstorm
so far, so good
soap opera
soccer
social security
solve (v)
some

sometimes
son
sophomore
sore
sorry
sound (v)
source
spacious
spamming
speak (v)
speak one's mind (v)
speaker
special
speech
speed
spend (v)
spinach
sponsor
sports
sports bag
sports car
St. Patrick
stamp
stand (endure) (v)
standard
start (v)
state
statement
station
stay (v)
steady
still
stomach
stop (v)
story
stove
street
stressed
stretcher
struggle (v)
student
stuff
stuffing
subscription
subway
successfully
such
sue (v)
sugar
suggest (v)
suit
Suit yourself!
suite
summer
sunny
supermarket

supervisor
suppose (v)
Supreme Court
sure
surgeon
surgery
surprise
surprised
swear (v)
sweat
sweet
swim (v)
swimming
switch (v)
syringe

T

table
tabloids
take (v)
take care of oneself (v)
take classes (v)
take a look (v)
take for granted (v)
take off (v)
tall
tapes
taste (v)
tavern
tea
televise (v)
television
tell (v)
temperature
tenant
terrible
terrific
thank you
Thanksgiving
that
That's true.
the
then
therefore
thigh
think (v)
thinner
this
thought
threaten (v)
throat
tickets
time
tip
toast

toe
tonight
too
too expensive
tooth
tough
tow (v)
tow away (v)
tow truck
toxic
toy
trademark
traditional
traffic
traffic jam
train
transportation
trash
travel (v)
travel agency
traveler's checks
treat (v)
trial
tricky
trillion
trip
trolley
try (v)
try on (v)
tuition
turkey
turn (v)
turn in (v)
turn on (v)
twice
type (v)

U
ugly
ultraviolet light
unacceptable
uncle
unconstitutional
under
understand (v)
understanding
unemployment
unexpected
unfurnished
unlimited
until
upcoming
uppercase
upset
urban transportation

use (v)
U.S. Census Bureau
usual
usually
utilities

V
vacation
vaccine
vacuum (v)
vegetable
very
veto (v)
video
viewer
violence
virus
visit (v)
volunteer (v)
vote (v)
voucher

W
wage
wait (v)
wake up (v)
walk (v)
wall
want (v)
warehouse
warm
warm up (v)
warn (v)
waste
watch
watch (v)
watch out (v)
water
weapon
wear (v)
weather
wedding
wedding reception
weekend
weight
welcome
welfare
well
well-liked
west
what?
What time is it?
when?
whenever

where?
which
while
who?
wholesaler
whom (v)
whose
why not?
why?
widow
widower
wife
windy
wine
wise
wish (v)
withdraw (v)
woe

woefully
wonderful
work
work (v)
world
worried
worry (v)
wrist
write (v)
write checks (v)

Y
yard sale
yesterday
yet
yield (v)
You're right.

INDUSTRY-SPECIFIC TERMS

Here are various areas of commerce, government, and nonprofit activities. Each has its particular terminology, and we've offered some of the more common terms. The industries covered are:

Advertising and Public Relations
Agriculture
Architecture and Construction
Automotive
Banking and Finance
Computer and Systems
Engineering
Entertainment, Journalism, and Media
Fashion
Government and Government Agencies
Insurance
Management Consulting
Mining and Petroleum
Nonprofit
Perfume and Fragrance
Pharmaceutical, Medical, and Dental
Publishing
Real Estate
Shipping and Distribution
Telecommunications
Textile
Toys
Watches, Scales, and Precision Instruments
Wine

ADVERTISING AND PUBLIC RELATIONS

account executive
ad
ad agency
ad style
ad time
advertise (v)
advertisement
advertising
advertising agency
advertising budget
advertising campaign
advertising message
advertising papers
advertising space
advertising strategy
advertising vehicle
air (v)
audience
baseline
block of commercials
brand-name promotion
broadcast (v)
broadcast times
brochure
campaign
catalog
commercial
commodity
competition
consumer research
cooperative advertising
cost per thousand
coupon
cover
daily press
depth of coverage
direct marketing
early adopter
effectiveness
endorsement
focus group
free shopper's papers
infomercial
in-house
insert
in-store campaign
introductory campaign
jingle
layout
leaflet
listenership
listening rate
logo
Madison Avenue

mail/letter campaign
market
market (v)
marketing
market research
mass marketing
media
media agent
media plan
merchandise
merchandise (v)
merchandising
misleading advertising
niche
opener
packaging
periodical
point-of-sale advertising
positioning
poster advertising
premium
presentation
press officer
press release
prime time
product
product information
product life cycle
professional publication
promote (v)
promotion
public relations
publicity
radio spot and TV ad
readership
sales
sales promotion
sample
sample products
selection
share
slogan
space
special offer
sponsor
sponsor (v)
sponsorship
story board
survey
target (v)
target group
target market
telemarketing
test market
trade show

trial
white space
word-of-mouth advertising

AGRICULTURE
acre
agronomy
area
arid
chemicals
cotton
crop(s)
cropland
cultivate (v)
cultivation
drought
export
farm
farm (v)
farmer
farm income
farming
feedstock
fertilize (v)
fertilizer(s)
grow (v)
harvest
harvest (v)
herbicide
husbandry
insecticide
irrigate (v)
irrigation
irrigation system
land
livestock
machinery
pesticides
plant
plant (v)
planting
plow (v)
potatoes
price
price supports
produce (v)
production
rice
seed (v)
seeds
seed stock
soil
soil conservation
store

subsidy
surplus
tariff
till (v)
tobacco
vegetables
wheat
yield

ARCHITECTURE AND CONSTRUCTION
aluminum
architect
art
asphalt
blueprint
brick
bricklayer
build (v)
builder
building
building materials
carpenter (master/apprentice)
cement
cement (v)
chart (v)
cinder blocks
computer design
concrete
construct (v)
construction
cool (v)
demolish (v)
design
design (v)
designer
destroy (v)
develop (v)
developer
dig (v)
draft
draft (v)
drafting
draw (v)
drawing
elevator
engineer
excavate (v)
excavation
fix (v)
fixture
glass
　　　frosted
　　　insulated
　　　Plexiglas™

see-through
safety
gravel
heat
heat (v)
heating and ventilation
implement (v)
iron
ironworks
joiner
joint
joist
land
lay (v)
light
lighting
material
measure (v)
metal
model
mortar
office layout
paint
paint (v)
painter
parking
plan (v)
plans
plasterer
plastic
plumber
refurbish (v)
renovate (v)
repair (v)
replace (v)
rock
steel
stone
structure
survey
survey (v)
surveyor
tile
tile (v)
weather (v)
welder
window
wire (v)
wood
cedar
ebony
mahogany
oak
pine
redwood

AUTOMOTIVE
ABS brakes
air bag
air cleaner
air filter
air vent
antilock brakes
ashtray
assembly line
automatic shift
automobile
auto show
axle
backlog
bearing
belt
blinker
body
body panel
body shop
brake
brake (v)
brake cylinder
bucket seats
bumper
bushing
buy (v)
camshaft
car
carburetor
car dealer
car maintenance
carpet
catalytic converter
CD player
chassis
child seat
chrome
cigarette lighter
climate control
clock
cockpit
competition
component
component stage
computer chip
connecting rod
console
consolidation
convertible
coolant
cooling system
cooling and heating system
cost competitiveness
crankshaft

cream puff
cross member
cruise control
cup holder
customer support
custom-made
cylinder
cylinder head
cylinder lining
dashboard
dealer
defog (v)
defogger
design
designer
diesel
differential
dimmer switch
displacement
distributor
door
door handle
door lock
door panel
drive (v)
driver's seat
drivetrain
electrical harness
electrical system
electronic system
emergency flasher
emission system
engine
engine block
engine cradle
engineer
engineering
Environmental Protection Agency (EPA)
exhaust
exhaust manifold
exhaust system
experimental design
exterior
fabricate (v)
fabrication
fan
fiberglass
fill (v)
finish
four-door
frame
fuel
fuel gauge
fuel pump
fuel tank

fuse
fuse box
garage
gasket
gas
gas cap
gas tank
gauge
gear
gear shift
glove compartment
headlight
headrest
heating system
high beam
hood
hood ornament
hubcap
indicator lights
instrument panel
intake manifold
interior
inventory
jack
jobber
key
labor
leather
lemon
lights
light truck
light vehicle
lock
lock (v)
lot
machine shop
machining
maintenance
make (v)
manual
miles per hour/kilometers per hour
miles per gallon/kilometers per gallon
mint condition
mirror
model
new model
noise
odometer
oil gauge
oil pressure
open (v)
overhead cam
paint
park (v)
parking

parking brake
part
parts distribution
parts manufacturer
passenger car
passenger's seat
pedal
pickup truck
piston
piston ring
platform
power brakes
power windows
price
price tag
radio
rear suspension
rearview mirror
repair shop
replacement part
reverse (v)
robot
rocker arm
run (v)
seal
seat
seat belt
sedan
service
service station
shift (v)
shop (v)
showroom
side mirror
signal
signal (v)
sound system
spare tire
spark plug
speedometer
sports car
stall (v)
stamping
start (v)
starter
start up
station wagon
steer (v)
steering wheel
stick shift
strut
sunroof
supplier
suspension
SUV (sports utility vehicle)
switch

system
tachometer
tire
tool
tool kit
torque
transmission
truck
trunk
turn (v)
turn into (v)
turn signal
twin cap
two-door
union
valve
van
vanity mirror
vehicle
vent
vibration
wagon
warning light
wheel
window
windshield
wipers

BANKING AND FINANCE

account
accrue (v)
acquire (v)
acquisition
asset
assets under management
automated teller machine (ATM)
back office
bailout
bond
bond market
borrow (v)
borrowing
bottom line
branch
branch manager
capital
cash
cash (v)
cashier
central bank
certificate of deposit (CD)
check
checking account
close (v)
commercial bank

commercial banking
commission
commodity
corporate bond
correspondent banking
cost of funds
credit
credit card
credit limit
credit line
currency
day trader
debt (short-term, long-term)
deficit
deflation
delinquency rate
deposit
deposit (v)
derivatives
down payment
due date
earnings
economy
efficiency ratio
exchange rate
fee
financial adviser
fiscal policy
foreign exchange
futures contract
go long/short (v)
hedge
hedge (v)
hedge fund
hedging
inflation
institutional investor
interest
interest rate (fixed, floating)
invest (v)
investment
investment bank
investment banking
investment services
letter of credit (L/C)
liability
liquid
liquidate (v)
lend (v)
loan (short-term, long-term, secured)
loan (v)
loan officer
loan volume
loss
merchant bank
merchant banking

merge (v)
merger
monetary policy
money
mortgage
mortgage (v)
mutual fund
net
net interest margin
nonrevolving credit
open an account (v)
open letter of credit (v)
overdraft
overdrawn
pay (v)
payment
percent
portfolio
portfolio manager
price
price (v)
price/earnings (p/e) ratio
private banking
profit
profit (v)
profit margin
recession
repayment
retail banking
revolving credit
safe-deposit box
save (v)
savings account
securitization
security/securities
share price
spread
stock market
stockholder
stocks
surplus
syndicate
syndicated loan
takeover
tax
tax (v)
teller
trade (v)
trader
transact (v)
transaction
transaction costs
transfer (v)
traveler's checks
treasury bonds
trust

trust (v)
trust officer
underwrite (v)
underwriter
wholesale banking
wire
wire (v)
withdraw (v)
withdrawal

ENGINEERING

calculus
chemical
civil
design
develop (v)
engineer
instrument
mathematics
mechanical
nuclear
science
structural
technology
test

ENTERTAINMENT, JOURNALISM, AND MEDIA
(See also Publishing or Advertising and Public Relations)

actor
artist
choreographer
cinema
column
columnist
commentary
contact
correspondent
dancer
director
edit (v)
edition
editor
editorial
editor-in-chief
feature story
headline
interpreter
journalism

journalist
music
musician
news (story)
perform (v)
performance
photographer
post-production
producer
production
radio
recording
rehearsal
report (v)
reporter
review
score
script
technician
television
translator
writer

FASHION
(See also Textile)

accessories
accessorize
appearance
beauty
bell-bottoms
belt
bias cut
blazer
blouse
boots
boutique
bow tie
bra
bust
cap
collar
collection
corset
couturier
cover (v)
cravat
design
design (v)
designer
dinner jacket
double-breasted suit
dress
dressing room

earmuffs
fabric
fake fur
fashion
fashion show
fur
garment
girdle
gloves
hat
haute couture
haute couturier
heel
hem
hem (v)
hemline
image
jacket
lapel
length
lingerie
metallics
miniskirt
model
model (v)
muff
necktie
nightgown
noncrease
overcoat
pad
padded
pajamas
pants
plastics
platform shoes
pleat
proportion
raincoat
ready-to-wear
relaxed
robe
runway
sash
scarf
seam (finished, unfinished)
season
separates
shawl
sheath
shirt
shoes
shoulder pads
show
show (v)
showroom

skirt
sleeve
socks
stiletto heel
stitch (v)
stitching
stockings
straight-leg
style
suit
sweater
tailor
tailor (v)
tailored
tailoring
tank top
three-piece suit
tie
trousers
T-shirt
undergarment
underwear
vest
waist
wardrobe
wedge (heel)

GOVERNMENT AND GOVERNMENT AGENCIES

administration
agency
arts
association
citizen
citizenship
college
commission
committee
community
cultural
delegation
department
development
economic
education
environment
form
government
governmental
grant
highway
housing
industrial part
information

institute
international
legislation
long-range
military
negotiate (v)
negotiation
nongovernment agency
nonprofit
office
park
plan
plan (v)
planner
policy
political
politics
population
procedure
proposal
public
public service
recommendation
region
regional
regional office
regulation
regulatory agency
report
representative
research
resources
road
rural
service
social
society
suburb
transportation
university
urban

INSURANCE
actuary
agent
annuity
broker
casualty
claim
commission
coverage
death benefit
deductible
endowment
face value

health
insure (v)
life
life expectancy
mortality
peril
policy
policy owner
premium
property
reinsurance
reserve
risk
risk management
term
underwriter
universal
variable annuity
whole life

MANAGEMENT CONSULTING
account
accounting executive
bill
bill (v)
entrepreneur
expert
fee
implement (v)
implementation
manage (v)
management
organize (v)
organization
organizational development
presentation
project
proposal
recommend (v)
recommendation
report
report (v)
specialize (v)
specialist
team build (v)
team building
time sheet
train (v)
training
value
value added

MINING AND PETROLEUM
blasting
chemical

coal
conveyor
cooling
copper
crosscut
crush (v)
crusher
crystal
deposit
diamond
dig (v)
digging
dredge (v)
dredging
drilling
earth
engineer
engineering
excavating
extraction
gas
gem
geologist
gold
hydraulic
iron
lead
metal
metallurgist
mine
mine (v)
mineral
natural gas
natural resources
oil
open-pit
ore
outcrop
pit
platform
power
processing
pump
pump (v)
pumping
quarry
quarry (v)
refine (v)
refinery
resources
safety
shaft
silver
sluice
sluicing
smelting

strip-mining
surface
tin
ton
truck
tunnel
tunnel (v)
tunneling
vein
uranium
water
waste
well
zinc

NONPROFIT
academic
analyst
associate
association
center
charity
college
consult (v)
consulting
contract
contract (v)
coordinate
council
database
develop (v)
development
directory
donation
educate (v)
education
educational
enterprise
fellowship
fine art
foundation
fund-raiser
fund-raising
gift
grant
information
institute
institute (v)
institution
interest group
international
issue (v)
laboratory
library
lobbying

museum
nonprofit group/not-for-profit group
organization
philanthropy
professional association
program
publish (v)
raise funds (v)
report
report (v)
research
research (v)
school
society
statistic
strategy
study
survey
survey (v)
university

PERFUME AND FRAGRANCE

aerosol
aftershave
air freshener
alcohol
aloe
aroma
base note
bath
bath oil
blush
citrus
cologne
compact
cosmetic(s)
cream(s)
deodorant
essential oils
eyeliner
eye shadow
floral
fragrance
fresh
freshener
herbal
lemon
lipstick
mascara
middle note
nose
oil
ointment
olfactory
orange

oriental
perfume
powder
powdery
rouge
salt
scent
smell
soap
spicy
toiletries
top note

PHARMACEUTICAL, MEDICAL, AND DENTAL

anesthesic
antibiotics
approval
approve (v)
capsule
checkup
clean (v)
cleaning
chemistry
clinical trial
disease
double-blind data
drug
drug trial (phase I, phase II, phase III)
exam
examine (v)
filling
generic drugs
hospital(s)
laboratory
manufacture (v)
magnetic resonance imaging (MRI)
over-the-counter
patent
patent (v)
patented drug
patient
pharmaceutical company
pharmacist
pharmacologist
pharmacy
pill
placebo
poison
prescribe (v)
prescription
prescription drug
proprietary drug
rash (skin)

release (v)
research
root canal
tablet
test
test (v)
testing
toxicology
treatment
veterinary drug
vitamins
X ray

PUBLISHING

acknowledgements
advance
advanced sales
appendix
art
asterisk
author
author's corrections
back ad
backlist
best-seller
binding
blockbuster
blurb
blow-in card
body
boldface type
book
book jacket
bookstore
border
box
broadsheet newspaper
bullet points
byline
caps (capital letters)
caption
chapter
circulation
color
color photograph
contents
contrast
copy editor
copyright
cover
cropping
dagger
deadline
dots per inch
double dagger

double-page spread
edit (v)
editing
editor
electronic publishing
endpapers
fact check
flush left/flush right
font
footnote
frontlist
galley
galley proof
glossary
glossy
graphic
hardcover
illustration
imprint
index
international paper sizes
introduction
international standard book number (ISBN)
international standard serial number (ISSN)
italics
jacket
justify
landscape
layout
legend
logo
loose-leaf
lowercase
magazine
manuscript
margins
masthead
mock-up
newspaper
newsstand
page(s)
page number
page proofs
pagination
paperback
paragraph
paragraph mark
percentage
pica
point
portrait
printing
prologue
proof
proofread (v)
proofreader

publisher
publishing
pulp
reference
reference marks
remaindering
reporter
resolution
royalty
section mark
sentence
softcover
subscript/superscript
subscription
tabloid
template
text
title
trade book
trim
typeface
watermark
word wrap
writer

REAL ESTATE
agent
agreement
air rights
amortization
annual percentage rate (APR)
apartment
appraisal
appraise (v)
assessment
assign (v)
assume
assumption
attached
attachment
auction
balloon mortgage
bankruptcy
bearing wall
bid (v)
binder
breach of contract
bridge loan
broker
building
building codes
building permit
buy (v)
capitalization

capital gains
cash flow
caveat emptor
closing
closing costs
collateral
commitment
condemnation
condominium (condo)
contract
convey (v)
conveyance
cooperative (co-op)
credit report
debt-to-income ratio
deed
default (v)
depreciation
diversified
down payment
easement
eminent domain
equity
escrow
foreclosure
first mortgage
flood insurance
free and clear
freehold
general contractor
hazard insurance
hotel
indemnity
industrial
industrial park
insurance
interest
jumbo loan or mortgage
land
landscaping
lease
lease (v)
lessee/lessor
let
lien
manufactured housing
mortgage
note
occupancy
office
option
owner
partition
points
power of attorney

prefabricated construction
prepayment penalty
principal
private mortgage insurance (PMI)
probate
promissory note
property
public sale
real estate
real estate agent
real estate investment trusts (REITs)
realtor
refinance (v)
rent
rent (v)
rental
renter
rescind (v)
residential
riparian rights
second mortgage
self-storage
sell (v)
settle (v)
shopping mall
sublet (v)
tenant
tenure
title
title insurance
title search
trust
utilities
vacant
warranty deed
zoning

SHIPPING AND DISTRIBUTION
agent
air freight
airport
anchor
barge
bill
bill (v)
bill of lading (BL)
boat
box
broker
bulk carrier
by air
by land
by sea
cargo

carload
carrier
certificate
charter
charter (v)
costs, insurance, and freight (CIF)
combine (v)
consign (v)
consignor
container
containerization
container ship
corrugated box
cost
crate
crew
customs
deliver (v)
delivery
delivery note
delivery time
depot
destination
dispatch
dispatch (v)
dock
dock (v)
double hulls
duty
estimate
estimate (v)
ferry
fleet
forklift
forward
forwarding
fragile
free on board (FOB)
freight
freight carrier
freight costs
freighter
freight weights
full containerload
goods
guaranteed arrival date
hazardous materials
hire (v)
hub
insurance
insure (v)
island
isothermal container
landing day
liner

load
load (v)
load capacity
loading
loader
loan
locks
lots
manager
manifest
merchant ship
message center
oil tanker
off-load (v)
order
order (v)
overdraft
package
package (v)
packaging
packing
pallet
partial carload
partial containerload
pick up (v)
port
profit
railroad
rails
rail yard
refrigerate (v)
refrigerated tank
refrigeration
reloading
rent (v)
route
route (v)
scrapping
sea
sea-lane
service
ship
ship (v)
shipper
station
storage
super tanker
surface
tank
tanker
taxes
tie-down
tonnage
track (v)
tracks (railroad)

traffic
traffic coordinator
train
transloading
transport
transport (v)
transport company
transporting
transporter
truck
truck (v)
trucking
van
union
union representative
unload (v)
warehouse
yard

TELECOMMUNICATIONS

analog
bandwidth
baud
cable
capacity
cellular
cellular phone
data
data transmission
dedicated line
digital
downlink
DSL line
e-commerce
e-mail
fax/facsimile
fiber-optical line
hertz
high-speed
identification number (ID number)
Internet
intranet
Internet service providers (ISPs)
keyboard
keypad
local area network (LAN)
line
link
liquid crystal display (LCD)
local call
long-distance call
megahertz
menu
mobile phone

modem
network
palmtop
password
personal digital assistant (PDA)
phone line
resolution
satellite
security
server
telecommunications
telegram
telephone
transmit (v)
transmission
uplink
videoconferencing
voice and data transmission
voicemail
Web
Web page
Web site
wireless
Worldwide Web (WWW)

TEXTILES
acidity
acrylic
alkalinity
apparel
artist
bonded types
braids
braided
brocade
cloth
clothing
color
composite fabrics
conventional method
converter
cotton
crimp
cutting
cutting room
damask
defect
design
dry-cleaning
dye
dye (v)
dyeing
elasticity
elongation

embroidered
engineer
fabric
fastness (of finishes and colors)
felt
fiber
fiber masses
fineness
finished cloth
flame-resistant
flax
flexibility
floral
garment
geometric
hand finishing
insulation
interlacing
jute
knit (v)
knitted
knitting
lace
laundering
layer
length
licensing
linen
loom
machinery
man-made fiber
manufacture
manufacturing operations
moisture absorption
natural fiber
needle
needle woven
net
newer construction methods
nylon
ornament
patterns
polyester
polyester filament
porosity
printed
printing
processing
production
quality control
quality label
rayon
reaction to heat, sunlight, chemicals
resistance to creases
resistance to pests

rug
sew (v)
sewing
silk
silk-screen (v)
spandex
specialization
spinning
stable-fiber
strength
structure
synthetic fabric
synthetic fibers
tapestry
technician
testing
texture
thread
trademark
traditional
treat (v)
uniform thickness
velvet
volume of production
water-repellent
weave
weave (v)
weave and yarn structure
weaving
weight per unit area
width
wool
worsted
woven
yarn
yard

TOYS
action figure
activity set
age compression
airplane
animal
articulation
art supplies
ball
battery
blocks
board game
boat
brand-name toy
building blocks
building toy
car
character

chemistry set
children
clay
computer game
creator
doll
education software
Frisbee
fun
fun (to have)
game
glue
hobby kit
hobbyhorse
hoop
infant toy
kaleidoscope
kit
kite
letter
marbles
microscope
mobile
model
musical toy
novelty
part
picture book
Peg-Board
plastic
play
play (v)
playing
playing cards
plush toys
preschool activity toy
puppet
puzzle
railroad
rattle
reissue
riding toy
rocket
rubber
science set
soldier
sports equipment
stuffed animal
stuffed toy
teddy bear
top
trading cards
train
vehicle
video game
wagon

wood
wood-burning set
yo-yo

WATCHES, SCALES, AND PRECISION INSTRUMENTS
analog
apparatus
balance
battery/batteries
brass
chain
chronograph
clock
coil
digital
display
friction
gear
gold
instrument
integrated circuit
jewels
laboratory
laser
mainspring
measurements
mechanism
miniature
miniaturization
motion
movements
optical
oscillate (v)
oscillation
pin
pivot
polished
precision
scale
self-winding
shaft
silver
spring
spring-driven
steel
stopwatch
time
time (v)
timepiece
torque
transistors
watch
weights

wheel
wristwatch

WINE
acidity
age (v)
aging
alcohol
aroma
barrel
Bordeaux
bottle
bottle (v)
bottled
brandy
bubbles
burgundy
cabernet sauvignon
casks
cellar
champagne
"character" of the wine
chardonnay
Chianti
clarifying
climate
color
cool
cork
cork (v)
crush (v)
crusher
drink (v)
dry
estate
ferment (v)
fermentation
flavor
flavor (v)
flavored wine
fortified wines
grape
grow (v)
harvest
herbs
humidity
label
label (v)
merlot
must
oak
pinot noir
port
precipitate
pulp

red wine
refine (v)
refrigerate (v)
refrigeration
region
Riesling
rosé wine
seeds
sherry
soil
sparkling wine
store (v)
sugar
sweet

table wine
tank
taste (v)
tasting
varietals
vermouth
vine
vineyard
vinifera grapes
vintage
white wine
wine
winery
yeast

INDEX

Adverbs of Negation 149
Adjectives 158
    Possessive 158
Articles 37
Capitalization 246
Comparative 130
Conditional 90
Coordinating Adverbs 225
Coordinating Conjunctions 225
Direct vs. Indirect Speech 200
Ever, Expressions with 160
Few vs. *a few* 39
For and *since* 66
Future Tense 79
    with *to be going to* 79
    with *will* 80
    Usage 81
    with Time Expressions 81
Gerund 169
Good vs. *Well* 133
Homonyms 92
Infinitive 178
Little vs. *A Little* 39
Modal Verbs 118
    Forms 118
    Usage 119
Negation 148
Not and *No* 149
Nouns 34, 157
    Possessive 157
Other, Expressions with 160
Participles 171
    Past 171
    Present 171
Passive Voice 189

Past Continuous 54
Past Perfect 67
Past Perfect Continuous 67
Past Tense, Simple 49
Phrasal Verbs 235
Prefixes 247
Prepositions 211
Present Continuous 24
Present Perfect 64
Present Perfect Continuous 66
Present Tense 22, 82
    Simple 22
    to Express Future 82
Pronouns 8, 158-160, 224
    Personal 8
    Impersonal 160
    Possessive 158
    Reflexive 159
    Relative 224
Quantity Expressions 39
Sentence, Elements of a 8
Sentences of Equivalency 133
Simple Past 49
Simple Present 22
Some vs. *Any* 149
Subjunctive 236
Subordinating Conjunctions 226
Suffixes 248
Superlative 131
To Be 11, 106
To Do 108
To Do vs. *to Make* 108
To Have 107
Used to 53